The Language of Touch

Also available from Bloomsbury

The Bloomsbury Companion to the Philosophy of Language, edited by
Manuel Garcia-Carpintero and Max Kolbel
The Bloomsbury Companion to Cognitive Linguistics, edited by Jeanette
Littlemore and John R. Taylor
Cognitive Grammar in Stylistics, by Marcello Giovanelli and Chloe Harrison
Mind Style and Cognitive Grammar, by Louise Nuttall
Mixed Metaphors, by Karen Sullivan

The Language of Touch

Philosophical Examinations in Linguistics and Haptic Studies

Edited by Mirt Komel

BLOOMSBURY ACADEMIC

LONDON • NEW YORK • OXFORD • NEW DELHI • SYDNEY

BLOOMSBURY ACADEMIC
Bloomsbury Publishing Plc
50 Bedford Square, London, WC1B 3DP, UK
1385 Broadway, New York, NY 10018, USA

BLOOMSBURY, BLOOMSBURY ACADEMIC and the Diana logo are trademarks
of Bloomsbury Publishing Plc

First published in Great Britain 2019

Cover design by Olivia D'Cruz
Cover image © Getty Images/SuperStock

A catalogue record for this book is available from the British Library.

A catalog record for this book is available from the Library of Congress.

ISBN: HB: 978-1-3500-5926-9
         ePDF: 978-1-3500-5927-6
         eBook: 978-1-3500-5928-3

Typeset by RefineCatch Limited, Bungay, Suffolk
Printed and bound in Great Britain

To find out more about our authors and books visit www.bloomsbury.com and sign up
for our newsletters.

Contents

Introduction

Mirt Komel

The question is not so much "to touch or not to touch," but rather what does the *not* in "not to touch" mean? What kind of touch does the negation imply? Is such a negated touch still conceivable as touching, if no actual touch happens?

Apart from being an obvious paraphrasing of Shakespeare's *Hamlet* and Heidegger's *Being and Time*, this introductory sentence's purpose is not merely a rhetorical word-play, but an attempt at transposing touch from its bodily, physical, empirical, and phenomenological existence towards its distinctively linguistic dimension. If we understand touch linguistically, then we can pose a variety of questions, which come down to: how does language structure touching?

Of course we are not the first nor, we imagine, will we be the last to raise this question. The first two extensive monographs that focused exclusively on touch also posed this question, implicitly or explicitly, although from two very different perspectives. It is one of those happy historical coincidences that the English translation of Jacques Derrida's *On Touching: Jean-Luc Nancy*, and *The Book of Touch* edited by Constance Classen, rolled off the presses in the same year, that is, 2005, a year that could be said to mark the birth of haptic studies strictly speaking—by which I mean: thinking of touch in its own terms and not, say, as a sense among other senses; a function of the body; a phenomenological curiosity; an existential question; and similar ways of appropriating touch in a different context where touch is not the sole or central object of inquiry.

Let me now reinforce and at the same time question the above demarcation line: Derrida originally published his book in French in the year 2000, but it was actually a reworking of an earlier essay from the beginning of the 1990s, itself published as *On the Work of Jean-Luc Nancy*, in English, as the introduction, to a special issue of the *Journal of Modern Critical Theory* dedicated to Nancy, whom Derrida himself labeled as the "first great thinker of touch." Interestingly, this label and the related interpretation of Nancy's work as the first haptic philosophy came well before Nancy himself explicitly addressed the issue of touch. This he did in his later works, most notably in his "essay on the resurrection of the body" *Noli me tangere* (2003) that related to his earlier work, focusing primarily on *Corpus* (1992). That is half of the reason why the English translation of Derrida's book marks the above-mentioned milestone, since it was only after Nancy actualized his philosophy as haptic, that all Derrida's speculative interpretations of Nancy as the "first great thinker of touch" actually came true.

The other half of the reason is that in order to have haptic studies "proper," philosophy did not suffice, since neither the starting point nor the aim of Derrida and Nancy's works was ever to constitute such a field, nor build their respective philosophies around touch, or anything similar. While, on the other hand, that was precisely the scope of Classen's editorial endeavor that aimed at constructing a "cultural history of touch". Let us not polemicize how much the book succeeded in this particular aspect, but what it indeed succeeded in was the establishment of "a culture of researching touch," thus elevating touch to become a respectable object of academic research (not at all a commonplace back in 2005). Many of the authors from *The Book of Touch* later focused on touch even more, either through their own monographs (such as, most notably, Mark Paterson's *The Senses of Touch*), or by editing special journal issues (for instance, David Howes with a special issue of *The Senses and Society* dedicated to the topic of *Remediating Touch*).

Apart from the happy historical coincidence there is one more important reason for paralleling the two books by Derrida and Classen already mentioned, since they paradigmatically, methodologically, and epistemologically defined all further inquiry on touch and formed the core of what is nowadays consolidating as haptic studies: all the current approaches towards touch follow—consciously or unconsciously, willingly or unwillingly—either Derrida's or Classen et al.'s thinking: touch is, in the final analysis, defined either by language (Derrida) or culture and society (Classen), or a combination of both (if you understand language to be the essential part of culture and society or if you understand language to be an essentially cultural and social phenomenon).

If this book claims anything then it claims to make a step forward from the current state of affairs in haptic studies by posing the opposite question from the one proposed at the beginning, namely, that our interest is not only in how does language structure touch, but also in how does touch structure language? And consequently, what is the specific haptic quality of language that allows such metaphoric articulations as "to be touched by a poetry," or, for that matter, "to be touched by a swearword"? And, if there is a haptic quality to language, are such metaphors really just metaphors?

Such questions could not have been raised either in ancient times or in the Middle Ages, but only afterwards and not without considering the linguistic turn that began at the beginning of the twentieth century with Ferdinand de Saussure and his followers, and that showed its full philosophical potential later on in the middle of the century with the structuralistic revolution, nowadays unavoidably referred to through the doubtful prefix "post-." However, the contribution that linguistics made to haptic studies is not a one-sided gift, and much like in touching where one supposedly cannot "touch without being touched back," haptic studies wants to touch linguistics back precisely through this book by discerning a tactile quality of language. Such an endeavor can put forward a completely different set of questions that are linguistically still pertinent: why are the minimal materialistic entities of language defined only in acoustic (phonemes) and visual (graphemes) terms, and not also in haptic ones?

These and similar questions are precisely those that we posed ourselves during the research project on touch and language for which we coined the term *haptolinguistics* and which was the springboard for the book on the *Language of Touch: Philosophical Examinations in Linguistics and Haptic Studies*. The academic circumstances in which this project was born are, I presume, not interesting for the reader of such a book, so let me cut this part off this introduction, and rather sketch the general framework and governing principle that structured our contributions.

My own contribution (Chapter 1) is meant to lay the fundamental approach towards a materialistic understanding of our topic through the development of a hapticity of language via Saussure's linguistics, Marx's conception of commodity, and Hegel's concept of concept, enhanced by Lacan's understanding of language as material, consolidated in the concept of *lalangue*. Tomi Bartole's contribution (Chapter 2) continues the linguistic line of inquiry by focusing on the history of phonetics through an anthropological examination of kinaesthesia and similar phenomena in order to demonstrate a distinctive haptic quality of language. Karmen Šterk continues the anthropological approach (Chapter 3), and takes on the more general problem regarding the material status of the symbolic, as developed from anthropologist Lévi-Strauss and as taken over by Lacan. Gregor Moder's contribution tries to take into account all of the above and founds such a concept of linguistic touch in the traditional philosophical tradition of ontology from Aristotle to Heidegger and Brentano (Chapter 4), while Goran Vranešević (Chapter 5) continues this endeavor by following another line of inquiry that takes us from Hegel's conception of language to Lacan's structural linguistics. On this basis, Bara Kolenc's contribution can develop the concept of haptolinguistics proper, the guiding principle of this book, through a series of parallel readings of Saussure and especially Marx, with whom she thinks about the materiality of language, thus repeating the initial chapter's endeavor. The second half of the book demonstrates the productivity of our general haptolinguistic framework through a series of case studies that reemploy all of the above-mentioned authors and approaches from classics like Augustine and Hegel to Lacan and contemporary post-structuralism: Rachel Aumiller's beautiful poetic take on the mother tongue (Chapter 7); Peter Klepec's handling of swearing and the peculiarly violent way that it touches upon us (Chapter 8); Jela Krečič's original interpretation of proper names and the way that touches upon our being (Chapter 9); Eva Vrtačič's curious case of *Doctor Who's* untouchable touch (Chapter 10); and, finally, Zack Sievers' conceptualization of screaming contagions through the exploitation of the haptic quality of contagion (Chapter 11).

Last but not least, since I am concluding with compliments and thanks: for better or worse we, the authors of this book, are very fond of the founders of Ljubljana's Lacanian School of Psychoanalysis, and therefore this book is theoretically indebted to Alenka Zupančič and Slavoj Žižek, but first and foremost to Mladen Dolar. However, moving inside the (post-)structuralistic paradigm, we always try to follow their own example that consists in a continuous endeavor to surpass one's own teachers, thus demonstrating that they were good teachers indeed. If Lacanian psychoanalysis traditionally focused on the gaze and the voice as two privileged objects which cause desire, then already this introduction of touch into the existing paradigm aims not only at continuing and prolonging it, but also at reshaping its very definition: if the gaze and the voice left the existing conceptions of language untouched, then touch, conceived linguistically, can touch upon language in a new, radical and previously inconceivable way.

To conclude: we hope, or at least I hope—that we as the authors of this collective enterprise hope—that the reader will find the content of this book as intellectually inspiring to read as it was for us to write.

1

The Wave of the Sign: Pyramidal Sign, Haptic Hieroglyphs, and the Touch of Language

Mirt Komel

Introduction

As I am going to discuss not only linguistic sign in connection to economic value on the one hand, and as a philosophical concept on the other—all mediated through the concept of touch as a common denominator—but also, at least at a certain point, Marx's reference to the hieroglyphs and Hegel's mention of the pyramids, let me start with an anecdotal remark.

The ancient Egyptian religious practices, architectural endeavors, and hieroglyphic language were, for a long period of time, considered as almost synonymous with the mysterious, the foreign, and the unknown. Contrary to the usual understanding that the Egyptians possessed a way to know things that were unknowable for an uninitiated mind, Hegel remarked somewhere that the "Egyptian mysteries were a riddle for the Egyptians themselves," implying that the practitioners of these mysteries held no special knowledge about the religion they practiced (cf. Stewart 2017). Perhaps we could say the same about our contemporary economic practices, especially if we consider the problems related to commodity fetishism as first analyzed by Marx. And even more, we could say the same also about language, especially if we take into account Lacan's distinctive linguistic take on psychoanalysis, as encompassed in his maxim "unconsciousness structured as a language."

As far as the ancient Egyptian language is concerned, its decipherment has undergone a decisive breakthrough, as it is well understood due to the discovery of the so-called Rosetta Stone during Napoleon's invasion of Egypt in 1799. This stone presents not only a hieroglyphic and demotic version of the same text, but also a Greek translation. I think touch can function as such a Rosetta Stone by helping translate certain materialistic economic mysteries into more palpable linguistic ones.

On a more conceptual note, let me lay all my cards on the table: what I want to make is a reinterpretation of the relation between the linguistic sign and economic value as defined by structural linguistics and dialectical materialism through the concept of touch, or rather and, more precisely, through the concept *as* touch; both were traditionally understood as separate and even opposing entities, while this contribution will provide a way of thinking of the two of them as identical.[1]

The haptic cut of the sign

Now, after laying my cards on the table let me take them back and restart by playing my best card for the current game, namely, a curious biblical metaphor that Saussure used in order to illustrate the definition of sign as the relation between the signifier and the signified: "Visualize the air in contact with a sheet of water; if the atmospheric pressure changes, the surface of the water will be broken up into a series of divisions, waves; the waves resemble the union or coupling of thought with phonic substance" (Saussure 1966: 112). The wave of the sign is therefore produced by the encounter between air and water, between the signifier and the signified—we will return to this definition of the sign after a short detour.

The purpose of Saussure's metaphor is to illustrate what Jean-Claude Milner, among others (cf. Benveniste 1971; Jakobson 1990; etc.), rightfully points out to be Saussure's innovation in respect to the traditional philosophical understanding of language (Plato, Aristotle, Stoics, Scholastics, Port-Royal Logic): if the sign was traditionally understood as an unilateral representation of thoughts or things ("speaking is an index of thinking", "smoke is an index of fire"—while the contrary is not true since "thinking is not an index of speaking" and neither is "fire an index of smoke"), then Saussure redefined the sign as a mutual relation between the phonic material and the ideas of thought where one reflects the other not by representation, but rather by mutual association: the signifier is associated with the signified as much as the signified is associated with the signifier (cf. Milner 2002). Now, to reinforce this point let us return briefly to Saussure's own wording with another comparison that precedes the metaphor of the wave: "Language could also be compared with a sheet of paper: thought is the front and the sound the back; one cannot cut the front without cutting the back at the same time; likewise in language, one can neither divide sound from thought nor thought from sound; the division could be accomplished only abstractedly, and the result would be either pure psychology or pure phonology" (Saussure 1966: 113). The whole passage ends with the identification of linguistics as precisely the methodological scissor operating the cut through which sign is produced not as a substance, as it is often misunderstood, but rather as *pure form*: "Linguistics then works in the borderland where the elements of sound and thought combine; *their combination produces a form, not a substance*" (Ibid.: 113). Thus, the important thing to remember for our own endeavor is that sign is form, while the signifier and the signified are not simply substance, but two different substances—phonic and thought material—and therefore governed by a similar logic, at least looking from the standpoint of touch, that governs the well-known Cartesian distinction between *res extensa* and *res cogitans*.[2]

If we now return to the metaphor of the sign as the wave and put the stress on what Saussure himself determined as the "contact between air and water": if the signifier (phonic material) is air, and if the signified (thought material) is water, then it is precisely their encounter that produces the sign in the form of wave, or vice versa, the sign as wave is the encounter of the signifier and the signified, of air and water. In this instance touch functions as the unifier of the otherwise distinct substances, since it is the contact between the two that produces the sign, that, again, itself is not a substance, but the *form* of this unity. However, if we consider Saussure's other metaphor, the one with the sheet of paper, we can discern another kind of logic, more in tune with the remark that the sign is not a substance, but rather a form: if the sign is a sheet of paper with two sides, the verso side the signifier and the recto side the signified, then touch functions precisely as the cut that enables the distinction between the signifier and the signified (phonic and thought material). Touch here does not function as the unifier enabling the contact between the signifier and the signified, as was the case in the previous metaphor with the wave, but rather as the instance that cuts through the sign and produces the distinction between the signifier and the signified.

So, to conclude this first round of the game: is touch an instance that unifies the signifier and the signified in the form of the sign, or does it rather cut through the sign, thus enabling the distinction between the two? To this the most direct answer is: both; touch can be identified with the solidus in the Saussurian axiom for the sign (S/s), the solidus that not only divides the two dimensions of the signifier and the signified, but also unites them in the sign.

The (un)touchable value

Now let us see what the possible consequences are for a critique of political economy based on such a tactile redefinition of the linguistic sign, considering not only Saussure's identification of sign with value, but, conversely, also Marx's own identification of value with sign. As we will see in a moment, the two of them can give us two very different perspectives on a common paradox present in the sign and the value as well—besides throwing some light and some shadow on the related problems with both Saussure's and Marx's endeavors while constructing their respective analogies.

Saussure himself understood the sign as "value" and made the parallel between political economy and structural linguistics by stating: "both sciences are concerned with a system for equating things of different orders – labor and wages in one and a signified and signifier in the other" (Saussure 1966: 79). Embarking on his train of thought one can further differentiate between diachronic linguistics, implying a temporal continuity in the development of a language, and synchronic linguistics or linguistics *stricto senso* that isolates language from history by defining it as a static system of signs; conversely, one can observe economic phenomena through a synchronic view of the contemporary market economy or its diachronic historical development. If we, however, focus on the synchronic structure of language and economy only, and consider the identification of the sign with value, where value functions as the common denominator of both structural linguistics and political economy, we can see not only the parallel but also the main discrepancy between Saussure's sign and Marx's value.

As it is known, or at least as it should be known in this context, Marx starts his *Capital* by analyzing commodity as the minimal element through which he develops the logic of value, itself conceptualized through the difference between exchange and use-value. We consider that where these touch is significant: a commodity is, at the same time, a tangible thing with its intrinsically practical or at least consumable use-value, but also an intangible object of exchange with what is considered as proper value, the difference between the former and the latter being that in the first instance we look at the thing as if it has a value on its own, while in the second we necessarily relate it to other objects in order to define its exchange-value (cf. Marx 2015: 27–30).[3] Similarly, Saussure states that in linguistics one must simultaneously observe the sign on its own, analyze the relation between the signifier and the signified, and consider the sign in relation to other signs by noting its peculiar character in the sense that it has sense only in relation to other signs. In short, and very broadly speaking, both sciences are "structuralistic" in their conception of sign/value since in both instances the object must be considered on its own and in relation to others at the same time—or speaking in Kantian terms: simultaneously "in itself" and "for itself" or "for others."

However, this is the point where the parallel between Saussure's identification of the sign with value ends, and it is Marx himself who marks the border: among the many commodities circulating on the apparently free market there is at least one that is far from free and disrupts the economic logic of value, namely, labor. Labor is, on the one hand, a commodity among others with is specific exchange-value, while on the other hand its use-value is precisely in its production of commodities and therefore, *mutatis mutandis*, the true source of surplus-value (cf. Marx 2015: 126–131). Samo Tomšič in his *Capitalist Unconscious* rightfully insisted on this border within Saussure's identification of the sign with value where there is no equivalent of the surplus-value in linguistics—at least not until Lacan's notorious theory of the surplus-pleasure (cf. Tomšič 2015: 64–78), as defined in the *Séminaire* dedicated to the *Other Side of Psychoanalysis* (cf. Lacan 1991).[4] I would like to explore the other problem of such a conception by considering Marx's own analogy between value and sign and the related linguistic border within the political-economic theory of value.

Re-reading the *Capital*, especially the chapter on the *Fetishism of commodities and the secret thereof*, we can find, among other things, the following passage that is related to the omission—or rather repression—of the traumatic role of labor when considering commodities in their own pleasurable terms: "Value, therefore, does not stalk about with a label describing what it is. It is value, rather, that converts every product into a social hieroglyphic"; and later on "we try to decipher the hieroglyphic to get behind the secret of our own social products; for to stamp an object of utility as a value, is just as much a social product as language." (Marx 2015: 49) In Saussure's example it was the twofold character of the sign that enabled the conversion of a linguistic entity into an economic commodity mediated by the concept of value, while in Marx's analogy it is value itself that transforms commodity into language, converting every product into a social hieroglyphic that we need to decipher in order to get behind its secret, since it is by stamping or rather inscribing value upon an object of utility that we transform it into a social product. Here language is understood as something that inscribes itself—and therefore we could add: touches upon—a tangible thing, thus transforming it into a hieroglyph that needs deciphering.

In short, if Saussure has a very elaborate theory of language and a very poor, merely analogical one of economy, then the same is true for Marx who has a very elaborate theory of value, but a very poor one regarding language, since he parallels language with value through a very elusive common denominator, namely, "society"; and, moreover, and more importantly for our own endeavor, he explicitly identifies language with a hieroglyphic scripture, thus understanding language as writing.

The sign as haptic pyramid

Let us make a short, relaxing, and I hope not too puzzling intermezzo by posing a very simple question: what is a hieroglyph?

A hieroglyph is a character used in the Egyptian writing system, which combines logographic, syllabic, and alphabetic elements, thus encompassing the three basic elements of language from the minimal to the maximal: character, syllable, and, phrase. I do not want to bore the reader with the linguistic details of Egyptian hieroglyphs but to focus on their status as a written system, and point out that it is precisely language understood as writing that enables Marx's analogy between value and language. When value is inscribed, as if it was written upon a given product, it immediately transforms it into an exchangeable commodity, that is itself understood as a hieroglyph, something unknown that needs to be deciphered; and in this instance we can see the exact reverse of Derrida's denunciation of linguistics as phonocentric.

Let me recapitulate Derrida's argument from *Voice and Phenomenon* (cf. Derrida 1978): the problem of Saussure's inaugural gesture of constituting linguistics as the science of language, *la langue*, leaving aside *la parole* as a specific utterance of speech (cf. Saussure 1966: 13–15), while at the same time clearly modeling his conception of sign on the spoken word as the very definition of signifier as phonic material demonstrates (cf. Jakobson 1978: 42), implies a certain privilege of the spoken word over the written one, thus understanding the latter only as a secondary tool for the former. This problematically phonocentric attitude can be, moreover, discerned not only in linguistics but also nothing less than in the whole history of classical philosophy from Plato to Hegel.[5]

From this perspective the problem of Marx's understanding of language appears to be quite the opposite of what it seemed as outlined above, namely, that in his analogy language is identified with writing while leaving aside the spoken word. However, when we dig further we can see that Marx's repression of speech returns a few pages later in the same chapter on commodity fetishism when we hear "commodities speak through the mouth of the economist," revealing that their true value lies in the exchange and not in the use-value of mere riches (Marx 2015: 53). A peculiar example of what, in Greek rhetoric, is labeled as *prosopopea*, dealt with in depth and length recently by Mladen Dolar in his own *Prosopopea* where he addressed, among various authors and themes, the above-mentioned parable of the "speaking commodities" (cf. Dolar 2006). Let us now recapitulate and reformulate Marx's own argument in connection to value and language: if the hieroglyphs as written language mask or hide the secret of our own social products that are in need of deciphering, then the deciphering enables us to hear the commodities speak through the economist's mouth; thus, we proceeded from a masking, secretive, foreign, unknown written language to the unmasked, unmistakable, understandable speech—a movement from neurosis and psychosis, one could say in classical psychoanalytical terms.[6] The relation between language and speech/writing and the related critique of phonocentrism can be applied to the relation between value and commodity by discerning a certain "value-centrism": with speech perceived as the original, and writing its secondary appendix, so is exchange-value perceived in the psychotic perspective of economy as the original, and commodity use-value as its mere consumable neurotic derivate.

Marx's reference to the Egyptian hieroglyphs as the fusion of value and sign in the form of a commodity, curiously echoes Hegel's own reference to the Egyptian pyramids while discussing the difference between sign and symbol in the paragraph §585, which is a part of the third part of the *Encyclopaedia* entitled *Philosophy of Mind* (preceded by the *Science of Logic* and the *Philosophy of Nature*): "The sign is some immediate intuition, representing a totally different import from what naturally belongs to it; it is the pyramid into which a foreign soul (*eine fremde Seele*) has been conveyed (*ist versetzt*: transposed, transplanted, transferred) and where it is conserved (*aufbewahrt*: kept, entrusted, guarded, deposited, consigned)" (Hegel 2000: 749). The sign is something foreign to the meaning it represents, and meaning is in turn defined as "a foreign soul" to the "pyramid" of the sign, while the symbol, introduced just after this passage, presents an ideal unity of meaning and representation. Here I am following Derrida's reading of this passage where he finds in Hegel an anticipation of what Saussure labeled as the "arbitrary nature of the sign" that can be discerned especially from two characteristics (cf. Derrida 1993: 97): the first is precisely this doubling of meaning, one immediate that is given to intuition, the other conveyed and conserved in the sign; while the later refers to the ancient "irreducibility of the soul and the body, the intelligible and the sensible, the *Vorstellung* (the concept or ideality signified) and the sensible body of the signifier", as represented by the distinction between soul-signified and pyramid-signifier.

Here we can palpably grasp—and the term I just employed is not coincidental—the role of touch as the instance that divides the signifier and the signified in its own terms of (un)touchability. If the primary function of touch, according to Jean-Luc Nancy, is to draw the dividing line between the touchable and the untouchable, where one cannot identify touch with either of the two, then touch fulfills the same role inside the sign itself, as we have seen through the function of the bar that divides the untouchable soul of the signified from the tangible pyramid of the signifier.[7]

However, this solution poses another set of questions, the principal among them being: how can we think this tactile moment—that can be discerned from our analysis and identified in the bar of the Saussurian axiom that divides the tactile sound material of the signifier from the untouchable thought material of the signified—is inside language itself?

The haptem of language

Reconsidering the linguistic definition of the sign once more we can discern a singular sensorial moment in the linguistic conception of the signifier, since it is defined as "phonic material," otherwise the primary object of phonetics.[8]

Already on this level we can see that there is a sensorial moment inside language, or rather, speech, namely, the acoustic one. As, on the other hand, and moving from Saussure toward Derrida, we can discern another sensorial moment in writing, namely, the visual one. These two minimal acoustic and graphic elements in language are defined in linguistics as "phonemes" and "graphemes" (cf. Jakobson 1978), and these two distinctive sensorial moments can be, furthermore, understood precisely as the two ways in which touch operates inside language itself.

Lacan coined the concept of *lalangue* in the seminar *Encore* (or: *More*) in order to demonstrate how language-based meaning arises from phonetic non-meaning, a poetic characteristic of language itself: "Language is without doubt made of *lalangue*. It is an elucubration of knowledge about *lalangue*" (Lacan

1975: 127); and developed it further and even more clearly later on in the *Synthome*: "That which characterizes *lalangue* the most are all the possible equivoques, like the one illustrated by *dieux* and *d'eux*" (Lacan 2005: 117). Lacan's *lalangue* can therefore be understood as the way in which "words touch each other," as Dolar puts it in his article *Touching Ground*, or more precisely the way in which words are being "contaminated by each other through their sound contacts, similarities, echoes, reverberations"; this is, furthermore, what "constitutes homonymy, the contingent sounding alike, which is at the basis of the mechanisms of the unconscious and which Lacan, in his later work, tried to pin down with *lalangue*" (cf. Dolar 2008: 96). However, this conception of *lalangue*, pertinent to the spoken word, can function also in the written one: as one can say that it is the phonemes (minimal phonic units) that touch each other from the standpoint of homonyms, so can one say that the graphemes (minimal graphic units) operate a similar role in writing from the standpoint of homographs.[9]

Moreover, I want to propose the coinage of *haptem* (minimal haptic unit) precisely to denote this touching that one can discern happening inside language itself. To be sure, language is defined by traditional linguistics as a system of differences—when one sign can have meaning only in relation to other signs, and this relational understanding of the sign is what is usually understood as "structure": from this perspective the phonemes and graphemes function as minimal material differentiating units without meaning in themselves (mere spoken sounds and written characters), but are nevertheless capable of producing meaning in their mutual interaction. The difference of the sign is, in short, analytically reducible to the difference between various phonemes and graphemes. The concept of haptem could similarly function as a minimal material differentiating unit in language that is, however, grounded neither in any acoustic nor in any visual representation (as phonemes and graphemes), but rather in tactility.

In the last analysis, if there is a tactile quality inherent in language, then the concept of haptem can provide a haptic conception of touch inside language itself, as, for instance, embodied in the braille system—a tactile binary system of reading for the blind or those with impaired vision.[10] In the future, this could potentially allow us to develop a braille system of haptems parallel to the two existing graphemes and phonemes, thus allowing us to literary grasp the tactile quality of language and promote further developments in linguistics, philosophy of language, and especially in haptic studies.

The touch of *begriff*

Now we can raise one final problem: if touch functions as the tactile precondition of production of meaning—the sensorial moment inside language itself split into the touching of phonemes and/or graphemes—then what about meaning itself, which is intrinsically connected to the concept of concept? Is it separated from touch and therefore strictly speaking untouchable?

To answer this question let us consider Hegel's reflections on the metaphor in his *Lectures on Aesthetics* (cf. Hegel 1988: 404): starting from a very general consideration about language he says that "every language already contains a mass of metaphors. They arise from the fact that a word which originally signifies only something sensuous is carried over into the spiritual sphere." The emphasis I would like to stress is on the "sensuous" that is "carried over" and thus not simply discarded, but rather retained and preserved in the "spiritual sphere", which is, as it is known, or should be known, Hegel's usual dialectical procedure of *Aufhebung*.[11] One of the examples given in order to demonstrate that metaphors contain a certain sensorial element, that is preserved in their spiritual meaning is precisely the concept of "concept", *begriff*: "If, for example, we are to take *begreifen* in a spiritual sense, then it does not occur to us at all to think of a perceptible grasping by the hand" (Hegel 1988: 404–405), as if by grasping the meaning inside the image employs an implicitly metaphorical use of the concept.[12]

I would like to argue that language as conceived by linguistics has an inherently dialectical tendency towards pure meaning, while in order to purify itself from any physical residuum it needs metaphors as an intermediate step from sensorial towards spiritual, while at the same time unavoidably retaining its sensorial character.[13] If, at least for Hegel, touch as a sensorial entity can become an abstract concept via its employment as metaphor because in the final analysis it was always already a concept (a conception of sensorial meaning—this is the logic governing the initial pages of the *Phenomenology of the Spirit*), then we could raise the converse question of where does the distinction between sensorial, metaphoric, and conceptual come from in the first place?

Since we need to leave this question for a later detailed analysis of Hegel's argument, it is not pertinent in this context; let me return and rephrase the idea of touch and language as developed thus far in linguistic terms from the standpoint of our initial endeavor. Touch, as the dividing and connecting line between the signifier and the signified inevitably contaminates both with its singular sensorial character, is discernable in the tactility of speech/writing as *lalangue* and in the concept of *begriff*.

Thus, as we can see, touch can be understood not only as the sensorial residuum present in language, identified with the concept of haptem proposed above, but also as the structuring instance of conceptual thinking itself.

Conclusion

If we now conclude by backtracking to the beginning: what can such a conception of touch teach us about the linguistic sign and economic value, and what can haptic studies therefore contribute to structural linguistics on the one hand and to the critique of political economy on the other?

We have seen, from a linguistic point of view, how Marx's analysis proceeded from writing to speech: in the first instance how the inscription of value upon tangible objects transforms them into unreadable social hieroglyphs, and how by being able to read this mysterious writing we can force these objects themselves to speak and confess that their true identity lies in their exchange-value. Modeled on Derrida's critique of philosophy in general and Saussurian linguistics in particular we applied the same critique to the economic view of value-centrism, the privileging of the exchange-value over use-value. Moreover, if the use-value is an intrinsic characteristic of tangible things, and if the exchange-value is a materialistic characteristic of commodities, we could apply what we developed as the (un)touchability of the sign to this split inside value itself so that the apparently tangible signifier coincides with the use-value, while the also apparently intangible signified with their exchange-value.

Now, if Marx's concept of labor as the source of surplus-value disrupts this simplistic economistic view in the same manner as Lacan's concept of surplus-enjoyment disrupts structural linguistics, then we propose to designate touch—as the divisional line that separates and unites the signifier and the signified based on the criteria of (un)touchability, that in the final analysis resulted in a tactile quality of not only language (*lalangue*), but also thinking (*begriff*)—as *surplus of touch*. If there is such a thing as the surplus of touch at work in both instances, then it is on at the limit between the neurotic identification of commodities as mere tangible things with the unavoidable conclusion at each consumption that "this is not it" on the one hand, and the psychotic voices of the commodities that find their equivalent in the invisible hand of the market, itself modeled upon the hand of God whose main characteristic is that it touches upon us without us being able to touch back.

We are not able to touch back in any other way but by conceptually grasping the concept of touch itself, that is, by conceiving touch not as much as a matter of the hand but of the mind, or rather, of both hand and mind at the same time.

Notes

1 Especially in the ancient Greek philosophical tradition which regarded the senses in general and touch in particular as grounded in the body, *sōma*, which differed from the soul, *psyché* (cf. Plato 1997; Aristotle 1984), while the Christian scholastic tradition, concerned primarily with the concept of the immortal soul, amplified this difference even more (cf. Aquineas; Augustine 1988).

2 Descartes' *Meditations* questioned the sensory bodily experience as a source of falsehood derived from the distinctively tangible *res extensa* ("physical-things"), which are defined in contrast to the otherwise volatile and untouchable *res cogitans* ("thought-things") as the sole source of certain truth (Descartes 1960: 17–23).

3 For a further interpretative analysis of Marx's logic of value in relation to the question of touch see Bara Kolenc's contribution in this book (Chapter 6).

4 For a detailed reading and interpretation of the somehow elusive relation between the Marxist concept of surplus value and the Lacanian concept of surplus of pleasure see also Alenka Zupančič's article: *When surplus enjoyment meets surplus value* (cf. Zupančič 2006).

5 Considering Derrida's insistence on the argument it is noteworthy that Saussure made a diametrically opposed claim, namely, that earlier theories of language as well as everyday understandings have always privileged writing over speech: "But the spoken word is so intimately bound to its written image that the latter manages to usurp the main role [. . .] This illusion, which has always existed, is reflected in many of the notions that are currently bandied about on the subject of language." (Saussure 1966: 23–24).

6 The standard definition and distinction between neurosis and psychosis as rendered by Freud in his *Psychopathologies* is that neurosis is characterized by a conflict between the ego and the unconscious, their battleground being the external reality to which the neurotic clings in his or her paradoxical fetishistic attitude, while analogously defining psychosis as the conflict between the ego and the external word, the latter eventually abolished in order to elevate the internal one as the sole solipsistic reality (cf. Freud 1987).

7 Interpreting the *Noli me tangere* scene between Jesus and Mary Magdalene from the New Testament Nancy makes the following elegant remark on touch: "This point is precisely the point where touching does not touch, must not touch in order to exercise its touch (its art, its tact, its grace): the point where the spacing without

dimension that separates what touching resemble, the divisional line between the touching and the touched and therefore the line inside touch itself." (Nancy 2003: 25).

8 For an extensive analysis of the history of phonetics and its relevance for haptic studies see the contribution by Tomi Bartole in this book (Chapter 2).

9 The conception of a certain tactile quality of writing can of course be first attributed to Derrida, or rather and more precisely, to his reading of Nancy in *On Touching: Jean-Luc Nancy* (cf. Derrida 2005); but as with Dolar in the above-mentioned article, who thought about the tactility of the spoken word while not considering the hapticity of writing, so also Derrida thought about the tactility of the written word without considering the haptic phonetics of the spoken one—I can see the value of both of these points of view applying at the same time.

10 Braille was invented by Louis Braille, who lost his sight in childhood, and in 1824 developed a tactile writing system for the French alphabet, which was also the first binary form of writing developed in modernity. Nowadays it is used for writing and reading by people who are blind or visually impaired, while the technological advancement is still developing various new and interesting possibilities for its usage.

11 Nancy points out in his *Speculative Remark: One of Hegel's Bons Mots* that there is no distinctively Hegelian dialectics without the concept of *Aufhebung*, which means "abolition" and "preservation" at the same time, thus enabling the dialectical progression of the concept; however, despite the fact that in the last instance anything can be *aufgehoben* there is at least one concept that cannot be, and that is the concept of *Aufhebung* itself (cf. Nancy 2001).

12 Hegel's dialectics here reflects the beginning of the *Phenomenology of the Spirit*, the section on *Certainty at the Level of Sense-Experience*, where the sensorial is retroactively turned into the conceptual: the original sensorial word can be the basis for the metaphor and the metaphor in turn for the conceptual since the very origin is already contaminated with the conceptual (cf. Hegel 2001: 33–38).

13 Derrida in his *White Mythology: Metaphor in the Text of Philosophy* will follow this line of argument in order to demonstrate that the metaphorical and metaphysical meanings are inseparable, that the metaphor clings to metaphysical conception as a linguistic shadow that philosophy cannot simply clean itself of (cf. Derrida 1974).

References

Benveniste, E. (1971), *Problems in General Linguistics*, Miami: UP.

Derrida, J. (1971), "Le puits et la pyramide. Introduction à la sémiologie du Hegel," *Marges de la philosophie*, Paris: Editions de Minuit: pp. 79–127.

Derrida, J. (1974): "White Mythology: The Metaphor in the Text of Philosophy," *New Literary History* 6/1: 5–74.

Derrida, J. (1978), *Writing and Difference*, London: Routledge.

Derrida, J. (2005), *On Touching: Jean-Luc Nancy*, Stanford: UP.

Descartes, R. (1960), *Discourse on Method and Meditations*, New York: Liberal Arts Press.

Dolar, M. (2006), *Prozopopeja*, Ljubljana: Društvo za teoretsko psihoanalizo.

Dolar, M. (2008), "Touching Ground," *Filozofski vestnik* 29/2: 79–100.

Hegel, G.W.F. (1988), *Aesthetics: Lectures on Fine Arts*, Oxford: Clarendon Press.

Hegel, G.W.F. (2000), *Enciclopedia delle scienze filosofice*, Milano: Bompiani.

Hegel, G.W.F. (2001), *Phenomenology of the Mind*, Blackmask online.

Jakobson, R. (1978), *Six Lectures on Sound and Meaning*, Cambridge: UP.

Jakobson, R. (1990), *On Language*. Harvard: UP.

Lacan, J. (1975), *Encore. Livre XX*, Paris: Seuil.

Lacan, J. (1991), *Le séminaire XVII : L'enverse de la psychoanalyse*, Paris: Seuil.

Lacan, J. (2005), *Le séminaire XXIII : Le sinthome*, Paris: Seuil.

Marx, K. (2015), *Capital: A Critique of Political Economy*, Moscow: Progress.

Milner, J.-C. (2002), *Le Périple structural*, Paris: Editions du Seuil.

Nancy, J.-L. (1992), *Corpus*, Paris: Métailié.

Nancy, J.-L. (2001), *The Speculative Remark: One of Hegel's Bons Mots*, Stanford: UP.

Nancy, J.-L. (2003), *Noli me tangere*, Paris: Bayard Editions.

Saussure, F. (1966), *Course in General Linguistics*, NY & Toronto & London: McGraw-Hill.

Stewart, J. (2017), *Hegel and the Egyptian Religion as a Mystery or Enigma: The Inner and the Outer*, Radcliffe Institute for Advanced Study, Harvard University, Cambridge, Mass., USA, pp.54–63.

Tomšič, S. (2015), *The Capitalist Unconscious*, London & New York: Verso.

Zupančič, A. (2006), "When surplus enjoyment meets surplus value," in: Clemens, J. & Grigg, R. (eds.), *Jacques Lacan and the Other side of psychoanalysis: Reflections on Seminar XVII*, Durham: Duke UP

2

The Structure of the Phonetical Touch: Unsettling the Mastery of Phonology Over Phonetics

Tomi Bartole

Introduction

This chapter approaches the traditional divide between phonetics and phonology through a haptic perspective. This divide could be said to be traditional both in the sense of being historically long-lasting and uninterrupted,[1] and in the sense of being grounded in the traditional dichotomy of the physical and the abstract. According to this dichotomy, phonetics is defined as the language science that deals with the anatomical and physical aspects of speech production, while phonology is defined as the language science that deals with the abstract aspect of language that is meaning production.

In addressing this divide I employ a haptic approach—an approach that is informed by the manifold forms of touch (Paterson 2007: ix). This approach is not, however, exogenous to linguistics. The history of linguistics reveals in fact that haptics is present throughout, although at different times and in different places its significance differs.[2] By attending to haptic aspects in the history of linguistics it is possible, I argue, to evince a haptic history of linguistics that at times informed and was informed by more general discussion on haptics. The goal of the chapter is not limited, however, to either the elicitation of haptic features or to the development of a haptic approach in itself, but extends the employment of the haptic approach in the unsettlement of the traditional relation between phonetics and phonology.

Such unsettlement could not but begin with the work of Roman Jakobson who portrayed this relation in its most radical sense as the mastery of phonology over phonetics, and conversely, the subjugation of phonetics to phonology.

Another reason to begin with Jakobson lies in his describing of phonetics and phonology as two different kinds of touch: the one physical, the other abstract, one occurring at the points of articulations,[3] the other occurring between signifier (sound) and signified (meaning). Between the phonetical and phonological touch thus conceived lies an unsurmountable gap. They could be said not to touch each other. In order to unsettle the traditional relation between phonetics and phonology I propose to interrogate the possibility of this apparent impossibility, namely, how these two kinds of touch might come to touch each other. Formulated this way, the question would seem to commit us to think of ways in which a physical touch would transcend its own material limits and come to touch the abstract. I would argue, however, for an alternative, more productive, way to proceed. While Jakobson does evince the difference between the two touches in terms of the physical and the abstract, he also grounds the difference between the two on the level of structure. An attentive reading of Jakobson in fact reveals that the physical/abstract divide is grounded in a more fundamental one: the presence/absence of a structure, where only a structure, and this is key, allows for differentiation. It is differentiation in fact that, according to Jakobson, allows phonemes, the smallest units bearing signifying value (Jakobson 1978: 3), to differentiate between meanings. But while for Jakobson phonology deals with phonemes, which are elements of a structure that allows for differentiation, phonetics, and their respective touches occurring in articulatory processes, on the other hand, lacks such structure and with it the possibility for differentiation and meaning creation. The corollary is that language can structure touch—language can differentiate and categorize different kinds of touch, and the existence of different kinds of touch is already predicated upon the fact of being approached through language (differentiation and language are just the same thing). I take my cue from this last of Jakobson's differentiations between phonetics and phonology to rearticulate the research question from how a physical touch might come into contact with an abstract one, to the question of whether the physical phonetic touch has a structure.

I attend to this question by way of revisiting recent research in phonetics. Firstly, I present the implication of research in phonetics that has been explicitly informed by kinaesthesia—the sensation of movement of body and limbs relating to sensations originating in muscles, tendons, and joints (Paterson 2007: ix). Secondly, I analyze the most recent phonological research in prosody, which includes features such as pitch, length, prominence, and timbre, because this has come to appreciate kinematic implications in meaning production and due to the fact that prosody implies a prosodic structure, which will serve as a clue in identifying the structure of the phonetical touch. I go on to address the question of what kind of structure a prosodic structure is, a question that has not been articulated before, and in answering the question I elicit the structure of the phonological touch, which I show to be dissimilar from the structure employed by Jakobson in the analysis of phonemes, but nonetheless allows for differentiation and thus meaning production. And finally, I conclude with the thought and suggestion that if touch does indeed structure language this is because touch is differential, that is, capable of, like the other two minimal material entities of language (phoneme and grapheme), producing differences.

Roman Jakobson and the mastery of phonology

Roman Jakobson's deliverance of the *Six Lectures on Sound and Meaning* in 1942–43 at the *Ecole Libre des Hautes Etudes* in New York, published in 1976, came to significantly influence French structuralism.[4] The aim of the *Lectures*, as the title suggests, was to address the question of the relation between the signifier (sound) and the signified (meaning). In particular, Jakobson aimed at revising Ferdinand de Saussure's thesis that the relation between these two is an arbitrary one, motivated only by social convention (see Saussure 1959: 65–70). On the other hand, Jakobson claimed that the relation is a necessary one, specifying that: "the only necessary relation between the two aspects [signifer/signified][5] is here an association based on contiguity, and thus on an external relation, whereas association based on resemblance (on an internal relation) is only occasional." (Jakobson 1978: 112)

A reading informed by haptics, that is, a perspective that is informed by the manifold forms of touch, allows us to gain a novel perspective into Jakobson's thesis as well as into the relation between phonetics and phonology. A haptic approach suggests that Jakobson's differentiation between phonetics and phonology could be read as the difference between two kinds of touch: phonetics is figured as a physical, simple, and meaningless touch, while phonology is figured as an abstract, complex, and meaningful touch.

Phonetical touch could be straightforwardly identified in Jakobson's description of phonetics: "Phonetics seeks to deduce sounds of our language from the various kinds of contact between the tongue and the palate, the teeth, lips, etc." (Jakobson 1978: 14). In this description, phonetical touch features as the manifold contacts occurring in the vocal tract at the places of articulation.

Phonological touch, on the other hand, could be identified in Jakobson's revision of Saussure's thesis, when he says that the relation between signifer and signified is "an association based on contiguity" (Jakobson 1978: 112). Although contiguity encompasses the meanings of bordering and being in contact, Jakobson's use of the concept belongs to psychology and thus includes the idea that ideas, memories, and experiences are linked by frequent experiences. However, once Jakobson applies this psychological concept to linguistics he comes to transform it through and into the implicit suggestion of a contact between the signifer and the signified.[6]

Jakobson could be said to reprimand phonetics for focusing (too much) on the contacts at the points of articulations (Jakobson 1978: 14) while suggesting instead a focus on the phoneme as the differentiating function in the phonological system of a given language, that is based on the contacts between signifiers and signified. As Jakobson (1978: 109) puts it: "Speech sounds cannot be understood, delimited, classified and explained except in the light of the tasks which they perform in language." In other words, Jakobson suggests that the physical, simple, and meaningless touches between articulators (phonetics) should be subordinated to the abstract, complex, and meaningful touches between signifer and signified (phonology). Or else, language structures touch, but touch does not structure language.

A haptic approach to Jakobson's theory reveals that touch and touching are significant categories employed in linguistics and that the two kinds of touch identified are hierarchically conceived. Through this hierarchy Jakobson institutes a boundary between phonetical and phonological contacts that is only mediated through the mastery of phonology and the subordination of phonetics. To put it into a haptic discourse, it could be said that for Jakobson touches found in phonetics and those found in phonology do not touch among themselves—they are incommensurable because phonetical touches are physical, simple, and meaningless while phonological touches are abstract, complex, and meaningful.

Throughout the *Lectures* Jakobson not only incessantly attacks phonetics, but does so because he believes the definition of phonetics is precisely what is wrong with it: "Speech sounds cannot be understood, delimited, classified and explained except in the light of the tasks which they perform in language." (Jakobson 1978: 109). His vision was to subordinate motor, acoustic, and auditory descriptions to structural analysis, which phonetics would hold an auxiliary position in relation to. The description of articulatory processes, according to Jakobson, should be seen only in the function of language where speech sounds are carriers of meaning (Jakobson 1978: 25, 109).

For Jakobson the paramount linguistic function of speech sound is differentiation. Phonology is endowed with differentiation because its object of study is phonemes—perceptually distinct units of sound in a specified language that distinguish the meaning of words (Jakobson 1978: 27–28, 32). Phonemes reside in a phonological system of reciprocal oppositions of a given language, in which different uses, that is to say difference produced by the system called structure, serve to discriminate between meanings (Jakobson 1978: 74, 85). For example, the signifer *cat* /kæt/ differs from the signifier *mat* /mæt/ in that the phoneme /k/ differs from /m/. According to Jakobson (1978: 85): "The phoneme is not to be identified with the sound, yet nor is it external to the sound; it is necessarily present in the sound, being both inherent in it and superposed upon it: it is what remains invariant behind the variations."

By placing phones (speech sounds) inside the phonological system of reciprocal oppositions, and thus turning them into phonemes, Jakobson no longer grounds the classification of speech sounds on phonetical description of anatomy and physics, but rather on the level of the signifier (Jakobson 1978: 72), that is, on the level of relationships between the physical forms of signs. Phonetics is called upon only a posteriori to describe, following the above example, the sound /k/ in *cat* as a voiceless velar stop and the sound /m/ in *mat* as a bilabial nasal. For Jakobson thus the subordination of phonetics to phonology stems from the fact that phonetics does not possess the linguistic function of differentiation and this is because, for Jakobson, phonetics does not have a structure in the sense that phonology does. The divide between phonetics and phonology, which was previously characterized as the divide between physical and abstract, is revealed to be a divide marked by the incapacity (phonetics) and capacity (phonology) for differentiation, which is at the same time an index of absence and presence respectively, of a structure that allows for such differentiation to occur.

The characteristics ascribed to the two kinds of touch are, however, amenable to the absence of a structure in the case of phonetical touch and the presence of a structure in the case of the phonological touch. This last point suggests that in order to recapture the contact point between phonetics and phonology, and their two kinds of touches, one should not proceed by way of demonstrating how physical touch, for example, transcends its own physicality and thus enters the sphere of abstractness, but rather by way of showing that the phonetical touch has a structure of its own, and further, that this structure has a relationship to signification comparable to that of the phonological touch.

Speaking is touching

Various forms of touch have been present throughout the history of phonetics, although at different times and in different places their significances differed. Kinaesthesia, one of the haptic forms, has recently vehemently entered into research in phonetics.[7] Kinaesthesia is the sensation of movement of body and limbs relating to sensations originating in muscles, tendons, and joints (Patterson 2007: ix) that occurs due to the interrelation of interposed layers of sensibilities throughout the body (Aristotle 2001; Merleau-Ponty 1964, 2002; Merleau-Ponty, Lefort and Lingis 1968).[8] Kinaesthesia thus represents a haptic complexity that encompasses beside a multiplicity of touches throughout the body also the motility of the body and the motility of touches. Jakobson's phonetical touch assumes in kinaesthesia the form of a series of touches registered as multilayered bodily sensations.

Loucks and Nil (2001) have recently conducted an assessment of physiological and behavioral evidence for the role of kinaesthesia in speech production by way of reviewing about a hundred researches. From the outset the authors recognize that speech production entails complex goal-oriented movements, which invariably involve the coordination of multiple joints or articulators. In order to make sense of these they foregrounded kinaesthesia as they believe this is potentially significant for theoretical questions in speech production research. It is quite soon revealed, however, that kinaesthesia represents no master descriptive or explanatory device of articulatory processes and that kinaesthesia itself is in need of description and explanation (Loucks and Nil 2001: 153).

The authors thus begin with a rather general thesis about kinaesthesia, which was first voiced by researchers gathered around McCloskey and Prochazka (1994) who, although opposed and contrasted with each other in matters of how kinaesthesia works, could at least agree on one point: "/o/ne can only control what one senses" (McCloskey and Prochazka 1994, Loucks and Nil 2001: 152, 165) or in another form, "one can voluntarily control only what one consciously perceives" (McCloskey and Prochazka 1994: 69). Kinaesthesia becomes then a vehicle to propose questions pertaining to the complexity of speech production at the base of which resides the question of voluntary, and thus conscious, control as speech production's condition of possibility.

Loucks and Nil are aware of the fact that what is known about kinaesthesia mainly derives from research with limbs, while kinaesthesia in speech production represents a specific form and a newer field of investigation. They concede that kinaesthesia is an integral factor in motor control, and while evidence for the role of kinaesthesia in speech motor control is more preliminary, it is reasonable to infer an important role for kinaesthesia based on the explicit inclusion of kinaesthetic information in theories of motor control and speech production (Loucks and Nil 2001: 161). The question of the importance of kinaesthesia in speech production is, however, quickly sidestepped by the question of how kinaesthesia works in speech production.

As exposed above, Loucks and Nil liken speech production to motor control (Loucks and Nil 2001: 161–162) and thus the question of how speech is produced is rearticulated as to how one controls motions. They refuse to explain motility's control according to either open-loop[9] or closed-loop[10] models of command, but rather suggest that both models are integrated and mediated by a "bridge." The so-called bridge is a feed-forward system, in which kinaesthetic information on current articulatory position and velocity (initial conditions) is used, to adjust upcoming motor commands to adapt ongoing movements to changes in the movement context. The feed-forward system is the predictive aspect and role of kinaesthesia that currently holds in kinaesthetic research the most possibility for inclusion of kinaesthetic information in theories/models of skilled movement, motor learning, and movement disorders (Loucks and Nil 2001: 162).

The predictive role, however, requires from the authors a new model on the base of which the predictiveness of kinaesthesia could be described. While they suggest there are many models with the help of which this could be achieved, they nevertheless propose the internal model concept, which consists of a neural representation that mimics the input/output characteristics of the motor system, allowing for predictive control over movement. This model in turn consists of a forward internal model, which predicts the outcome of a movement, and of an inverse internal model, which predicts the motor command needed to make the movement (Loucks and Nil 2001: 162).[11]

On this aspect it is possible to elicit three key points: hearing is critical in learning not words alone, but whole sentences, which represents speech proper; the closed-loop feedback allows for multi-modality that allows hearing to play a role in motor control; and multi-modality allows for desired acoustic output or auditory percept to be integrated into the motor control system.

This last point is key to understanding kinaesthesia as motor control in speech production because Loucks and Nil further claim, that the desired acoustic output/auditory percept carries within itself information on articulatory positions, that is, kinaesthetic information. Kinaesthetic articulatory information is no longer held solely in people's heads, nor in their bodies, but this knowledge is also encompassed within speech sounds themselves. Not only do speech sounds carry meaning as Jakobson would have it (1978: 25), but also the knowledge for their own production. As a corollary, the knowledge encompassed in speech sounds is inalienable from speech production in which speech sounds are made. It would not be inaccurate therefore, to say that the kinaesthetic knowledge in speech sounds is produced in the movements between articulatory (and) kinaesthetic motions and the speech sounds, but once these motions are stopped the knowledge appears to reside in the speech sounds, which are presented as the locus-objective of desired and thus goal-oriented movements (see Loucks and Nil 2001: 153) founded in the control of motility. According to this view, motility is lost to control, precisely when the latter manages to make sense of the former.[12]

At this point I return to Jakobson who emphasizes that linguistic sounds have two aspects, the motor and the acoustic, and when asking himself whether the immediate goal of the phonatory act is either the acoustic or the motor phenomenon, he replies that it is "obviously [...] the acoustic phenomenon which the speaker aims at producing, and it is only the acoustic phenomenon which is directly accessible to the listener" (Jakobson 1978: 5).

What is in the acoustic aspect of sounds that gives information to kinaesthetic articulation? What does one "hear" in speech sounds that, in the selfsame process, makes articulation possible? How does one access articulatory kinaesthetic knowledge through acoustic information? I suggest Jakobson provides a clue to where to look for an answer. For Jakobson speech sounds do not possess meaning in themselves, but it is rather the different uses that they are put to that allow one to discriminate between meanings (Jakobson 1978: 74, 85). In foregrounding the phoneme as the quanta of language—the smallest units bearing signifying value (Jakobson 1978: 3), which is operative inside the phonological system of oppositions—meaning is the elicitation of certain meaning-relations (ex. *cat*) and the foreclosing of others (ex. *mat*). This is why for Jakobson the phonemes, the sounds that are able to distinguish words, are neither to be identified with sounds nor are they external to them. They are present in sounds because they are both inherent in them and superposed upon them, meaning, phonemes are what remains invariant behind sound variations (Jakobson 1978: 85).

I suggest that Jakobson's clue for finding articulatory kinaesthetic knowledge in the acoustic aspect of speech sounds is relations, and more recent research suggests that the relations that inform kinaesthetic knowledge are to be looked for on a supra-segmental level, the level of speech proper, that is, on the phonological level of prosody.

Prosody, or towards the structure of phonetical touch

Prosody is a phonological term that refers to the supra-segmental structure of the utterance and it is commonly known as the musical aspect of speech as it includes phenomena such as pitch, duration, and loudness. Prosody encodes prominence, which serves to highlight important or new information and it is also used for rhythmic purposes, as well as phrasal organization, which serves to group words together into appropriate chunks, as in the examples: "She knew David thought about the present," and "She knew, David thought, about the present." Significantly, these chunks are used both by the listeners and the speakers for language processing, that is, in conveying, as well as in deducing the meaning of utterances (Krivokapić 2014: 1–2).

Krivokapić's and others' research on prosody that I address here is informed by articulatory phonology (henceforth AP) (Browman and Goldstein 1986, 1992, 1995), a linguistic theory that identifies theoretical discrepancies between phonetics and phonology and aims to unify them by way of treating these as low- and high-dimensional descriptions of a single system in which the physical system (phonetics) constrains the underlying abstract system (phonology), thus making the units of control at the abstract planning level the same as those at the physical level.

AP establishes a relationship between phonetics and phonology dissimilar from that of Jakobson's. While AP is an actual attempt to bring phonetics and phonology together, Jakobson has never aimed to do this. AP, on the other hand, ascribes to phonetics a prominent role.[13] The role of phonetics is in fact to constrain or limit the abstract level, thus delimiting the conditions of possibility of the whole system. The physical limits simultaneously stand for the converging points between the abstract level of planning articulations and the physical level of possible execution.

In AP the plan of utterance is formatted as a gestural score, which provides the input to a physically based model of speech production, where gestures are phonologically relevant events of the vocal tract. There are three types of gestures: constriction, tone, and clock-slowing gestures. I focus on the latest because these invoke, as I show below, Jakobson's relational phonemes. The prosodic spatio-temporal effects, such as lengthening, strengthening, and stops, differ from constriction and tone gestures in a significant way—these are effects non-related to specific articulators, but their concreteness consists in the modulation of spatial and temporal properties of articulatory gestures, including constriction and tone (Saltzman et al. 2008). It could be said that clock-slowing gestures are devoid of their own substance and exist only in the effects they bring about. As such, these gestures are not identifiable with the articulators—and this is really the point of resemblance with Jakobson's relational phonemes: clock-slowing gestures reside within the articulators, but are not parts of them.[14] The clock-slowing gestures could be said, similarly to phonemes in relation to sounds, to transcend articulatory gestures, while simultaneously being immanent to them.

Although prosody is expressed in speech through tonal and temporal properties, recent studies have found a fourth set of articulatory gestures, namely, body gestures. Research in prosody shows in fact that manual and oral gestures lengthen under prominence and at prosodic boundary,[15] indicating that the effects of prosodic structure extend beyond the vocal tract to include body movement (Krivokapić, Tiede and Tyrone 2017). Although body movement could be seen as a mere appendix to articulation, that is, a non-essential feature, as far as articulation could be said to be achieved without it, researchers have suggested instead that speech and body gestures "act jointly" or are "tightly integrated" in forming a prosodic boundary.[16] Such a suggestion is based on experimental observations of co-occurrence and exact coordination of speech, body gestures and the effect of prosodic structure on such coordination and, most importantly, the durations of body gestures (temporal lengthening).[17] This finding is articulated through the idea of extendability of the effects of prosodic structure beyond the vocal tract to manual gestures (Krivokapić 2014: 7; Krivokapić, Tiede & Tyrone 2015, 2017: 1–5).

The idea of the extension of the prosodic structure reaching beyond the vocal tract to include body movement is informed, however, not by kinaesthetic research, but rather by kinematic, which is grounded in classical mechanics and also called the geometry of motion. The premises of classical mechanics allow the separation of articulatory movements from bodily movements as if the vocal tract were not part of the latter. In the next step, the two motile areas of the body are conjoined through the capacity of the prosodic structure to extend.

The mediating function of the prosodic structure thus appears in the form of an extension—an extension, however, that is always preceded by the geometry of motion and its precept of *partes extra partes*, i.e. to exist alongside, beyond each other, exterior to each other, and most importantly, without interdependence. In kinematics, geometry is applied metaphorically to bodily motions, which allows the instantiation of corresponding areas of motility such as the vocal and the body (which excludes the vocal).

If the abstract level controls the physical and if the physical level provides the limits of the former, which limits also stand for the corresponding points between the abstract and the physical level where control is enacted, it follows that the function of control performed by the abstract level is blind and fundamentally grounded in a hidden hapto-centrism (see Derrida 2000). The extendability of the abstract level as a function of control is thus a capacity created by the suppression of kinaesthesia, as a function of control through the contacts of sensibilities in the bodily movements.

The abstract level of prosodic structure, through its capacity to extend, unites geometrically established areas of the motive body as different parts interact differently among themselves. It comes as no surprise then that the prosodic structure is defined as a hierarchical structure. I would suggest, however, that a kinaesthetically informed approach, instead of a kinematic one, to prosody, could evince a different kind of structure from that of a hierarchy.

Milner notes that any kind of structuralism is founded on the premise that speech is structured and has a structure. In all its forms structuralism has always tended, as a science, to reduction and minimalism in that it strived to reduce the amount of properties of an element of the system to a bare minimum (Milner 2003: 127–128).[18]

Although Jakobson, for example, reduced all speech sounds to the phoneme, his structuralism is not radically minimalist because grounded in a two-dimensional system incorporating the paradigmatic (substitution) and syntagmatic (positioning) axis. This system is usually expressed in a table and the properties of an element are determined by both axes (see Milner 2003: 137). Neither is a prosodic structure minimalist as this is hierarchically organized (Argyro et al. 2014: 62–63). The utterances are hierarchically phrased and the lower units are grouped into smaller phrases which in turn are grouped into larger phrases through several levels (Hayes 1989: 201).[19]

For AP the low-dimensional descriptions (phonetics) represent the limits of high-dimensional descriptions (phonology) and thus simultaneously the limits of the whole hierarchical prosodic structure. If the physical (phonetics) is thus conceived in terms of a delimited range of possibilities for the abstract then the physical is cut open to produce a temporal space called abstractness. On the level of kinematics, for example, the bodily areas of motility are dissected in order for the abstract level of prosodic structure to extend into and come to encompass them all.

On the level of planning articulations, AP conceives of the speaker as a planner aware of its (physical) articulatory possibilities who after planning at an abstract level executes his or her plans by way of returning to the physical one. Coincidentally, prosodic research and phonetic research informed by kinaesthesia are captivated by the idea of prediction or control, and by the activity of making predictions through the formulation of theories and models. In the same process of studying linguistic phenomena linguists tend to construe the speaking subject in the image of their own linguistic science.

Kinematics is a body geometrically broken apart that is only reassembled by the abstract level that is, paradoxically, born from the body's fissures and cracks. The very possibility of the abstract level stems from a first intervention of the geometrical abstractness, where abstractness is a feature of language par excellence, into the body that breaks this segmented parts. This is true both for the areas of motility (vocal, body) and for the general motility that engender sounds. Unlike kinematics, the haptic form of kinaesthesia does not allow for such breaks to occur, because this does not consist of distinct areas of movement, but rather of a continuous bodily movement of sensibilities. Most telling in this regard is Jakobson's amusement at the discovery of X-rays and their application to phonetics. When the workings of the vocal apparatus were made finally visible he saw the proof that the distinction between positional and transitional sounds is untenable because all sounds were in fact transitional, that is, they were constantly in movement (Jakobson 1978: 11). This did not prevent Jakobson, however, from continuing to rely on the phoneme as the true principle of language organization, in which he followed Saussure who predicted the results brought by the X-rays in saying that: "Even if we could record all the movements of the mouth and larynx in producing a chain of sounds it would still be impossible to discover the subdivisions in this sequence of articulatory movements; we would not know where one sound began and where another ended." (Saussure in Jakobson 1978: 10)

I would not agree with Saussure because what it takes to discover the beginnings and endings of sounds is to listen, and research in prosody has shown that this is precisely what the speaker, as well as the listener, do. I take, however, my cue from Saussure's expression *chain of sounds* to foreground what I claim to be the structure of a kinaesthetically informed prosody, which I suggest to conceive as a phonatory act that is limited not by the physical level, as in the case of kinematics, but by the actual speaking act, in which length, internal boundaries, and duration are delimited by the spoken sentence. In this view the structure assumes a minimal form of the chain of sounds delimited by the sentence as act. The prosodic phonetical touches are spatiotemporal effects, such as lengthening, strengthening, and stops—effects of the structure, which concreteness consists in the modulation of spatial and temporal properties, that is to say, kinaesthetic properties of articulatory gestures that include constriction and tone. Such a chain would be commensurable with the spoken sentence and minimally conceived as the chain of elements that composes it, where changes in the former bring about changes in the latter and vice versa. In short, the chain is one-dimensional, short, concluded in itself, and unstratified (see Milner 2003: 138–139).

Articulatory action is then motion and motion is kinaesthetic motion, but also the sentence is structured as a chain of motions. Kinaesthetic motion activates the differential property of the elements by actively making distinctions through the form of hiatuses[20] and junctures. In the case of the hiatus, each and every last element in the chain sentence (every element is at least once the last in the series), actively makes distinctions, which affects the elements and the chain as a whole retroactively. In the case of junctures, elements in the chain sentence fail to make (expected) distinctions.

Conclusion

Research in prosody makes ample use of controlled experiments in which the subjects are given in advance written sentences with punctuation that they are supposed to read—"stimulus sentences" (see Byrd, Krivokapić and Lee 2006; Katsika et al. 2014; Krivokapić and Byrd 2012; Krivokapić 2006; Krivokapić et al. 2016).[21] Stimulus sentences have the form of planned acts that are imposed upon the subjects, which create the analytical situation to observe the executions of articulatory plans. Such analytical situations, however, do not allow for freedom of expression and fail to be properly appreciated as significant linguistic aspects, because given sentences are closed in themselves and given in advance to be meticulously and consciously studied and trained in before execution.

In the sentence, "If the body is the house of the spirit, then I (being 165 centimeters tall), am a studio," notice how *house* ceases to stand for a building for human habitation, especially one that consists of a ground floor and one or more upper storeys. Instead, *house* comes to stand for home or in general a category that subsumes all habitations including small flats, workrooms and ateliers that are not even exclusive to humans only.[22] In regard to failure, consider the following example of a person saying, "Tu es ma mère" (You are my mother) and "Tuer ma mère" (To kill my mother). A slight difference in articulatory space and kinaesthetic temporality— /ty/ /ɛ/ and /tɥe/—brings about a radical transformation in the meaning the speaker intended to convey.[23]

At the same time, these kinds of failures radically transform the analytical categories of intentionality and speech planning employed both in research in prosody as well as in phonetics informed by kinaesthetics because kinaesthetic articulations come to be embedded, as Jakobson suggested in a somewhat different fashion, in a structure that allows for differentiation and thus for meaning production. If for the two mentioned language sciences intentionality and speech planning were questions pertaining to the possibility and modus of articulation, and were conceived as abstract devices that allow speakers to execute possible articulations, now intentionality and speech planning refer to the possibility and modus of conveying meanings and are conceived as effects (hiatus/juncture) of the chain of kinaesthetic movements.

Phonetical and phonological touches do indeed touch each other, but they do not touch each other directly. They touch indirectly through their perspective structures and their perspective ways of differentiation by way of which they at once create and subvert meaning. This is why contacts between phonetical and phonological touch could be ultimately registered on the level of speech and discourse.

The quest to elicit the structure of phonetical touches in the end revealed itself to have the form of a recovery. I initially departed from Jakobson's suggestion of phonetics's subjugation to phonology—the former needing to reside in the function of language where phonemes are carriers of meaning (Jakobson 1978: 25, 109), because only these adhere to the paramount linguistic functions of differentiation (Jakobson 1978: 27–28, 32). Then, by showing that phonatory touches, conceived kinaesthetically as a chain of touches that produce effects amenable to hiatuses and junctions, have all the making of phonemes because having a structure, I have returned to Jakobson's very precepts. Through the recovery of the structure of phonetical touch, however, these precepts ceased to stand in for the function of phonology's mastery over phonetics, and instead they rather acquired the function of elicitory devices because the identification of the structure of phonetical touches really was an elicitation through Jakobson's work. He himself pointed out the transitivity of phonetical touches in his commentary upon the visualization of articulatory processes made possible by the X-rays and he himself brought about Saussure's citation in which the latter highlighted the "chain of sounds".

Notes

1   Tillman says that the word "phonetic" was used for the first time, in the modern sense, in 1797 by the Danish Egyptologist George Zoega who used the adjective

phoneticus in connection with the question as to what sound-forms in ancient Egypt's hieroglyphic signs on the obelisks stood for (Tillman 1995: 401).

2 For example, in the first millennia BC Pānini employed touch categories to describe the production of certain sounds (Kemp 1995: 371–372). In *Poetics* Aristotle described speech sounds without vowels with the term *prosbole* (having contact) (Aristotle 1456b20–1457a30; see also Kemp 1995: 372). Early modern inspections of speech sounds were done through tactility, like touching the Adam's apple, and in the nineteenth century devices were used to translate tactile perception into visual representations (Tillman 1995: 404, 414–415).

3 The point of contact between active articulators and a passive location.

4 Lévi-Strauss, the progenitor of structural anthropology, was also amongst the audience.

5 The linguistic sign is for Saussure a two-sided entity encompassing the signifier and the signified that recall each other (Saussure 1959: 66).

6 The form of this contact or rather contacts could be identified, according to Jakobson's articulation, in repetition.

7 Although kinaesthesia in the modern sense is a term that appeared in the late nineteenth century, its implications could already be appreciated in the relations between internal and external articulatory processes, on the one hand, and breath and voice, one the other hand, evinced by Pānini, an ancient Sanskrit linguist, grammarian, revered scholar in Hinduism, and father of Indian linguistics who dealt with phonetics in the first millennia BC (Kemp 1995: 371).

8 In *De Anima* (*Pery Psyche*, "On the Soul"), Aristotle wrote that among the "five senses touch seems to be the most enigmatic", because the medium, the object and the organ of touch do not correspond to the schema of the other senses. Through a series of thought experiment he comes to refuse the schema used to analyze the other four senses and proposes instead that the body, as well as the objects that come into contact with it, be conceived as multiply layered and that the heart should be conceived as the organ of touch, and also of all other senses. The complication of the limit of touch, as in wearing a glove, makes touch recede into the flesh as the medium. The proper medium of touch is not detached from the body as it is in other senses, but is part of the body itself, the flesh, which connects the surface, the skin, with interiority, with the inner sense, the seat of sense, its heart (cf. Aristotle 2011; see also Dolar 2008: 85). In short, for Aristotle, touch belongs to the flesh, *sarx*, as opposed to *soma*, the body (Dolar 2008: 84–85). Merleau-Ponty's notion of *la chair*, the flesh, as opposed to the "body", is a very Aristotelian move to start with, although Aristotle is never quoted, and rarely mentioned, while Dillon (1997: 146) claims that Merleau-Ponty appropriates the notion of flesh from Sartre.

9 The open-loop system is a control system in which an input alters the output, but the output has no feedback loop and therefore no effect on the input.

10 The closed-loop system is a control system in which an input alters the output, where the output has a feedback loop and thus an effect on the input.

11 The strongest evidence for the predictive capacity of internal models comes from grip force studies, while several current computational speech models also posit that internal models are operative in the predictive control of speech production (Loucks and Nil 2001: 162).

12 In the *Theaetetus*, Plato highlights a similar paradox when exploring perception through the case of colors. For Plato color is not something, but rather a motion occurring between the touching (strikes against) of the eye and the touched (struck against) of the colored object. The problem surfaces when one wants to describe things-movements, because: "/i/n order that we may not put a stop to them [all things] in the speech, every answer becomes similarly correct – to say 'This is so' and 'This is not s'. But one must not even say 'so', for 'so' would no longer be in motion, nor in turn 'not so', for not even this is a motion. [...] But those who speak this speech must set down some different language [...]" (Plato 183 A, B, 1.50–1.511). For the implications of touch and motility, see Moder's contribution in this book (Chapter 4).

13 Notwithstanding the "low/high dimensional descriptions of a single system," which otherwise hints at a dichotomy that has not been overcome yet.

14 For sake of comparison I propose here Jakobson's words concerning the relation between phonemes and sounds: "The phoneme is not to be identified with the sound, yet nor is it external to the sound; it is necessarily present in the sound, being both inherent in it and superposed upon it: it is what remains invariant behind the variations" (Jakobson (1978: 85). Moreover, prosody is similar to Jakobson's phonemes in that prosody also differs from language to language (Krivokapić, Tiede and Tyrone 2017: 1).

15 Prosodic boundaries are pauses or breaks in speech. The International Phonetic Alphabet has symbols for a minor | and for a major prosodic break ‖, which in terms of orthography and punctuation could be rendered, assuming these are used to represent prosody rather than grammatical structure, with the comma and full stop respectively.

16 See Goran Vranešević's contribution in this book (Chapter 5) for a discussion about the coextensiveness of the body and the signifier.

17 Research has demonstrated that the close connection between the production and perception of prosodic-boundary strength shows that listeners are able to perceive subtle differences choreographed in the articulatory kinematics (Krivokapić and Byrd 2012).

18 Milner's book, *Le Périple Structural: Figures et paradgime* has not been translated into English. I make use of the Slovenian translation.

19 In this sense the attempt of AP to overcome the phonetics/phonology dichotomy is amenable to Jakobson's mastery of phonology over phonetics.

20 Hiatus is a term also used in prosody for a break between two vowels coming together but not in the same syllable, as in *the ear* and *cooperate*.

21 Subjects usually receive instructions of this kind: "During the experiment, please read the question silently, and the answers aloud. Please read carefully, paying attention to punctuation. Below are the sentences you will be reading. Please familiarise yourself with the question and answer. You can do so by reading them aloud or to yourself." (Krivokapić and Byrd 2012: 339).

22 It is not by coincidence that I have proposed a joke as vignette. I have suggested elsewhere (Bartole 2011) that Freud touching the foreheads of his patients during hypnosis had a structure and effect comparable to those found in jokes by Freud himself.

23 From a psychoanalytical perspective, for example, it is not even important whether the subject "actually meant" to kill the mother, because by the simple fact of saying it, he or she already said more than he or she wanted to and thus pointed at the unconscious desire. See Mirt Komel's contribution in this book (Chapter 1) and Komel 2016: 122–123 for a Lacanian take on the same question.

References

Aristotle (1991), "Poetics", in J. Barnes (ed.), *The Complete Works of Aristotle, The Revised Oxford Translation, Volume Two*, Princeton: Princeton UP.

Aristotle (2011), *De Anima*. Newburyport: Focus Publishing.

Bartole, T. (2011), "Freud on Touch: Thinking Sexuality in Anthropology," *Esercizi Filosofici* 6: 376–387.

Browman, C. P. and L. M. Goldstein (1986), "Towards an Articulatory Phonology," *Phonology Yearbook* 3, 219–252.

Browman, C. P. and L. M. Goldstein (1992), "Articulatory Phonology: An overview," *Phonetica* 49, 155–180.

Browman, C. P. and L. M. Goldstein (1995), "Dynamics and Articulatory Phonology," In R. F. Port and T. Van Gelder (eds.), *Mind as Motion: Explorations in the Dynamics of Cognition*, 175–193, Cambridge: The MIT Press.

Byrd, D., J. Krivokapić and S. Lee (2006), "How Far, How Long: On the Temporal Scope of Prosodic Boundary Effects," *The Journal of the Acoustical Society of America* 120 (3): 1589–1599.

Derrida, J. (2005 [2000]), *On Touching: Jean-Luc Nancy*, Stanford: Stanford UP.

Dillon, M. C. (1997), *Merleau-Ponty's Ontology*, Evanston: Northwestern UP.

Dolar, M. (2008), "Touching Ground," *Filozofski vestnik* 29 (2): 79–100.

Hayes, B. (1989), "The Prosodic Hierarchy in Meter," in P. Kiparsky and G. Youmans (eds.), *Phonetics and Phonology, Volume 1: Rhythm and Meter*, 201–259, New York: Academic Press.

Jakobson, R. (1978 [1976]), *Six Lectures on Sound and Meaning*, Cambridge, London: MIT Press.

Katsika, A., J. Krivokapić, C. Mooshammer, M. Tiede and L. Goldstein (2014), "The Coordination of Boundary Tones and its Interaction with Prominence," *Journal of Phonetics* 1 (44): 62–82.

Kemp (1995), "Phonetics: Precursors to Modern Approaches," in E. F. K. Koerner and R. E. Asher (eds.), *Concise History of the Langauge Sciences: From the Sumerians to the Cognitivists*, 371–388, Oxford, New York, Tokyo: Pergamon.

Krivokapić, J. (2006), "Prosodic Planning: Effects of Phrasal Length and Complexity on Pause Duration," *Journal of Phonetics* 35: 162–179.

Krivokapić, J. (2014), "Gestural Coordination at Prosodic Boundaries and its Role for Prosodic Structure and Speech Planning Processes," *Communicative Rhythms in Brain and Behaviour. Theme Issue of the Philosophical Transactions of the Royal Society B (Biology)* 369 (1658): 1–10.

Krivokapić, J. and D. Byrd (2012), "Prosodic Boundary Strength: An Articulatory and Perceptual Study," *Journal of Phonetics* 40 (3): 430–442.

Krivokapić, J., M. Tiede and M. Tyrone (2015), "A Kinematic Analysis of Prosodic Structure in Speech and Manual Gestures," *Proceedings of ICPhS 2015*, Glasgow, United Kingdom.

Krivokapić, J., Tiede, M., Tyrone, M., & D. Goldenberg, (2016), "Speech and Manual Gesture Coordination in a Pointing Task." *Proceedings of Speech Prosody 2016*, Boston.

Krivokapić, J., M. Tiede and M. Tyrone (2017), "A Kinematic Study of Prosodic Structure in Articulatory and Manual Gestures: Results from a Novel Method of Data Collection," *Laboratory Phonology: Journal of the Association for Laboratory Phonology* 8(1): 1–26.

Loucks, T. M. J. and L. F. de Nil (2001), "Assessing the Physiological and Behavioural Evidence for the Role of Kinaesthesia in Speech Production," *Journal of Speech-Language pathology and Audiology* 25 (3): 152–169.

Merleau-Ponty, M. (1964), *The Primacy of Perception*. Evanston, Illinois: Nortwestern UP.

Merleau-Ponty M. (2002), *Phenomenology of Perception*. London: Routledge.

Merleau-Ponty, M., C. Lefort, and A. Lingis (1968), *The Visible and the Invisible: Followed by Working Notes*, Evanston: Northwestern UP.

Milner, J.-C. (2003), *Strukturalizem: Liki in paradigme*. Ljubljana: Krtina.

Nam, H., E. Saltzman, J. Krivokapić and L. Goldstein. (2008), "Modeling the Durational Difference of Stressed vs. Unstressed Syllables," *Proceedings of the 8th Phonetic Conference of China* (PCC 2008), Beijing.

Paterson, M. (2007), *The Senses of Touch: Haptics, Affects and Technologies*, Oxford: Berg.

Plato (1984), *The Being of the Beautiful: Plato's Theaetetus, Sophist, and Statesman.* Chicago, London: University of Chicago Press.

Saussure, F. de (1959 [1893]), "Nature of the Linguistics Sign," in P. Meisel and H. Saussy (eds.), *Course in General Linguistics*, 65–70, New York: Columbia UP.

Tillmann, H. G. (1995), "Early Modern Instrumental Phonetics," in E. F. K. Koerner and R. E. Asher (eds.), *Concise History of the Langauge Sciences: From the Sumerians to the Cognitivists*, 401–416, Oxford, New York, Tokyo: Pergamon.

3

Surplus of Touch: From the Forest of Symbols to the Jungle of Touch

Karmen Šterk

Introduction

The carnal history of humanity has seen it all: touch defined as the purest and the ugliest; the substance of truth and the vehicle of magic; the realm of pleasure and the province of the uncanny. Moreover, the language of science and poetry seem to collide most viciously on the subject of touch, as if it were the human sense most open to explanation and/or to being expressed when searching for meaning. Both philosophical and artistic references to Doubting Thomas claim touch to be the only sense beyond and beneath our symbolic reality of language, making it thus quite incomprehensible.

To use the anthropological metaphor of human reality: with the senses—all but touch—anything can be easily understood and reduced to the symbolic dimension of language, a well-structured and peaceful realm of a forest of symbols, whereas touch defies symbolization and utterance, thus remaining erratic and un/touch/catch/able.

The human world is seen as a forest, docile, unperturbed, and ordered, while the jungle of touch is passionate, twitchy, and messy. Now let us see how deep the rabbit hole that connects the two worlds can take us.

Anthropological predicament

Some basic presumptions behind our introduction lead us back to ancient Greek tradition which perceived touch as the one true basic sense which could overrule and/or confirm all the other senses (cf. Komel 2016), thus making touch the only authentic bodily sense of an otherwise fictionalized language-like reality. This argument can be paralleled with the persistent dyad in the very core of anthropology; what in the human body is natural (authentic, primordial, universal) and what, on the other hand, is cultural (arbitrary, superimposed, relative)? Can we simply conceive touch as "natural", and the other senses as "cultural"?

As soon as we start arguing the aforementioned hypothesis, we encounter an epistemological predicament: every natural fact needs symbolic representation, not only in order to be recognized as having cultural existence, but primarily in order to be defined as "natural." So does the body. By the same token, every "natural" (physical) fact needs an ideal (metaphysical) justification that provides a referential frame within which both, symbolic and natural, are thought of as belonging to an all-encompassing, coherent, and homogeneous order of things. That is to say, and this is the basic epistemological premise of the anthropological predicament concerning nature, that "natural facts" (biology, corporeality, touch etc.) are concepts and not things in themselves. They are always culturally defined through science, religion, mythology, or some other cosmology, which in a given time holds the mandate over explaining why things are as they are. Natural facts are thus not really discovered, they are invented, essentialized, and defined through the use of any given (cosmological) paradigm.

If touch lies within the jurisdiction of "natural," it must thus adhere to the laws of the discursive in order to be properly grasped (say, through scientific discourse). And since what both science and common knowledge refer to when saying "natural" is in fact the sedimentation of the discursive, the dialectics of nature and culture becomes in fact an internal dialectic of culture. Culture both produces and regulates what is referred to as "nature" (cf. Zupančič 2017: 40). The province of touch as belonging to human affairs is inconceivable, simply invisible without a certain paradigm, which is, in final analysis, an ideological paradigm, and as such bound by defined political, economic, and historical constraints. This paradigm is the way ideology is inscribed into observed reality, and by which the senses get to be assigned a cognitive mode. To put it bluntly: precisely by investing them with very existence, "natural" or other, the ideology inevitably distorts the senses into something they are not. In other words: as there is no such thing as "Immaculate Conception," we cannot conceive of immaculate perception either.

Hence, when discussing "natural" facts, if presuming touch to be one of them, we are always already discussing their discursive emanations, their symbolic framework, employed in the construction of what is called a "natural" (thus presumably neutral) fact. Worse even: the so-called natural sense is so intertwined with its discursive framework and pertaining definition that the pair can only be distinguished analytically. Along the lines of different scientific disciplines (not to mention other cosmologies), we are given the possibility of various analytical structures, which inhibits us in having any non-distorted, neutral knowledge. As demonstrated by Foucault's theory of knowledge (cf. Gordon 1984), something that could be termed "neutral knowledge" does not exist; the fantasy of neutral knowledge is a product of some institutionalized power and always serves to legitimize that power itself.[1]

Humanities and social sciences are about concepts, i.e. ideas, not about things, facts, or observable ontological entities. Things are always symbolically mediated (cognitive in nature), never directly expressed (naturally sensed). Something is recognized as being a human sense only in retrospect, retroactively, when it is articulated in a preexisting socially constructed cognitive model of the human body. When defining the human body as always already invested with symbolic connotations, Cohen states: "Strictly speaking, 'the body' does not naturally exist. Or to put it more affirmatively: 'the body' only exists within a political ontology that distinguishes the human organism both from its life-world and from 'the person' to whom 'it' supposedly belongs." And further on: "Only our bio-politics, and not 'our nature', makes 'the body' seem natural to us" (Cohen 2008: 119). Human reality, then, is a field of symbolically structured representations, since "it is the world of words that creates the world of things." Lacan (1977: 65) puts this in different terms: "There is no meaning or meaning bearer behind language that is not itself a language-like phenomenon" (Wheeler 2000: 44).

In short, if touch is mediated by an always already given epistemology based on the cultural division between culture and nature, and by the use of language that itself pertains to culture, there can be only one conclusion we can draw thus far: touch is a symbol.

Linguistic predicament

Words can be embodied, a lesson extended from Austin's performativity of utterance (cf. 1975) and the symbolic performativity of Levi-Strauss and V. Turner (cf. 1970). What about vice versa? Touch as the embodied sense—can we reduce it to language?

In structuralism, language has so important a status that it can be puzzling; it is a precondition of culture, a result of culture, and a part of culture. Language is, obviously, all over the place, and if overlapping, then overlapping only within itself, within its borders. As if there is too much language to hold a coherent structure. Levi-Strauss in his famous dictum (cf. Levi-Strauss 1963) asserts that all human cognitive processes consist of the "appropriation of the world by words," transforming it into the realm of signifiers. By every (new) word we reduce the unknown, the so-called *mana*, to something understandable, and when all the reality is reduced to meaningful signifiers, we shall reach the end product of cognition, and we will know everything about everything. Such a teleological declaration leads to an ending of one thing only—structuralism itself. It was too full of language to withstand postmodern times.

Touch seems to be plagued by the same predicaments; it is regarded as one of the human senses, the common denominator of them all, in addition to being their leftover after all words fail. Perhaps this is the reason why naïve (as well as some academic, cf. Walton 2016) notions conceive of the rise of knowledge and civilization as the progress from tangible to presumable, from solipsistic to reflexive, from physical to symbolic. As Freud put it: "The first human who hurled an insult instead of a stone was the founder of civilization" (Freud 1986b: 36). The process of "civilizing" can be seen as a transformation of violence, of physical, natural, erratic, and haptic, into a symbolic and cultural phantasm of an ordered, placid universe. Putting touch ("a stone") to words ("an insult") attempts to "find-and-replace" tangibility with a cultural, convenient, comparable measure—a signifier. The modern bans on touching, being adorned either in hygiene regimes or political correctness, can be perceived as an imperative to "find-and-repress" or translate all real, quasi-natural relations into a symbolically structured universe (cf. Dolar 2008). Moreover, the cosmologies that insist on non-touching, making touch a gruesome abject (the uncanny, horrible no-longer-an-object and not-yet-a-subject (cf. Freud 1986a, Kristeva 1982)), serve as a denial of the very existence of the Real (in the Lacanian sense of the word).[2]

Be that as it may, of all the senses, touch is always something exceptional; betwixt or between, a common denominator, a single dispositive or an a-perceivable negative. From Aristotle onwards, touch is kind of a zero level of the senses, all other being its metaphor or metonymy (cf. Roodenburg 2016). Within the context of searching for linguistic epistemologies of the senses, let us put it this way: all other senses can be reduced to words plus the unspeakable excess, which can (within the analytical framework of the senses) only be conceived of as a sense of touch, which makes touch the irreducible reminder of the use of language. This is, if anything, the uniqueness of touch if compared to the other senses. The sameness of it would presume the equal formula: touch is a sense composed of "the sensible," as represented in language, plus some sort of excess. When the two structural propositions are combined, all the senses are commensurable (cf. Kuhn 2000), have a common denominator (the signifiers' zero level of sense), while the formulas for touch include one additional excess— or perhaps an excess of a different kind?

To elaborate on the above let us start again at the beginning.

It seems convenient that Levi-Strauss discusses the beginning of the appropriation of the universe by means of language most exhaustively when tackling a subject belonging to the realm where all words fail: discussing magic and the "spirit of the gift" in his famous introduction to Marcel Mauss; for being utmost elucidating, we cite a lengthy fragment:

> Whatever may have been the moment and the circumstances of its appearance in the ascent of animal life, language can only have arisen all at once. Things cannot have begun to signify gradually. In the wake of a transformation [...] a shift occurred from a stage when nothing had a meaning to another stage when everything had meaning. Actually, that apparently banal remark is important, because that radical change has no counterpart in the field of knowledge, which develops slowly and progressively. In other words, at the moment when the entire universe all at once became significant, it was none the better known for being so, even if it is true that the emergence of language must have hastened the rhythm of the development of knowledge. So there is a fundamental opposition, in the history of the human mind, between symbolism, which is characteristically discontinuous, and knowledge, characterised by continuity. Let us consider what follows from that. It follows that the two categories of the signifier and the signified came to be constituted simultaneously and inter-dependently, as complementary units; whereas knowledge, that is, the intellectual process which enables us to identify certain aspects of the signifier and certain aspects of the signified, one by reference to the other—we could even say the process which enables us to choose, from the entirety of the signifier and from the entirety of the signified, those parts which present the most satisfying relations of mutual agreement – only got started very slowly. [...] The universe signified long before people began to know what it signified; no doubt that goes without saying. But, from the foregoing analysis, it also emerges that from the beginning, the universe signified the totality of what humankind can expect to know about it.
>
> (Levi-Strauss 1987: 59–60)

At the beginning, then, there was a fundamental discord between what is meaningful and what is already recognized. The reality was divided into established, firm signs surrounded by the floating, uncontrollable, and incomprehensible, reduced to one common signifier, *mana*. As Levi-Strauss continues (cf. Levi-Strauss

1987: 62–63): "In man's effort to understand the world, he always disposes of a surplus of signification (which he shares out among things in accordance with the laws of symbolic thinking, which it is the task of ethnologists and linguists to study)." That "distribution of a supplementary ration," as he puts it, is "absolutely necessary to ensure that, in total, the available signifier and the mapped-out signified may remain in the relationship of complementarity which is the very condition of the exercise of symbolic thinking." Such notions as *mana* "represent nothing more or less than that floating signifier which is the disability of all finite thought (but also the surety of all art, all poetry, every mythic and aesthetic invention), even though scientific knowledge is capable, if not of staunching it, at least of controlling it partially." In other words, while accepting Mauss's concept that social and cultural phenomena can be "assimilated to language," he sees in "*mana, wakan, orenda,* and other notions of the same type, the conscious expression of a semantic function, whose role is to enable symbolic thinking to operate despite the contradiction inherent in it." From here, the apparently insoluble antinomies of concepts such as *mana* (force and action; quality and state; substantive, adjective and verb all at once; abstract and concrete; omnipresent and localized, etc.) are unified together, but precisely because it is none of those things. The concept of *mana*, therefore, is pure "form, or to be more accurate, a symbol in its pure state, therefore liable to take on any symbolic content." In short, in any given system of symbols, it would just be "a zero symbolic value, that is, a sign marking the necessity of a supplementary symbolic content over and above that which the signified already contains, which can be any value at all."

Levi-Strauss' "any value at all" seems to resonate with the notorious ambiguity of the meaning ascribed to touch in the modern philosophy of senses, whereby touch represents "over and above" what words can express: touch is, in this sense, a similar contradictory category, that can encompass any given meaning precisely because it is itself void of meaning and thus a "zero symbolic sign".

Psychoanalytical predicament

While Levi-Straussian cosmology presupposes the existence of two levels—the level of the signifiers (language), and the level of the signified (always already established universe), for Lacan in the last analysis, there is no other reality but language.[3]

In linguistic psychoanalysis, to become a human being is irreversibly linked only to being able to define oneself in both ways: in terms of language, and as a being of language; this symbolic incarnation via signification has its side effect in the form of an indivisible remainder (Žižek 2007) in any symbolization; there always remains something that cannot be articulated in language. If an individual is to become a social subject, a being of language, he or she must become a language-like phenomenon. The difference is crucial and manifold: while previously contemplating Levi-Straussian split reality (signifiers vs. signified), we are now dealing with a split subject: "there is always a disjunction, according to Lacan, between the subject of enunciation and the subject of the utterance; in other words, the subject who speaks and the subject who is spoken" (Homer 2005: 45). To be recognized as a subject means to sacrifice some presymbolic existence, an essence that can never be articulated in terms of symbolic medium.

All of this forces us to acknowledge a double gap: a gap in the subject and a gap in the Symbolic Order; the former is established through the ritual of forced choice, meaning that the subject has to choose between becoming irreversibly un-whole upon entering the realm of symbolic mediation (*ipso facto* sacrificing its very essence) or remaining a silent feral child of nature. The outcome of the first choice is a "split subject" (defined by Lacan as the mathem $), while the outcome of the second one is entrapment in an unhuman presymbolic objective reality. The antagonism of these two gaps, the gap in the subject and the gap in Symbolic Order, is purely topological. What we have here is the same element put in two registers: the surplus of signification (*mana*) is a way in which the internal void of the subject is expressed in language. To put it differently: if there existed a way of communicating in an utterance, not only its enunciated content (what is being said) but also the level of enunciation (the position from where it is being said), then this would be a possibility for how someone could signal that there is something else in him or her, something authentic (tangible) rather than just his/her language-like presence of body and mind.[4]

Levi-Strauss's conception of *mana*—what cannot be articulated in language, yet pertains to the subject—can be translated into what Lacan called *object petit a*, "object cause of desire," which is not something substantial, something we can simply find and thus satisfy our desire, but rather the function of masking the lack in a subject, the very lack that makes him/her a desiring subject. Object cause of desire is "the formless remainder of the Real which, precisely, resists subjectivization: *objet a* is not merely the objectal correlative to the subject, it is the subject itself in its 'impossible' objectal existence" (Žižek 2007: 102). In short, and very schematically speaking, the "object a" is the intersection between the subject and the Real, the way in which the subject relates to the Real, otherwise inaccessible through language or the senses.

The Real in Lacan's theory stands for thing-in-itself, the realm beyond symbolization and images: "The Real is a kind of ubiquitous undifferentiated mass from which we must distinguish ourselves, as subjects, through the process of symbolization" (Homer 2005: 83). However, it is not conceived as preceding the Symbolic, it is that which absolutely resists symbolization, and can be defined as such only retroactively; a traumatic remainder, the excess, the residue that cannot be transformed through language, the Thing we did not lose, something we could not distance from, through the process of alienation through language. The Real, then, is to be understood as a traumatic reminder that resists symbolization, and it is precisely the resistance to symbolization that lends it its traumatic quality. To elucidate what is this "retroactive primacy" of the Real, let us compare it to the Ancient Greek conception of *soma*. As with Lacan (whereby the Real is defined only via mediation of the Symbolic and not as something which precedes the Symbolic, but rather as a leftover), Homer also understood *soma* not as always already being a human body: "The word *soma* means precisely a body from which life has fled, the husk or shell of a once-living being" (Vernant 1991: 62). The concept of *soma*, then, is never a mere physical entity, not something we start living with, but something which remains after we have lived it through—an uncanny fleshy leftover, itself depleted of life.

The attentive reader noticed that all along we were always already discussing touch: analogous to the Lacanian conception of object a as belonging to the Real, touch *qua* object a (the reminder, an excess of the senses after being translated into language) is not something we start living with, adding other senses as we go on living in language. Rather, touch is a secondary compromised reaction; it is a leftover of symbolization, and a remaining of what could not be transformed into any other sense. As such, touch would represent the real kernel, retroactively formed, after the leap of faith we took when entering the promised world of a meaningful symbolic reality.

Lacanian object a is nothing but a parallax (cf. Žižek 2010) of the previously mentioned anthropological conception of *mana*. Let us apply the theoretical frameworks above to the analysis of touch as having an excess signification unparalleled with the touch as an excess of all other senses. In short, what is the *mana* of touch? While in the structural paradigm of *mana* it denotes the universe not yet known, too distant to be "touched by words," object a refers to the inner core of a subject, from which having a distance (by words) is impossible. In the first case, we deal with something we have not (yet) attained, in the second we deal with something we find impossible to lose. Levi-Straussian "surplus of signification," "over and above that which the signified already contains," the outer rim of what "humankind can expect to know" (Levi-Strauss 1987: 61) is also already the inner condition, the internal void of signification (object a), upon which the fullness of language as a symbolic system is founded. With this turning of the surplus that is out there into a lack, which is within a subject of language itself, the collision happens, which can only be defined as "romantic love," whereby one gives what one does not have to someone that does not exist (cf. Žižek 2002). For an illustration of this point let me refer to every Lacanist's favorite tale of the only right answer to the traumatic question of: "Darling, why do you love me?" It would be wrong to start enumerating all the positive characteristics of the beloved person: "I love you because you have beautiful hair, a nice pair of legs, because you cook so well, because you make my life comfortable, because you are never late, because you provide me the opportunity to beget a family, etc." Whatever one says is never enough; it is not really the answer. Even more, it does not sound like a compliment, but more like an insult. The feeling of being in love presupposes that the beloved will remain beloved, no matter what—even if without all of these "positive" properties, for a true love only love (itself) is a true reason. Thus, the only possible answer to the above question is: "I do not know what it is; there is something about you that is incommensurable, some X."

This X, the mysterious core of the beloved, is named object a, it speaks as if saying "I love you more than everything," meaning that there is something more in you that I am in love with, some inexplicable *mana* that follows you as well as surpasses you; it transcends, as well as precedes, all tangible proportions of you. Not only contemporary pop-culture,[5] but also, and especially, classical romantic poetry is filled with the illustrations of this *mana* as object a being both too far and too close. This is also the point where any "experience beyond experience" overlaps with the reminder of the surplus closeness of that what one "cannot touch, because it is too near" before the intervention of language.

Which brings us to a simple provisory conclusion, implied already by Levi-Strauss in his discussion of *mana*: touch, being irreducible to symbolization, resistant to commensurability, language and/or other senses, could nonetheless be conveyed by poetry.

Predicament of poetry

To recapitulate: if all the senses can be reduced to language and a minimum amount of touch (touch as a zero level of the senses), and touch is, moreover, commensurable with language as such in its extreme variant as poetry (touch as one of the senses including its surplus of meaning in the form of *mana* or object a), then both interpretations bring us to an awkward conclusion: touch is an even more language-like phenomenon than other senses can ever be, a surplus of language in itself.

Trying to elaborate on this twist, let us start with Lacan's essay "Logical Time and the Assertion of Anticipated Certainty" (Lacan 2006: 161–175). In this essay, quite analogous to the Levi-Straussian proposal on how our knowledge of reality progresses, Lacan develops three modalities of logical time: an instant of the glance, time for understanding, and moment of concluding (ibid., 173).[6] At first, then, we are observing a particular "objectal reality," i.e. the level of the signified. This is followed by the intervention of words, the symbolic medium, language—the signifier. In the third step the former two become united in sensible interpretation—the sign.

So far so good. But what if our glance encounters the Levi-Straussian *mana* as "surplus of signification," understood as the Lacanian object a? Such emanations, proposes Lacan, yield no logical sequence; they appear as if the three elements of logical time have collided into a single moment. All that we need is an instant of the glance, there is no need for time for understanding, nor is there any use for the moment of concluding for it has always already been implied in the moment of looking. A single glance explains everything, between a glance and a conclusion there is no room left for an intervention of language. When this happens, the words, along with poetry and art, are always both insufficient and redundant at the same time, being too little and too much at once.

What we encounter is the sublime uncanniness of the "too-close-to-touch," coinciding with capital capitulation of judgment where all words fail. The implosion of the three logical times in one moment consists of the subject's encountering the traumatic reminder, the precluded object a, a kernel of the subject's being which had to be sacrificed in order for him or her to become a subject. At once we are dealing with fullness without any lack, with subject *qua* whole as well as Symbolic Order *qua* whole. What we are dealing with from that moment on is reintegration of culture within nature, wherein the world collides with the Thing that it is only supposed to represent. Hegel proposed a very elegant shortcut to articulate this collision in the form of an "infinite judgment": "Spirit is a bone." Hence, we would like to add a new infinite judgment that is more in tune with the problem of touch and language we are dealing with here: "Language is a touch."

Only in reality, which is not a language-like reality, one could claim a pure, complete understanding without anything leftover. Perhaps precisely in this manner we ought to understand Saussure's (2006) enigmatic proposition that the gist of all communication is misunderstanding, for if we understood, if all concluding was already invested in a glance, the language as a system of signifiers, signifies, and signs, all communication even, is rendered useless, serves no purpose. The unspeakable has no purpose in the symbolic reality, moreover, it shuts it down; its magnitude is beyond linguistic explanation. It is beyond humanity. How else can one understand Adorno's famous "no poetry after Auschwitz?"

Touch is composed of more than mere language, a surplus of language: it is a shared phantasm that there is something beyond and beneath the shared reality of human beings. Touch is supposed to indicate where our true unfeigned subjectivity could be situated, i.e. where my essence, my "true nature," is. To obscure the fact that it is not somewhere outside the field of anything we can speak about, we made its immediacy uncanny, we designated it as a double negation, whereby touch stands not only as a nonlinguistic part of a language-like universe, but moreover as negation, devoid of any relations to the language. The phantasm of touch as being outside the spoken word is shattered precisely when "words touch,"⁷ where we can detect, inside language itself, a signal of "the real event" (the collision of three logical times as discussed earlier), when all our understanding is reduced to the prelinguistic sense of touch.

When a phantasmatic (language-structured) universe is thrown out of joint, the human body breaks down. Surplus of touch is what becomes of language when the subject passes out. Or is, at least, so "touched by words" that it displays bodily, tangible reactions. This presents in very diverse states from autistic catatonia to phantom pain, but it can, of course, have more benign representations for which we use metaphors, such as: "to tremble," "to feel one's hair standing on end," "to have one's heart in one's mouth," "to have a lump in one's throat," "to grow pale," "to make one's flesh crawl." By these figures of speech we hint at the unspeakable that has touched our flesh, and which renders flight, denial, repression, and not poetry. Physical experience of the feeling of touch serves to indicate the proximity of the Thing, while its uncanny dimension provides the means to scare us away, to prevent the impossible encounter, to avoid the happening of the unimaginable outside all language. But what we are dealing with here is not a mere emptiness of words, but emptiness occupied by lack of words, a structural void, the background upon which speech can emerge against (Žižek 2002: 77). To put it differently: when "words touch" this is no supplementary satisfaction, since such a touch supplements something, which was already missing from its place in the original symbolic framework. And only because it is void and excess at the same time, touch cannot convey, translate, explain, or be in any way reduced to words, or art, or poetry, or, for that matter, to other senses. This is the reason why touch is the only sense that is not only essentially incommensurable, but also irrefutable, indisputable, and thus presumably the only authentic signal of our subjectivity, which sets us apart as individual human beings, in the otherwise shared phantasm of humanity.

However, the surplus touch outside words is opposed not so much to the other senses, as to the structure of language inasmuch as the structure constitutes a language. The surplus of touch without translation into language is not an untouchability, the undefined, free-floating zone, unattached to any symbolic chain of signifiers, but rather an untouchable prerequisite of the ability to touch. The full lack of language over touch is a parallax of an ability to touch as a fully language-like phenomenon. Or to use another conception altogether: if language is cultural, and human touch is the *mana* or object a of language in its inability to grasp the Real, then the surplus of touch is inhuman, already pertaining to humanity as such, rather than simply nonhuman.[8]

Conclusion

Nothing that pertains to touch is external to language. It can, however, appear as a placeholder for the inconsistency of a symbolic patchwork of reality. Since when Lacan defines the birthplace of a subject within symbolization and attributes to this process an objectal reminder of the Real, object a, he also states that full and complete symbolization would have resulted in a structure without a subject.

Such a structure can only be thought of in terms of Levi-Strauss's theory of *mana*, placed on the periphery, on the outer limit of language that exists without reference neither to the subject nor to language. As soon as one proposes *mana* to be an indivisible reminder, when one conceives that "every process of conceptualisation, of rational apprehension, of symbolization, every attempt by *logos* to seize reality, produces a reminder" (Žižek 2017: 17; italics orig.), only then the immanence of the subject becomes possible. For "subject can occur only where there is a radical rip in the texture of reality, when reality is not a 'flat' collection of objects but implies a radical crack" (ibid.: 43). To put it in more simple terms; if one is to withstand the fallacy of symbolic reality dominated by social and cultural fictions, one must also presuppose the existence of a solid, true authenticity, warranted by the objects, which could take the place of object a as the reminder of the Real. Touch can very well fill the role of such an object since it traverses both registers; it can be signifier and signified at once.

The empiricist's and the idealist's statements are both equally true: "If you want me to believe, I have to touch it," as well as "If you want me to touch it, I have to believe it." As such, the authenticity of touch is the biggest fiction of them all, since it serves to over-determine other fictions, such as the fiction of the senses making sense of anything but language.

Notes

1 The problem of how to think knowledge independently from power is not a very modern idea in itself: it was first posed by the enlightenment movement in order to counter Christian theology, which was, at the time, perceived as *the* seat of power and knowledge.

2 Lacan's RSI scheme aspires to encompass the whole of human experience into three concepts: the Symbolic, defined through the subject's link to language; the Imaginary, or the subject's sensorial experience of the world; and the Real, defined as the kernel of reality that eludes any linguistic or sensorial grasp.

3 And this is one of the key reasons why Jean-Claude Milner labeled Lacan's later work as characterized by a distinctive "hyperstructuralism" (cf. Milner 2002).

4 For a further elaboration of touch and language in relation to the traditional philosophical body–mind dichotomy see Bara Kolenc's contribution in this book (Chapter 6).

5 See, for instance, the movie *Her* (2013) where the protagonist (played by Joaquin Phoenix) falls in love with an intangible software program, present in reality only through her hardcore voice (that of Scarlett Johansen); or the reenactment of this same moment in the new *Blade Runner 2049* (2017), where the protagonist (played by Ryan Gosling) again falls in love with an intangible software program, who has not only a voice, but also an image (that of Ana de Armas).

6 Those modalities are developed out of a riddle three prisoners must solve without communicating to each other and which is solvable only if two conditions are met: that all three belong to the same realm of the Symbolic, and that the absence of an event is always already present in its absence, that the absence of signifier always already has a signification like all other signifiers. So goes Lacan: "A prison warden summons three choice prisoners and announces to them the following: For reasons I need not make known to you now, I must free one of you. In order to decide which, I will entrust the outcome to a test that you will, I hope, agree to undergo. There are three of you present. I have here five disks differing only in colour: three white and two black. Without letting you know which I will have chosen, I will fasten one of them to each of you between the shoulders, outside, that is, your direct visual field [...] You will then be left at your leisure to consider you companions and their

respective disks, without being allowed, of course, to communicate among yourselves the results of your inspection [...] The first to be able to deduce his own colour will be the one to benefit from the discharging measure at my disposal. But his conclusion must be founded upon logical and not simply probabilistic grounds [...] As soon as one of you is ready to formulate such a conclusion he will pass through this door so that he may be judged individually on the basis of his response" (Lacan, 2007: 161).

7   For a further elaboration of this conception see Mirt Komel's contribution in this book (Chapter 1).

8   If we are to venture into another horizon, which would bring us closer to a so-called transhumanist perspective, we might conclude that both humanity and inhumanity are but masks of the void, which separates us from animals, and which forces us to realize that a human being is not something more than an animal, but something less; it lacks the naturalness and authenticity of "being a body." It is possible to conceive of touch as something outside language, irreducibly linked to nature only from the standpoint of nature itself, where there is no divide between culture and nature; everything is nature. This would necessitate the inverse epistemological premises from those we started from at the beginning.

References

Austin, J. (1975), *How to Do Things with Words*, Cambridge: Harvard UP.

Cohen, E. (2008), "A Body Worth Having? Or, A System of Natural Governance," *Theory, Culture & Society* 25(3): 103–129.

Dolar, M. (2008), "Touching Ground," *Filozofski vestnik* 2(29): 79–100.

Foucault, M. (1984), "Power/Knowledge," in: C. Gordon (ed.), *Selected Interviews and Other Writings 1972–1977*, London: Harvester Press.

Freud, S. (1986a), "The 'Uncanny,'" in: *The Complete Psychological Works* of *Sigmund Freud*, Standard Edition (vol. XVII), London: The Hogarth Press, pp. 217–256.

Freud, S. (1986b), "Some Points for a Comparative Study of Organic and Histerical Motor Paralyses," in: *The Complete Psychological Works* of *Sigmund Freud*, Standard Edition (vol. I), London: The Hogarth Press, pp.155–171.

Homer, S. (2005), *Jacques Lacan*, London and New York: Routledge.

Komel, M. (2016), "A Touchy Subject," *Družboslovne razprave* 22(82): 115–125.

Kristeva, J. (1982), *Powers of Horror: An Essay on Abjection*, New York, Columbia UP.

Kuhn, T. S. (2000), *The Road Since Structure*, Chicago: University of Chicago Press

Lacan, J. (2007), *Ecrits*, New York, London: W. W. Norton & Co.

Levi-Strauss, C. (1963), *Structural Anthropology*, New York: Basic Books.

Levi-Strauss, C. (1987), *Introduction to the Work of Marcel Mauss*, London: Routledge & Kegan Paul.

Milner, J.-C. (2002), *Le Périple Structural*, Paris: Editions du Seuil.

Roodenburg, H. (2016), *A Cultural History of the Senses in the Renaissance*, London: Bloomsbury Academic.

Saussure, F. (2006), *Writings in General Linguistics*, Oxford: Oxford UP.

Turner, V. (1970), *The Forest of Symbols*, Ithaca: Cornell UP.

Vernant, J. P. (1991), *Mortals and Immortals: Collected Essays*, Princeton: Princeton UP.

Walton, S. (2016), *In The Realm of the Senses: A Materialist Theory of Seeing and Feeling*, New York: Zero Books.

Wheeler, S. C. (2000), *Deconstruction as Analytic Philosophy*, Stanford: Stanford UP.

Žižek, S. (2002), *Did Somebody Say Totalitarianism?* London: Verso.

Žižek, S. (2005), *Interrogating the Real*, New York, London: Continuum.

Žižek, S. (2007), *The Indivisible Remainder*, London: Verso.

Žižek, S. (2010), *Parallax View*, Cambridge, Mass.: MIT Press.

Žižek, S. (2017), *Incontinence of the Void*. Cambridge, Mass., London: MIT Press.

Zupančič, A. (2017), *What is Sex?* Cambridge, Mass., London: MIT Press.

4

Ontology of Touch: From Aristotle to Brentano

Gregor Moder

Introduction

Before presenting an attempt at an *ontology of touch*, I want to point out that ontology has always been closely related to the study of language. This is not simply the claim that any ontological consideration must necessarily be expressed by some language and within some language, and is therefore inevitably limited by that particular language. That would define the relationship between language and being only by way of negation. On the contrary, metaphysics, both ancient and modern, has consistently acknowledged that language determines being in an affirmative, productive, or constructive manner. Long before Heidegger insisted that "language is the house of being" (Heidegger 1998: 239 and *passim*) and that (human) being therefore creatively dwells in language, Aristotle famously declared in *Metaphysics*: "There are several senses in which a thing may be said to 'be'" (*Metaphysics* VII.1, 1028a10). It is important to note that Aristotle did not think this was merely a matter of homonymy, of the ambiguity of language. On the contrary, the several senses all relate to one general, overarching sense which Aristotle conceived as substance. But our initial interest lies in the wording used repeatedly across *Metaphysics*, in the phrasing that already presupposes a close relation between language and being: "a thing may be said to 'be.'" We shall read this as in the strong or affirmative sense, where language is the horizon of what there is and in what sense it is. When we discuss being *qua* being—which is Aristotle's own formulation of the task of metaphysics—we are guided by language itself.

Within Aristotle's body of work, the relation between language and ontology is perhaps even more clear in his logical work, *Categories*, which is preoccupied to an extent with categorizing things that are (*ta onta*). In concordance with *Metaphysics*, the central category of being is substance; it is the only independent one, and all other categories—like quality and quantity—are relative to substance.[1] Aristotle divides what he calls "things that are said" (*ta legomena*) into ten types, and it is a matter of some controversy whether he is talking about purely linguistic categories, or about logical categories, or else about things that exist in themselves, independently of any language or logic. Émile Benveniste argued that Aristotle's distinctions "are primarily categories of language and that, in fact, Aristotle, reasoning in the absolute, is simply identifying certain fundamental categories of the language in which he thought" (Benveniste 1971: 57). Benveniste added, quite astutely, that the concept of substance (*ousia*) points to substantives, and explained other categories as linguistic categories of adjectives, adverbs, and verbs (Benveniste 1971: 60). One should note that Benveniste was not the first to propose the possibility of a linguistic interpretation of Aristotle's categories. The nineteenth-century Aristotelian Friedrich Adolf Trendelenburg describes the "kinship [*Verwandtschaft*] of logical categories to grammatical ones" and suggests the very same pairs of categories as Benveniste from substance–substantive onwards (Trendelenburg 1846: 23). Benveniste, however, is much more radical in this regard, and goes as far as to conclude that Aristotle's logical categories, or categories of thought, are derived from the categories of language *unbeknownst to Aristotle himself*: "[Aristotle] thought he was defining the attributes of objects but he was really setting up linguistic entities" (Benveniste 1971: 61). For Benveniste, Aristotle merely thought that he was referring to real objects, whereas in truth he was referring to particulars of the Greek grammar.

At the other end of the spectrum of interpretations of Aristotle's categories we can find philosophers who seek to disentangle the clearly evident relation between Greek grammar and Aristotle's logic and/or ontology, defending the realism of Aristotle's categories. In this chapter, however, we will pursue a path that neither reduces (onto)logical categories—to purely grammatical instances, nor separates completely between language and reality in order to claim that language is nothing but means for a realist ontology. Instead, we shall adopt a stance which can be discerned from Jacques Derrida's response to Benveniste: "Without having reduced thought to language in a fashion similar to Benveniste's, Aristotle tried to direct his analysis back to the point of emergence, which is to say back to the common root of the couple language/thought. This point is the locus of 'being'. Aristotle's categories are at one and the same time language and thought categories" (Derrida 1976: 535). In other words, Aristotle's "being *qua* being" inhabits, or dwells in, the intersection of language and thought. Leaving no room for doubt, Derrida affirms: "The system of categories is the system of the ways in which being is construed" (Derrida 1976: 536). Derrida's reading of

Aristotle's categories thus brings us back to the constructive, even creative understanding of the relationship between ontology and language.

Bearing in mind the nexus of ontology, logic, and language, our attempt at presenting that which one could call the *ontology of touch* will inevitably lead us to include abstract logical, grammatical, and even mathematical perspectives. In part, and in turn, this investigation will inevitably become a grammar of touch, a logic of touch, and even a mathematics of touch. The reason I choose the term ontology as a prevailing, all-encompassing one is because of the centrality of ontology in the metaphysical thought of Artistotle, both in his own works and through the works of his modern followers. It was Aristotle, writing within the specifically Greek historical conjuncture, following his predecessors, who put being at the heart of logical and grammatical investigations.

The sensible, the geometrical, and the conceptual touch

Broadly speaking, a discussion of touch falls into one of three main categories. Firstly, there is everything that surrounds the sense of touch, tactility, especially touching something with hands or with another part of the body. Since the object of touch may very well be another hand or another body, or another human being in general, we can include all sensuality (bodies touching bodies) and a good portion of sensitivity (being touched, being touchy) in this category. This category also includes the metaphorical understanding of the sensual or physical, since to be touched also means to be emotionally moved, to be hurt, to be perturbed; there is an analogy between physically touching and emotionally "touching." Furthermore, the English word feeling, related etymologically to the Latin *palpare* (something is palpable because it can be touched), seems to favor the haptic sense above all other senses; to *feel* a material is to touch it. In a way, the sense of touch can serve as the synecdoche for sense as such.

Secondly, touch can designate spatial proximity of objects or beings, quite independently of the question of the tactile sense. For instance, in considering landscape one can say that a mountain top is touching the sky; *in abstracto* in geometry, a tangent is so named because it is a line that "touches" a circle: it coincides with it in exactly one point; and in human relations, like in the phrase "to stay in touch" insofar as this means "to stay in close relation to one another." From an empiricist perspective, this second genre of touch seems to be metaphorical at its very core, because the spatial proximity can also be expressed easily in other terms. Using the word "touch" instead of describing "vicinity," "proximity," or "connection" between the mountain and the sky makes the expression somewhat poetic: a mountain certainly does not want or desire to touch anything at all. However, these other terms seem to be equally metaphorical. The idea of the proximity of mountain top and sky seems to fully rely on the sense of sight, and so one could argue that any spatial proximity expressed in language is a metaphorical use of the proximity as a relation native to the sense of sight. One could argue—as indeed some have—that geometry is an elaborated abstraction from the visible, a metaphorical representation fundamentally enrooted in what was gained by our mind from the sense of sight. But in arguing this we would needlessly favor the sense of sight over the other senses; we know very well that proximity (or distance), depth, and other spatial properties are detected by other senses as well (and in some creatures, such as bats, not by sight at all) including the sense of touch. On the other hand, this entire empiricist debate might easily be dismissed by rationalists: is geometry not precisely the conclusive argument that shows us that it is our mind that structures what can be perceived as sensual content, and not the other way around? Are the rational geometrical shapes and relations not precisely what we are looking for, and finding, in nature? Are we not designing and building objects (buildings) in nature according to geometrical shapes, formed in our minds? And is a geometrical space not infinitely richer and more perfect than any natural, sensible space? In any case—whether we deduce geometry from the sensual or from the rational, or if we understand, with Kant, space and time as pure forms of our inner sense—we argue that geometrical concepts comprise their own field of objects that can be said to touch and be touched. In this context, the use of the term "touch" is perhaps a metonymy or a synecdoche, so that touch functions as the metonymy for intuition (Kant's *Anschauung*) as such: one could argue that physical proximity of two objects, perceptible by many senses, is expressed in geometry as belonging to one specific sense: touch.

And thirdly, the use of the term touch can be purely metaphorical, as is the case when we refer to the highest cognitive capabilities of our mind. For instance, we can say that the professor touched upon an interesting topic or question in his or her discourse. Such use of language is metaphorical to a greater degree than in the case of the analogy between physical and emotional touching, because emotions (or better, feelings) could be seen as senses of the psyche. There is an analogy between "briefly discussing" something and "touching on" it, and it seems that this analogy rests upon the idea that discussing something or talking about something is similar to "spending time in the proximity of something." If we follow these analogies through, we come to a perhaps surprising conclusion that apparently, there is an equivalence between *talking* and *touching*. Of course, other senses are used as analogies or metaphors to represent the activity of the mind, too, for instance in phrases like "I see your point," "I hear you," and "this idea stinks." Such phrases point to equivalences between understanding and seeing, between acknowledgment and hearing, and between rejecting (or accepting) ideas and rejecting (or accepting) food.

Now, for all senses we can describe a passive or an active relationship between the subject of sense (that which senses: sees, hears, smells, and tastes) and the object of sense (that which is sensed: is seen, heard, smelled, or tasted). It is only with the sense of touch, however, that we are immediately immersed in a mutual relationship that works as something like Newton's third law of equal but opposite forces: to touch inevitably means also to be touched, and the object that we touch is touching us in return. But there is one more peculiarity of the sense of touch that makes it stand out from all the other senses; to a greater degree than the other senses, to touch something or someone implies a transformation or displacement either of ourselves, of the object of touch, or both. This plasticity specific to the sense of touch corresponds perfectly to the plasticity of understanding and reason. In many languages, even the most complex concepts are expressed as an analogy of the tangible, and among these, two are especially worthy of our attention: firstly, the concept of *contingency* as a concept in a potential encounter, and secondly the concept of *grasping* as the concept of comprehending.

In short, "touch" can relate to any of the three major categories; either to the sense of touch, or to the geometrical representation of proximity (contact), or to the plasticity of understanding. In this chapter we shall argue that these categories are not merely homonymous, that they are not using, by pure chance, the very same signifier for entirely different notions, but rather represent three different stages of posing the same problem that requires of us to consider the ontology of touch. Let us begin by turning to Aristotle's account of the *sense* of touch.

The sense of touch in Aristotle

With Aristotle usually comes hierarchy, and this is true both with the senses as well as with the sensible; touch appears as the most primitive sense: "The primary form of perception which belongs to all animals is touch" (*De anima*, II.2, 413b3–4). Touch is so basic that some animals even have only that sense: "without touch, none of the other senses are present, though touch is present without the others; for many animals have neither sight nor hearing nor a sense of smell"

(II.3, 415a3–6). However, the primacy of touch is not only negative, because touch is also the most necessary sense for Aristotle: "some animals have all [senses], others have some of them, and others have one, the most necessary, touch" (II.2, 414a2–4). Here we come to the important point. The necessity of touch does not merely mean that all animals happen to have the sense of touch; it means also that, firstly, all senses are dependent on touch, and secondly, an animal, deprived of the sense of touch, is destroyed. As for the second point, Aristotle writes:

> An excess in the objects of touch, on the other hand (for instance cases of hot or cold or hard) will destroy the animal. For an excess in any object of perception will destroy the sensory organ, [but] an excess in the objects of touch destroys not only the sensory organ, but the animal as well, because this alone an animal must have.
>
> (III.13, 435b13–19)

Looking directly at the sun will destroy our sensory organs, eyes, but it will not kill us. This is similar for other senses as well; being completely deprived of the sense of touch, however, is the death of an animal. On this point, Aristotle keeps affirming that "the other senses an animal has not for the sake of existing, but for the sake of existing well" (III.13, 435a15–21). Aristotle goes at great lengths to point out that the sense of taste may seem to be equally important as the sense of touch, but if this is indeed so, it is because taste is already a kind of touch, or else it is coupled with touch. This allows Aristotle to claim that the very existence of an animal is bound to its sense of touch. In this, we can already detect a tacit ontological claim—to exist is to touch, to be touched, and to be in touch.

As for the claim that all senses depend on the sense of touch, it is connected to Aristotle's detailed analysis of the question of the *medium* through which a sense perceives its sensible objects. Let us take a look at the example of sight, where Aristotle, first of all, argues that a medium is absolutely necessary for it to function, contrary to what materialists may think.

> Democritus is wrong to think that if the intervening medium were a void, even an ant in heaven would be seen clearly. For this is impossible, since seeing comes to be when what is capable of perceiving is affected by something. Hence, while it is impossible that it be affected by the very colour seen, what remains, surely, is that it be affected by the intervening medium. Consequently, there must be an intervening medium. If it were a void, it is not that things would not be seen clearly, but rather that nothing would be seen at all.
>
> (II.7, 419a15–21)

Without the medium, senses would not have some sort of direct, immediate, and clear access to the sensible object, but on the contrary, they would be cut off from the object completely. According to our modern knowledge, this is in fact true for the sense of hearing: in a void, a completely empty space, sound cannot travel to our organ of hearing, and so there is no sound. What we hear, when we do hear sounds, is the vibration of the molecules of air (or other medium) causing the vibration of the eardrum. But we can hardly argue that Aristotle's explanation works for sight because the movement of light is not made possible by air (or water etc.); if anything, air (water, glass, etc.) obstructs or at least distorts the visible. However, since we are only interested in the possible link between Aristotle's understanding of senses and his ontology, such inaccuracies are not our primary concern. Instead, what interests us is Aristotle's idea that a sense organ must be *affected* by something in order to perceive, either through a medium like air, or directly; and the idea that void is not capable of affection. Another term that Aristotle uses for such affection is *movement*; when explaining how it is that we see an object, he argues that it is because "colour moves the transparent, e.g., air, and the sensory organ is moved by this" (II.7, 419a13–14). Color moves the air, and the air moves the eye. Speaking in general, perception is only possible through a medium, which is why to perceive is to be affected, to be moved. But then Aristotle comes to the very special case of the sense of touch:

> Elements other than earth can bring about sensory organs, but these all produce perception by perceiving through something else, that is, through a medium, whereas touch occurs by touching objects of touch—whence its name. And indeed, the other sensory organs also perceive by touch—but through something else. Only touch seems to perceive through itself.
>
> (III.13, 435a15–20)

"To affect," "to move"—these are simply different expressions for one and the same operation: "to touch." This finally allows Aristotle to claim that all senses perceive by touching their objects through some medium; touch is the only sense that remains within itself when perceiving. Even seeing is possible only insofar as our eyes are affected, moved, or *touched*, by a medium which is itself touched by the visible object. In fact, even with today's knowledge of how sight operates, we could agree with Aristotle to an extent and argue that we only see insofar as the light, reflected from a visible object, *touches* our eyes. But, again, the most important point for our analysis is the idea that Aristotle's account of the senses reserves a privileged spot for the sense of touch, because "only touch perceives through itself." In some sense, touch works without a medium, and Aristotle employs his notorious example of the shield to prove it:

> [T]he object of touch differs from the objects of sight and hearing, since we perceive these latter because the medium affects us in some way, whereas we perceive the objects of touch not in virtue of having been affected by the medium but simultaneously with the medium, as when someone is struck through a shield. For it is not the case that the shield hit its wearer after it was struck; rather, both coincided in being struck simultaneously.
>
> (II.2, 423b8–17)

As on other points, we may argue that Aristotle is quite mistaken in the assumption of the simultaneity of the hits. However, the important point that he is trying to make, I think, is not that touching works without the passage of time, instantaneously and immediately. The point that he is trying to make, I argue, is that where touch is concerned, there is no mediation in that there is nothing that needs to "carry" the tangible to us (as is the case with hearing, where the sound is carried by the medium of air, water, or wire etc.) because when we perceive by touching, we are already in direct contact with the tangible. In other words, Aristotle is not trying to make the ridiculous argument that shields are useless on the battlefield because they have no effect on our perception of the blow. Aristotle is making the argument that touch is only explained with itself and through itself—and in this sense, without a medium (and only in this particular sense as if without the shield); touch is its own medium.

This leads us to one final assertion Aristotle makes about the sense of touch: "[Touch] is the sense which is most precise in humans. For in the other senses humans are surpassed by many other animals, whereas in the case of touch humans differ from the others in being by a long measure more precise. Humans are, accordingly, the most intelligent of animals." (II.9, 421a17–23) Apparently, there is a connection between the sense of touch and intelligence: it is the precision in the sense of touch that makes humans the most intelligent of all animals! As Cynthia Freeland pointed out, this assertion should be read *cum grano salis*; in other works, Aristotle attributes superior intelligence in humans to other properties—to standing upright, to having a large brain with which they can cool their complex organs of perception located in the head (*sic*!), to having acute hearing etc. (Freeland 2003: 234). However, we should not underestimate the importance of such an assertion, especially given that Plato's metaphor of the cave, as well as other metaphors and analogies, and the very idea of idea, make such dramatic use of the sense of sight, and given that it is Aristotle himself who argues, in the opening of *Metaphysics,* that it is the sense of *sight* that is most useful and appropriate for knowing and discerning. The argument in favor of the primacy of touch should be read together with the (tacit) ontological claim of *De Anima,* that to be is to touch and to be moved is to be touched. S. H. Rosen argued that "*De Anima,* which contains Aristotle's fullest account of the process of thinking (as distinct from the objects, or the results, of thought, or from the logical rules whereby that process is governed), rests fundamentally upon an analogy between thought and touch" (Rosen 1961: 129). Even though Rosen concludes that Aristotle failed to demonstrate that the sense which best serves as an analogy for thought is indeed touch, he points to several key phrases, including the comparison of the soul to the hand: "Consequently, the soul is just as the hand is; for the hand is a tool of tools, and reason is a form of forms, and perception a form of the objects of perception" (III.8, 432a1–3). If it is indeed possible to claim that the soul is like the hand, and to understand is to (move or affect by) touch, then this is only possible because in general, existence is tangibility. Rosen writes quite directly: "[T]he account of thought is inseparable from Aristotle's conception of Being itself, of the *way* in which things are. Things are touchable; i.e. they are discriminable through aesthetic-noetic touch" (Rosen 1961: 133). In *De Anima,* it seems, Aristotle truly argues for the ontology of touch.

The fear of the void

Let us now leave the crust of the empirical, of the sensible, and finally enter the domain of the ontology proper. Our task will be to show that Aristotle's ontology is not only analogous to the sense of touch, but that it should be explained as an ontology of touch and the tangible, as ontology of contact. In this, we follow what Mirt Komel argues about the metaphor of touch, namely, that it is strictly speaking not a metaphor at all: "if metaphors can touch their listeners or readers, then it is because they are not metaphors at all, but rather the haptic, almost projectile projections of language" (Komel: 2016 124). Komel makes this argument specifically within the domain of language, but we shall adopt it in ontology as well, since—as we have argued at the very beginning of this chapter— ontology is perhaps nothing but a variation of linguistics. One could suggest, furthermore, that it is precisely the ontological thrust of linguistics itself that allows for Komel's claim that language does not touch us in a metaphorical, but in a literal way. It is precisely insofar as linguistics intervenes in ontology that the metaphor of touch becomes a literal touch.[2]

Our main focus in this section will be on Aristotle's *Physics*, known for its abhorrence of the void and its explanation of movement, the central characteristic of the physical world, without the concept of void. We shall argue that what interests Aristotle in the debate about void, is the distinction between the continuity and the discontinuity of beings, and that Aristotle adamantly argues for continuity, rejecting the existence of any intervals of void between beings, thus in principle offering ground to the claim that a being must always be in direct contact with another being, embracing a plenist ontology, based on *contact*.

First of all, one should note that for Aristotle, the question of the void arises insofar as this concept was used by some to explain *movement or change*. Aristotle uses the same expression for both locomotion and mutation, which emphasizes the opposition of both to *permanence*; as a result, Aristotle's treatment of the void must explain both aspects of alteration. Secondly, for Aristotle, mutability is not simply one of the many aspects of nature as such, but rather the very key to its understanding: "Since nature is a principle of change and alteration, and our inquiry is about nature, it must not escape us what CHANGE is: for if it is not known, it must be that nature is not known either" (*Physics*, III.1, 200b12–14). Aristotle's attempt to explain alteration without reference to the concept of the void has immense ontological consequences. On the one hand, Aristotle agrees with the pre-Socratic thinkers of Elea, like Parmenides and Zeno, that nothing can come out of nothing, but on the other hand, Aristotle does not want to conclude that there is no such thing as motion or change—which is the radical consequence of the Eleatic concept of being. For Aristotle, it is permissible to speak of existence not only when we are dealing with something actual, but also when we are concerned with mixed entities which involve a degree of potential to move or change.

Aristotle denies that a concept of the void is necessary to explain change; according to him, a fullness is capable of transforming itself, and locomotion happens with simultaneous replacement of entities. But Aristotle goes further than this and argues that not only does one not need void in order to explain motion, but that motion would in fact be impossible in a void: "Though some say that there is void because it is necessary if there is to be change, in fact, if one considers carefully, it is rather the opposite that results: that if there is void it is not possible for anything to move" (IV.8, 214b28–31). The reason why void would prevent and not enable motion is that void allows for no differences and therefore also for no change: "Just as some say that the earth is at rest because of symmetry, so in the void too [a body] must be at rest, there being nowhere for it to move to more or less [than anywhere else], since the void, as such, admits no differences" (IV.8, 214b31–34). This argument is, of course, a parallel argument to the one Aristotle makes in *De Anima* where he claims that an object placed in a void would not be visible, since it would be impossible for it to affect us, to touch—through a medium—our sensory organ. We find ourselves, again, on the field of plenism, where to affect a body necessarily implies to have contact with (to touch) that body (at least through mediation of another body).

But there is one further reason Aristotle is so suspicious of the void: we could call it a mathematical reason. He argues that if we were to try to explain motion by reference to the void, we would be committing the mistake of counting with proportion to zero (dividing by zero). Aristotle goes to great lengths to make this point; he claims that an object moving through air will be faster than an object moving through water, and even faster if it moved through some even "thinner" medium. Void, however, is a different story. "But the void has no proportion in which it is exceeded by body, any more than nothing has to number. [. . .] For this reason, too, it is that a line does not exceed a point, unless the line is composed of points. In the same way, the void cannot bear any proportion to what is a plenum" (IV.8, 215b12–20). For Aristotle, zero cannot be in proportion to a natural number, no more than a line can be in proportion to a dimensionless point, or a void to a plenum.

Thus we come to one of the most interesting parts of *Physics*, Aristotle's attempt to resolve Zeno's paradoxes without accepting the concept of the void, a dimensionless point, or a proportion to zero. For Aristotle, Zeno's paradoxes are not just a trivial exercise in the application of mathematics. It is clear to everyone— including Zeno himself—that if someone is moving at certain speed from point A to point B, they will also get there in a certain amount of time; that Achilles will *de facto* catch the turtle; and that there is a difference between an arrow in motion and an arrow at rest. But what we are lacking is a proper ontological (*de jure*) explanation of what, if anything, is movement. The mathematical operation of calculating velocity and distance is quite trivial, and Aristotle's task is not simply to refute Zeno by pointing this out. The problem for Aristotle lies precisely in the fact that he *agrees with Zeno*, that the mathematical solution does not really address the *de jure* (philosophical) problem of movement. How so?

Let us consider the simplest of Zeno's paradoxes. If one is to move from point A to point B, one first has to pass through the middle point between A and B; let us call it point M. But before getting to M, one must get to the middle point between A and M, and so *ad infinitum*. Conclusion: one can never get to point B, since there is always another point to pass before we get to the one we chose as the current goal. Knowledge of very basic mathematics is quite sufficient to reject Zeno's conclusion; contrary to what is often believed, there is no need to use infinitesimal calculus.[3] Aristotle understands, however, that the problem described by Zeno is not a mathematical problem, but a philosophical one. What Zeno seems to be suggesting is that our concept of time and space, as consisting of points, is insufficient to explain movement as such—even though it leads to adequate and precise mathematical calculations. We know that one, empirically, *de facto*, gets from place A to place B—this is why walking around does not refute Parmenides' or Zeno's claim that there is, ultimately, *de jure*, no such thing as movement. We know, just as Zeno did, that it is quite simple to calculate the time required for Achilles to catch the tortoise—but the question is what exactly do we mean when we say that we move? The problem that Zeno describes with his paradoxes can be reduced to this: what exactly allows us to claim that we have ever moved from that point A in the first place? If we want to proceed, to move, we would have to make the leap from one point to *the next point*—but this is precisely what is impossible, because, as everyone knows, there is always another point between any two given points. There is no such thing as "the next point," or "the closest point," or "the adjoining point" on the interval between A and B. A point does not "touch" or "contact" another point. There is no way to construct a line if we only have points, because there is no amount of points that will add up to a line, just as there is no amount of zeros that one would have to add to get to one $(0 + 0 + 0 +. . . = 1)$. In principle, this is the same problem that Zeno hints at in the Achilles paradox and more properly describes in the paradox of the flying arrow. How can we claim that the arrow is moving, when it is clear that if we observe it at any given point in time (in an instantaneous "now") it is at rest? How can a series of rests, even if it is infinite, amount to movement?[4]

To resolve this paradox, Aristotle takes the radical step and abandons the whole idea that time or place could be observed in dimensionless instances like points or nows. As I argue, this is completely consistent with Aristotle's general rejection of the void: *points are, namely, incapable of touch*, and this is why Aristotle's ontology cannot rely on them. Two distinct points (on a line, or a time-line, for instance) can never touch or be in contact with one another, be adjoining one another, because there is always another point between them. A point can never be said to be touching a line or a plane either, because such an intersection, a coincidence of the two, would in fact be one and the same point, and would not amount to two distinct points. In this particular sense—if a point can never touch another point—we could claim that a concept of a point is inseparable from a concept of void. It is not that a point is "surrounded by" void, but rather that a point is nothing but the void itself, considered at a specific location. A point is not a body, it is not an entity, but simply the delimitation, the "there-ness" of an entity. We can never proceed to a concept of a body or a line or something continuous if all we have is a concept of the point. In fact, this is basically the logical background of Aristotle's argument that the void prevents movement: insofar as the void is truly the void, and not just a quantifiably delimited space devoid of specific quality, the void is itself untouchable, ungraspable, and even illogical.[5]

Aristotle thus agrees with Zeno and Parmenides that ontology must not allow for the existence of the void, the nothingness, the zero, but neither can it rely on the point or the now. Aristotle's account of movement therefore rests on the idea of a continuum: an arrow in flight cannot be said to be at rest at any given moment ("now"), because time is not composed of moments ("nows"). Time itself is a continuous interval, and if we break it into parts, those parts are also continuous intervals (of certain length or duration, even if infinitesimally small). We can never observe the flying arrow in a given "now," because movement is not a collection of "nows." We can only observe the flying arrow in a particular interval, and even if that interval is infinitesimally small, it still has its duration, it is still continuous, and the arrow is still moving. And so, the basis for a proper ontological account of movement is laid; Aristotle applies his distinction between existence in actuality and existence in potentiality, and he argues that if we observe an arrow in flight and an arrow at rest, in the same interval, they can both be said to exist, but the flying arrow has a different degree of actuality if compared to the arrow at rest.

At this point, we shall depart from Aristotle's ontology. In order to explain movement, he had to give up the mathematical concept of a point, which seems a very high price to pay. Instead, we will look to Aristotle scholars, particularly to Franz Brentano, who revisited the problem and proposed a solution that bridges the gap between a plenist ontology and the mathematical representation of movement in dimensionless points. In effect, what Brentano suggests is nothing short of a miracle: a concept of a point-in-movement, of a continuous point, and therefore of a point capable of touch.

The touching point

To be sure, the problem described here is certainly not a problem for mathematics. Mathematics has long since abandoned the idea that its terms should be regarded as abstractions from the real world of human experience, as abstractions from intuition. As far as mathematics is concerned, it is quite enough to demonstrate that its terms are consistent with its primordial assertions (axioms), and there is no need to worry about any possible application of those terms to the science of nature or to the science of the spirit. Philosophy, and especially phenomenology and ontology, however, must at least attempt to bridge the gap between our experience of the real world and the mathematical representation. Specifically, the problem that faces ontology can be rendered thus: how is it that we can represent a moving object as resting at a point in time and still produce reliably accurate calculations? How is it that mathematical representation of movement "works" even though it represents movement as consisting of (an uncountable infinity of) rests?

Brentano's solution to this problem—a philosophical problem, not a mathematical one—is based on the idea that a point should always be considered as a border (a boundary).[6] For Brentano, a point does not exist "in itself," but only insofar as it is considered as a boundary of an observed interval or continuum, or a border between two or more intervals or continua. Even though a point is never attached to another point and is in this sense even the very concept of detachment, it is, within Brentano's understanding of space, always already attached to some continuum and thus makes a part of it. In other words, as soon as we have a point, we already have a continuum—a line—that the point belongs to as its boundary. This injunction allows Brentano to treat a point as a part of a continuum without having to further justify their correlation. And it allows him much more: it allows him to consider continuum at work even in its non-continuous part: a point.

Brentano argues that the property of the continuum as a whole is inherited by the point which belongs to the continuum as its part. In order to explain this, he introduces a concept of *plerosis*, or fullness of a point. Brentano invites us to compare a disk of completely blue color to a disk sliced into four quadrants: white, blue, red, and yellow. The center of the sectored disk, if observed as the outer boundary of the blue sector, has only a quarter of the *plerosis*, compared to the full *plerosis* of the center of the completely blue disk (Brentano 2010: 8). The concept of *plerosis* thus allows us to treat the very same point differently, depending on the continuum it belongs to as part. In fact, the concept of *plerosis* allows us to draw not only one, but infinitely many straight lines between two points, even within the framework of the Euclidean geometry—each line only with a fraction of *plerosis* (Brentano 2010: 8).

Introducing this concept allowed Brentano to solve a very specific problem he had with mathematical representation. If we split a line AB into two halves, the point C in the middle has to belong to either of the halves, *but not to both*. For mathematics, this is not a problem at all, we simply define one half as a closed interval AC (which means that it *includes* its final point, C), the other half as an open interval CB (which means that it *excludes* its beginning point, C). For Brentano, whose concept of the continuum should correspond to phenomenological intuition, the very idea of an open interval is an abomination: how can we claim that we have *defined* an interval if this interval has no *boundary*? Brentano writes:

> One of the two lines into which the line would be split upon division would therefore have an end point, but the other no beginning point. This inference has been quite correctly drawn by Bolzano, who was led thereby to his monstrous doctrine that there would exist bodies with and without surfaces (...) He ought, rather, to have had his attention drawn by such consequences to the fact that the whole conception of the line and of other continua as sets of points runs counter to the concept of contact and thereby abolishes precisely what makes up the essence of the continuum.
>
> (Brentano 2010: 105).

It is clear from these words that Brentano is profoundly an Aristotelian: a body without a surface—which is basically what the mathematical concept of open intervals leads to—is a monstrosity precisely because it contradicts the very concept of *contact*, which makes up the essence of the continuum. We are clearly still in the field of the ontology of touch. But with the concept of *plerosis*, we can now finally explain that while it is correct to observe a moving object like a flying arrow in a certain point in time (in a "now"), it is not correct to say that the arrow is at rest in that point, because the point does not exist independently of the continuum of movement it belongs to. In Brentano's words: "every boundary, because it exists only in the context of the continuum to which it belongs as boundary, must itself show up differences in reflection of differences in this continuum" (Brentano 2010: 18). With *plerosis*, Brentano allows us to construct a miraculous point-in-movement, or movement which is present even in its non-continuous part, even in a dimensionless point. With *plerosis*, a point becomes capable of touch. If time truly consists of "nows," then a now is not an isolated point and it does not exist in itself but already involves the continuum reaching to the past and to the future. Implications of this premise are vast; Husserl's and Heidegger's phenomenology, to state only the obvious, profoundly depend on it.

Conclusion

The general aim of this chapter was to demonstrate, firstly, that Aristotle's account of the senses, his account of movement and change in nature, and his ontology in general, all depend on the concept of touch. Without contact, there is no sensation (even no sight); without contact, there is no movement; and since there is no gap or void in being, existence always means existence-in-contact-with. Insofar as the underlying premise for this chapter was Derrida's argument that language and thought share the common root, located in "being," then the ontology of touch, such as we can detect it at work in Aristotle, shares the common root with the linguistics of touch. Just as Aristotle argued that thinking corresponds to touching, it is, in a certain sense, justifiable to claim that to speak is to touch.

Secondly, our aim in this chapter was to return to a little-known attempt by Franz Brentano to bridge a gap between Aristotle's concept of the continuum based on his ontology of touch and the mathematical understanding of a continuum. Brentano's solution, according to which a continuum can only be thought of as consisting of parts which are in contact, even if those parts are themselves not continua, does not remain without a certain split with mathematics. Nevertheless, it is useful to us because it produces a formula according to which a finite, and even non-continuous, part inherits properties of the infinite whole it belongs to as a part. In other words, Brentano offers us a formula according to which we can talk about the *infinite whole at work in its finite part*. While it is not the task of this chapter to expand on this proposition, we will be permitted to briefly outline a possible direction of further analyses. The plasticity Aristotle points out with regard to the sense of touch—namely the fact that touch is the only sense where to perceive also means to be perceived—reaches a completely new level with Brentano's concept of the relationship between the boundary and the continuum. In Brentano's ontology of touch, just as in Aristotle's, there are no gaps in being, or, being as such is continuous. However, it is only in Brentano's ontology that the overall "horizontal" continuity of being is traversed "vertically" with an agreement between the continuous whole and the non-continuous part. It is only this second level of the plasticity which allows us to properly address the peculiar nature of language to express in terms of touch such profoundly contradictory concepts as that of *contingency* and *grasping*, which could, respectively, be explained as the relation between Aristotelian concepts of accident and substance, or as the Hegelian idea of the relationship between the contingency of the series of particular historical events and the necessity of history as a whole.

Notes

1   S. Marc Cohen even argues that in order to "understand the problems and project of Aristotle's *Metaphysics*, it is best to begin with (. . .) the *Categories*" (Cohen 2016).

2   Incidentally, it is curious that in order to separate between the metaphorical and the literal sense of the word "touch" we must resort to a purely linguistic distinction between the spirit and the letter (*littera*).

3   If we understand Zeno's paradox of Achilles (which is basically the same as the paradox of splitting the distance in half) as the problem of finding the sum of infinitely many infinitesimally short intervals, it may seem that one requires the infinitesimal calculus to properly calculate the sum and to refute the paradox. However, once we know the velocity and the distance (or the difference between velocities and the distance between Achilles and the tortoise), we already have all the required data to calculate the time necessary for Achilles to catch the tortoise. For each operation of splitting the distance in half, even if this sequence never ends, there is the operation of splitting the time required in half. Thus the abstract splitting of distances has absolutely no effect on the duration required to catch the tortoise.

4   Of course, contemporary mathematics distinguishes between a countable infinity (infinity of the set of natural numbers) and uncountable infinity (infinity of the set of real numbers, but also of the points on a line). Aristotle and Zeno did not have a concept of such distinction, and we shall not further pursue it at this point. Suffice to say that even with the assertion that a line is a set of points of uncountably infinite cardinality, one still cannot claim that one can get to a line by "adding" points.

5   Perhaps surprisingly, the etymology of the word "logic" points back to gathering, collecting, selecting—which are all actions of the hand and belong to the domain of touch. The void is thus precisely that which is illogical: void is that which is uncollectible, ungatherable, untouchable. Inasmuch as the Greek word *legein* also means to speak—to gather and collect words in sentences—the void is also that which is unspeakable (silence).

6   Brentano's explicit rejection of Cantor's concept of the continuum and of Dedekind's cuts is not a mathematical rejection. For Brentano, the concept of something continuous is an abstraction from our intuition; therefore, Cantor's concept of the continuum is simply not a phenomenological concept. The editors of the English edition of Brentano's phenomenological considerations of continuum write: "Once we recognise the distinction between the mathematical and the phenomenological conceptions of continua, it should be clear that there is no conflict at all between the theories of descriptive psychology (in the sense of Brentano) and the theories of pure mathematics (in the sense of Dedekind) or the theories of mathematical physics (in the sense of Einstein)" (Körner and Chisholm 2010: xii).

References

Aristotle (2016), *De Anima*, trans. by Christopher Shields, Oxford: Clarendon Press.

Benveniste, É. (1971), "Categories of Thought and Language," in *Problems in General Linguistics*, trans. by Mary Elizabeth Meek, Coral Gables: University of Miami Press, 54–63.

Brentano, F. (2010), *Philosophical Investigations on Space, Time and the Continuum*, trans. by Barry Smith, London: Routledge.

Derrida, J. (1976), "The Supplement of Copula: Philosophy before Linguistics," *The Georgia Review*, 30: 3, 527–564.

Freeland, Cynthia (2003), "Aristotle on the Sense of Touch," in: Nussbaum, M. and Oksenberg Rorty, A. (eds.), *Essays on Aristotle's De Anima*, Oxford: Clarendon Press, 227–248.

Heidegger, Martin (1998), *Pathmarks*, trans. by Frank A. Capuzzi, Cambridge: Cambridge UP.

Komel, Mirt (2016), "A touchy subject: the tactile metaphor of touch," *Družboslovne razprave*, 32: 82, 115–125.

Körner, S. and R. M. Chisholm (2010), "Editors' Introduction to the English Edition," in: Brentano, F., *Philosophical Investigations on Space, Time and the Continuum*, trans. by Barry Smith, London: Routledge.

Rosen, S. H. (1961), "Thought and Touch: A Note on Aristotle's De Anima," *Phronesis*, 6, 127–137.

Trendelenburg, Adolf (1846), *Geschichte der Kategorienlehre*, Berlin: G. Bethge.

5

Anatomical Aporia: Speculative Unity of Touch and Language

Goran Vranešević

Introduction

This contribution will deal with a rudimentary speculative question: is there a common ground between touch and language? While touching is an engaging subject, in itself, it represents a field of inquiry where, in spite of long-held curiosity there still seems to be little known. Being present everywhere, it is as if touch is too evident to be taken as a fundamental topic of philosophical inquiry. But rather than offer a coherent overview of different perspectives, concepts, and ideas which have been articulated around the phenomena of touching—ranging from various researches on its tangible qualities, discussions on the sensual dimension itself, more focused phenomenological investigations (Merleau-Ponty), and certain anthropological studies about the haptic realm—my endeavor shall focus on the aporias of touch, a tradition going back to Aristotle, who famously elaborated on the idea of touch in his *On the Soul*.

The obscurities of the tangible, which are not there to be solved or to be done with, but enable us to think (and grasp) it, are initially condensed in the perception of the sense itself, which requires an exterior object to become palpable. However, while vision has color as its sensible object, hearing sound and taste flavor, touch is missing its object. Being objectless, touching is by definition only a potentiality, as the finger cannot directly contact the surface itself, touch is on hand only in relation to the "untouchable limit" (Derrida 2005: 297) that marks the gap between the intention and the deed; the touch is thus liminal, relating to a position at, or on both sides of, a boundary or threshold. Furthermore, the essence of an object of touch remains inaccessible or even absent, as its only function is to stand as untouchable. Hence, in the same manner as visible and invisible are inscribed into the sight, "touch is concerned with both tangible and intangible" (Aristotle 1957: 424a11–14) whereby the field of touchable has a wider scope. In the terminology of a Marxist account of class struggle, touch has to be thought of as a fundamental antagonism, not a relation or a conflict between different senses, as Aristotle hypothesized, but a constitutive principle, primarily structuring the relationship of senses.

To expound such an antagonism, it is not enough to deal with touch in all its apparent manifestations. It is paramount to take touch under scrutiny where it lacks any exterior content or object, where it only persists as a sign of its absence. Such an inscription into the field of language is a purely speculative maneuver: the external, physical realm becomes internalized and subjective and the internal becomes externalized, materialized, and objective. But contrary to expectations, the result of this procedure is not the emergence of a discursive medium where the inherent antagonism of touch can be resolved; by encompassing both of these aspects touch represents the point where thought emerges.

Touching for a principle of unity

To get a clearer insight into the structure or—by looking under the skin of pure materiality—the bloodstream of touching, a slight detour through the systematic confusion of Hegel's fragmentary theory on the sense of touch will be necessary. Naturally, he follows Aristotle, whose *Physics* he characterizes as being "far more a Philosophy of Nature than it is a physics" (Hegel 2004: 2), in positing the sense of touch as the first essential capacity of sensation, which we all share. In various parts of *Encyclopedia of the Philosophical Sciences*, Hegel espouses the sense of touch in the context of nature's *Aufhebung* or sublation,[1] where the sense apparatus as such is observed from two equivalent perspectives. At the physiological level, the structural principle of sensibility resides in the task of translating the external conditions into the inner ideal form—"sensibility as an outward process" (Hegel 1970: 137). Such a process enables an individual to separate themselves from determinateness and become aware of themselves in a particular moment, becoming a particular moment of self-determination, a self-differentiated entity. In this constellation touch is the most general and abstract, while hearing and sight are regarded as the most expressive point of the inwardness. In this manner, that which is touched acquires selfhood (ibid.: 156) as it introduces a particular form into the indistinctness of matter. However, the sublation of "the nature which first developed itself as its sense of touch" (ibid.: 160) or feeling as such, is not a one-act trick. There is a more substantial twist present if one considers the sense of touch from the anthropological level, where a reversal of roles occurs. The sequence of events follows the logic from the "relative abstraction of sensation to the relative concreteness of feeling" (Hegel 1978: 486), sight now being the most general and abstract sense, and touch presented as the most specific and concrete sense. Such a reversal is exemplified in "the hand as the element wherein one essentially recognizes the human" (Hegel 2007: 160). Hegel continues, that the human activity reveals itself corporeally in the hand,[2] not simply because of the ability to manipulate its surroundings and represent oneself, but because touch as the elementary embodiment of feeling performed by the hand is determined as a sign. If applied to the twofold procedure of touching: physiologically touch is too abstract to be something, enduring as a leftover of the body, but anthropologically, it is too concrete to be manifested, a material surplus, thus functioning as the "insubstantiality of substance." Both approaches thus do not merely reflect two incompatible facets of the sense of touch, but moreover express the function of the sign itself.

If we apply a bare bones approach, excluding specific (natural) conditions and extrinsic determinations from deliberation, we are left with a notion of touch presented as the cut between standpoints, even a viewpoint that is presented as "I" and its opposite, manifested as the "non-I," which mutually delimit themselves. Clearly, we can recognize the basic twofold outline of Fichte's *Science of Knowledge* (*Wissenschaftslehre)* here (cf. Fichte 1991). The activity of the "I" is a tense relation to itself: a drive to persist in its particular place of "I-ness" while simultaneously striving for an otherness of the "non-I." However, it is the activity of the "I", the resistance to the outer sphere, that establishes the prerequisite conditions for "non-I" to emerge as something placed outside. The "non-I" is thus not a preexisting state but a condition realized through a variance in "I," which means that the latter is determined by external causes only inasmuch as it is the "I" itself that enables them to affect it. In this sense, the "I" undermines the notion that he himself can be portrayed as the absolute foundation, according to which it is "only in and through the 'I's' absolute positing that the 'I' first comes into existence" (Zöller 1998: 47). By mediating the self-sufficiency of the "I" through its self-posited exterior surface presented as "non-I", the "I" produces an inherent discrepancy usually found in the horror genre, for instance George Langelaan's *The Fly* (1957), where as a result of a scientific procedure, an individual becomes attached to a fly on the molecular level and must transpose this change onto his exterior. This manifestation is not realized because the being of the fly prevailed. On the contrary, it seems as if the disfigured appearance would be the only form that preserves the unity of the subject. Such a discrepancy, where a gap between appearance and being materializes on the surface, is nevertheless constitutive of the subject that is attached to the field of appearance. If we substitute such abstract principles with a general perspective on touching, it is with such variance that a perceived external stimulus is formed as feeling, the feeling of being touched.

Hegel confronted this fundamental separation of exterior sense impressions and subjective thoughts embedded into perception in his famous essay *The Difference Between the Systems of Fichte and Schelling*, where he rigorously expounded their inadequacy, and with it also generic empiricist inferences based on sensuous information. He therefore committed himself to the annulment of its oppositional character into a unitary form (cf. Hegel 1977). The appearance of the "I" is liable to be treated just as appearance which is hidden behind its true form. Instead, Hegel makes a speculative move by positing them on the same level: the true and only being is the appearance established through the movement of reflection, self-actualization of the "I". While Fichte's "I" stumbled over its own subjective endeavor, in a differential structure, it is through sublation of such contrast that the subject truly assumes the form of substance. The phenomena of touching has a similar issue. Even though it is mostly linked to a perceived external reality, which is incorporated into the sense apparatus, the logic must be reversed, as the reality has in some sense to appear to itself: it is here that Hegel articulates touching within the framework of self-positing. The relation to the outside is not conceived as a mediation of two substantialized extremes, as they are "nothing in themselves," but on the insight that their meaning is more or less a movement of vanishing, "they are what they are only in this middle and touching" (Hegel 2008: 125; §141). Both sides are sustained merely as expressions (*Äusserung*), which is "nothing but a self-sublation" (ibid., 126), while the truth of this process is the thought of the movement which collapses into an undifferentiated unity realized as a concept (*ihr Begriff, als Begriff*)[3]. In this context, it is possible to characterize the idea of *Begriff* as a sentence, wherein meaning negates the words. For this reason, the moment of touch has to be simultaneously comprehended as a "practice" that does not just establish a grip on things but also grasps them.

Sign and language

Equipped with this understanding, we can make another step and juxtapose Hegel's insight into the first emergence of an object elaborated in the *Jena*

Lectures, with his theory of language, which is posited as the mediating principle between "external indeterminacy of Nature" and "internal concreteness of Spirit." Standing as "the first potency of consciousness" and the "immediate mediation" of Nature and Spirit, language is the unique link or hinge by which the external becomes internalized and subjective, and the internal becomes externalized and objective, not because it is able to bridge the differences between both, but because language has a life of its own. By expressing the movement or self-relation of the form itself, it does not just "make us say the opposite of what we mean" (Nuzzo 2006: 78), but more importantly enables us to grasp how touch is a prerequisite for thinking. But even if such a linguistic suture of touch and thought is essential, it still does not explain how an object of touch emerges. As in so many other instances, Hegel's approach can offer a unique perspective to unravel this issue.

As customary with Hegel, he presents an arbitrary object, let's say a lion in its immediacy, which is initially received by being heard or seen by a bystander in a particular form. Thus, an empirically rich external existence of a lion receives a general form as an idea, which subsists as *Erinnerung*. In common use, this can be translated as remembrance, a leftover thought, but more specifically, it signifies a re-internalization, a return to oneself.[4] It thereby gains a certain meaning; the picture of a lion slumbering on a savanna. In such a rich descriptive form, the lion stands as a symbol. However, such blissful existence is short lived. To grasp the image of a lion, it needs to be imprinted into the idea by being externalized (*Äusserung*), which means that the presented content is *Aufgehoben* (negated)[5] and "counts as a sign" (Hegel 1983: 88), not as what it is. If we slightly adjust Hegel's ultimate point to his later writings, the other side of the inwardness of the sign, treated as an idea, is still present in the Jena period, but in the *Encyclopedia* this point is refined by externalizing the sign in the form of a material trace left when it is expressed into an auditory form.[6] The moment the lion is named, it is pushed into the realm of signification. Or, in Hegel's words: "immediate inwardness; it must also enter into existence (*Daseyn*), become an object, so that on the contrary this inwardness is made external—a return to being (*Seyn*). This is language, as the name-giving power" (Hegel 1983: 89). The lion is now "not merely something yellow, having feet, etc., something on its own, (existing) independently. Rather, it is a name, a sound made by my voice, something entirely different from what it is in being looked at, and this [as named] is its true being" (Ibid.). What is left of the lion? The name of the lion, which is extremely close to another name, i.e. of the father, that likewise does not require a material backup in the image or the notion, as the name alone is enough to understand it.[7] By asking: "What is this? We answer, it is a lion" (ibid.). It becomes embedded in language. An arbitrary sign of the lion is liberated from the confines of the material conditions of the initial signified essence, or as elegantly described by Jure Simoniti, "the immediacy of the sign is emancipated of the content" (2008: 96), and thereby enables thought to arise.

In passing from the notion (*Vorstellung*) of the object to its enunciation in a sentence, Hegel does not simply show the journey of a lion from the intuition (*Anschauung*) to its concept (*Begriff*), but displays the extent of his sacrifice on this odyssey. The lion's arrival to himself is a tragic one, almost as tragic as the fate of king Oedipus. Bereft of its meat and bones, it stands there as a sign of its lost substantiality. However, it is only now, when we have completely exhausted its meaning and lost every reference to its external determinations, when it is only its own absence, that we can truly touch the lion—by thinking it (the point when the arbitrary sign is deprived of the adequate content of the signified object). And the same reasoning can be applied to the sense of touch as such. The individuals' separation from external determinateness is actually the separation from the immediacy of the touch. Since the physical force of a contact is inadequate in establishing its meaning for itself, the sense of touch first has to anesthetize its own physicality to cause a sensation of touch as a particular moment of self-differentiation or alienation—a sign of touch as an intuition (*Anchauung*) devoid of self-posited content can only gain sense/meaning through an inscription into the medium of language.

A finger is not enough to touch

There is a plethora of ways that one can be touched, whether it be intimately or *ex officio*, emotionally or in a somatic manner; but, touch can also signify a rhetorical device of alluding to or briefly speaking on something and can even express the state of senselessness. It may thus seem that the sense of a touch can be reflected in an attentive word, whereby it communicates a meaningful and graceful message to the one whose ears it was meant for. That is certainly possible, but touch is in essence not a mere discursive expression but an antagonism of such a framework, working at the outskirts of the symbolic realm: curious gazes that touch us like the nerve of a tooth, intimate recollections that touch us by surprise, even an inter-passive sight of a touched audience in the theater. Touch itself therefore is not something an individual can prepare for as it undermines the structure within which it emerges. In this manner, touch can befall a random passerby only when it is devoid of any meaning.

Such a contingent act disturbs the translation of outer content of affects into the internal process of cognition, which would enable a neutral field of inquiry. The wholeness of the body is contaminated by a gesture, but in turn the body itself becomes untouchable, strained by the meaninglessness of the latter. While normal skin is already endowed with a vague biological role of a limit, the same biological function along with reasoning is made obsolete by a random external contact—this scene can be presented as an overlapping of two limits, boundaries, explicitly depicted with the figure of the Terminator whose skin is embedded onto an artificial endoskeleton and vice versa. The plot is well known. A cyborg with human-like exterior appearance is brought back from the future with a simple task, to eliminate the resistance leader's mother, Sarah Connor, and prevent the formation of the resistance; however, with the help of a soldier from this future, she succeeds in exterminating the cyborg and also in conceiving her son, but thereby setting in motion the inevitable consequences; a clear instance of self-fulfilling prophecy. While the appearance and actions of the Terminator cause fear and even despair, the only instance of unfathomable doubt in reality itself is brought about by a mere touch of the Terminator's lifeless arm on Sarah's shoulder. To surmount the aforementioned intractable tension of limits, a sublation of this fundamental difference is needed, and this can only be achieved through a contrasting form of touch. A speculative thought suffices to reestablish some purpose, by overlapping the passing occurrence of touch with the body: the moment of reason becomes embedded into the genesis of the body. Upright posture attests to that as it enabled a sudden evolutionary transformation of anatomy and thereby not just setting free the hands, but simultaneously also granting the freedom of the mind. This is one way to read Lacan's quip that one thinks with the feet, because they touch the ground.[8] Such an episode has always already happened, though it is not present, but it nevertheless constitutes the form by means of which the human kind is *ex post facto* casually structured. We can say the same about sense perception itself, which would fall into arbitrariness if taken in the immediate form, efficiently depicted by Jan Brueghel the Elder's painting *The Senses of Hearing, Touch, and Taste* (1618), and can thus only be manifested in the senselessness of words. The consequences are dramatic: the bodily sphere and the spiritual lose their independent sovereignty, inasmuch as a linguistic quality becomes entangled with the function of tangibility.

The history of fingerprinting is probably the most obvious example of how the absent touch is inscribed as a sign into language. It was not always self-evident that every person is gifted with his own particular set of fingerprints, friction ridges on everyone's hand.[9] While fingerprints have become recognized as a culturally common method to distinguish between individuals, it is less well known that US courts also allow footprints as evidence material. They are most commonly used in the military and for flight personnel, as friction ridges are more resistant inside boots. But it was only in the nineteenth century that the fingerprints became a unique identifying sign of a subject, which reduced the arbitrariness of a complex set of human characteristics to a single impression of the finger. The finger itself is not adequate to be anything else but a stain on paper. It is only when the finger is estranged (*entfremdet*) within a name that the fingerprint touches the owner of the latter. A similar logic is present in Lacan's elaboration of the function of the veil. He explains it by using Pliny the Elder's tale of the contest between Zeuxis and Pharrhasios to determine which of them is the greater artist. When Zeuxis unveiled his painting of grapes, they appeared so real that birds flew down to peck at them. But when Pharrhasios, whose painting was concealed behind a curtain, asked Zeuxis to pull aside that curtain, the curtain itself turned out to be a painted illusion.[10] There is nothing behind the veil except what we put in it, a certain sign. In this instance, the artist touched upon the impoverishing principle of the sign. The wealth of artistic expression thus resides in the simplification of color and tone, and abolishment of intensity, whereby the tie between the representation and its manifestation is preserved but, in the materiality of the latter, is also broken apart. A suitable example would be Malevich's formalistic painting *White on White*, though Hegel's concise remark that the task of philosophy can be explicated as "painting gray in gray" (1991: 23) presents a far more elaborate interpretation. Only after the world is portrayed is it possible to discern the subtle spacing between the two layers of coating and thereby make the structure of thinking visible or even possible.[11]

With this in mind, let us return to the initial question of the common core of language and touch, which are inherently tied together in an object of touch—a sign. The latter can only stand as untouchable and thus indicating the other, negative aspect of touching. However, the prefix *un-* (e.g., Unmethod) is not merely the expression of the complementary other side of a touch, but also touch tainted with its absence. Instead of emphasizing such intricacies, it is more convenient to outline the nature of this structure through a different context: how are the touchable and untouchable realms related in the circumstance of a revolution? While Robespierre allowed Saint-Just to bring him flowers and touch him intimately, the first thing that Jacques-Louis David swore after his arrest was that he did not even touch him. Both formed a close relationship with Robespierre, but with opposite reasoning. Of course there is something intimate in touching; the question remains if it is an individual act. Plato through Socrates would argue that it is Eros who brings bodies (back) together, touching into a single soul, which is accordingly an act which "unites unitively" (Lacan 2015: 20), but the question is then, how does the untouchable touch. Derrida sees in this the question of tact, as "to not touch a loved one enough is to be lacking in tact; however, to touch him, and to touch him too much, to touch him too quick, is also tactless" (Derrida 2005: 80). By utilizing Hegel's speculative idea of the sign, let us make a speculation. What specifically made the revolutionary company function is not determined by the same logic. On one hand, Robespierre was a sign of the revolution for David, who after his fall effortlessly exchanged him for Napoleon, while on the other hand, for Saint-Just, Robespierre was the ideal of a man, which is why he felt obliged to exhibit his affection towards him.[12] The figure of an idea cannot be touched, while an ideal must be worshiped.[13] Such a distinguishing feature of a person that can be at the same time expressed in the form of fondness and loyalty is ingrained in the platonic tradition.[14]

This inquiry can be further paved by Derrida, who in *On Touching* cunningly asked if "eyes can manage to touch, to press together like lips?" (2005: 2). Being of the same kind and anticipating the same outcome, do both of them come into contact with each other? Certainly, a deliberation that may seem redundant and absurd, but it discloses a specific feature of touching, which is not based on the usual search for the common point, a surface, but on a discrepancy where the connecting bond is an interruption in the form of a failed encounter. The similarity with the phenomena of the gaze is evident.

The function of the gaze, as described by Lacan in the *The Four Fundamental Concepts of Psychoanalysis*, is not the ability to convert the form of an outer heterogeneous object into a recognizable image. Any appearance of a connection between an object and an organ of vision is namely established through a detour. Firstly, it is paramount to establish a distinction between what is seen (the imaginary visible world of our perceptions) and the gaze (cause of desire, or more pretentiously said, a stare of the world itself), which is excluded from our field of vision. Accordingly, the gaze is always already redoubled, inscribed into the object as the spot which cannot be perceived. While the materiality of object itself is not enough to establish its own existence, it needs a material backup whereby the outer realm depends on the presence of the gaze within itself. There are numerous implications contained in such an interpretation, but our focus has already been established. How does touch intervene in this framework? To touch a picture with one's eye requires a gaze. While the materialism of the eye is still steeped in the image, still hangs on a splinter of significance, the subject's gaze is always already inscribed into the perceived object itself, in the guise of its "blind spot," that which is "in the object more than object itself," the point from which the object itself returns the gaze. Lacan is even more straightforward: "Sure, the picture is in my eye, but me, I am also in the picture" (Lacan 1998: 63). The lips can be attached to a specific person, with specific traits, in a specific relationship with another person with similar orientation as himself, but their lips can only touch, when they overcome the immediate meaning of touch in the coincidence of love. This is why Badiou claims that love is not a contract between two narcissists, but a sort of nullification of their separate identity with which both entered into the relationship.[15] A similar argument was put forward by a young Hegel, especially in his time in Bern and Frankfurt, where he sought to expound a principle of unity in love and beauty.[16]

A touch or a kiss; I shall know when you give it to me

While there is a wealth of ideas embedded in the topic of love, our interest will be drawn to a specific perspective where Novalis's fingerprints are clearly noticeable. In his *Logological Fragments* he offers a description of the first kiss, not just as a kiss as such, but standing as a sign of a crossroad. In this respect, Novalis regards it as the principle of philosophy, or more specifically, "the origin of a new world, with which a chronological order starts" (Novalis 1997: 59). Such a comment about philosophy could only be a product of a poetic mind, but it also constitutes the most immediate depiction of touch as such. Not just a reflection of a union of two surfaces or a failed meeting of desires, but more importantly, the annulled potentiality and the emergence of thought.

However, any allegory of the first kiss can only offer an inadequate portrayal if it is not read together with Longus' proto-pastoral *Daphnis and Chloe*, which is also more suitable for offering useful speculations about the conundrum of the (un)touchable. Briefly summarized: it is a story of two children abandoned at birth, who were brought up by farmers who found them in the thicket. They grew up together and had a relatively uneventful life, until an incident, if we can characterize it as that. Daphnis fell into a muddy pit and was bravely rescued by Chloe. They immediately started to feel emotions for each other, which of course culminated in their first kiss. After a dare, Chloe, eager to kiss Daphnis, "simply and artlessly" delivered the kiss, with which she "inflamed his heart" (Longus 1989: 9). Daphne, on the other hand, felt it as a sting, rather than a kiss:

> What has Chloe's kiss done to me? Her lips are tenderer than roses, her mouth is sweeter than a honeycomb, but her kiss is sharper than the sting of a bee. I have

often kissed my kids: I have often kissed newly-born puppies, and the little calf which Dorcon gave me: but this kiss is something new. My pulse beats high: my heart leaps: my soul melts: and yet I wish to kiss again. O bitter victory!

(Ibid.: 9–10)

Their touch of the lips redefined the meaning of their relationship. The moment that their intuition is translated into thought material is the moment it loses the anchoring point in a certain image of the relationship and changes into something else. Their common ground is no longer a possibility on the horizon, but the materiality of the sign.

The incident at the pit was not the sole romantic stimulus that directly led to their kiss. A certain amount of work had to be done to establish the prerequisite conditions. After the events that transpired at the pit, Chloe and Daphnis went to wash themselves: "When she washed his back, his skin yielded softly to her touch, so that she kept touching herself stealthily to find out whether he was more velvety that she" (Ibid., 13). Later on, she persuaded him to have another wash, "she watched him while he washed, and after watching she touched him, and again she came away in admiration, and this admiration was the beginning of love" (Ibid.). We intentionally omitted this detail, as a curious mind is quickly misled by such imagery and would put too much emphasis on it. Just to clarify, her self-touch, this auto-affection, was instrumental in laying the foundation for their encounter, but it amounted to nothing else but empty positing which is more in vein with Fichte's early conceptualization of the absolute "I." By postulating its own existence, the "I" organizes a self-mediating procedure, whereby the founding act itself undermines the notion that such an act could be actualized in a pure form, as it needs to introduce an external other to implement it. The latter fails to recognize its own shortcoming and thus establishes a differentiated antagonistic structure that is never overcome. In this state, Chloe would merely exhibit affection and not love. Such a discrepancy is a result of the absence of an inner inhibition which is established only with the kiss whereby the empty positing collides (*Anstoss*) with the motivation that inaugurated the procedure of positing.

There are countless anecdotes, incidents, and stories from Lacan's practice, however one in particular stands out in its subversive nature, where the prohibition of touch is brought to its logical conclusion. One of Lacan's patients[17] was once in a session recollecting a dream to him. Herself a survivor of Nazi occupation, she would constantly dream of how she woke up every morning at five o'clock, which was the precise time that the Gestapo came to carry away the

Jews from their houses. The moment she concluded her thought, Lacan jumped from his chair, walked over to her and extremely gently caressed her cheek. An unusually tender gesture especially for him, but she understood it, rightly, as a purely linguistic act: "Gestapo" became "*geste à peau*," a gesture on the skin, a gesture which refurbished her anguish into something else. To interpret this effect as a product of the physical contact would fail to recognize the radicality of this act. Any serious analysis has to turn the focus to this simple homophone, which sufficed to transform an undesirable act and touch the analysand. It is hard to find a clearer example of the materiality of the signifier in the subject's speech. By setting aside the heft of the meaning behind the youthful encounter with the Gestapo, and shifting the focus to a contingent sign which was embedded into the memory of the analysand, words themselves become emancipated and lived their life independently of their initial host. What touched her was not embedded in the physical contact, but in the alienation of the sign: the structure of the sentence. The failure to articulate an authentic answer to a central subjective antagonism turns out to institute an immediate palpable touch.[18]

Conclusion

In retrospect, the answer to the principal conundrum seems even vaguer than it initially appeared. In order to deal with the supposed dualism of the touchable and the untouchable, a speculative maneuver is required; an act which does not inhere in the abstract idea which encompasses both aspects, but endures as an inherent paradox of language. The latter is brought about in its own deficit (lack of meaning); in the point of touch, which is essentially missing in the structure of language. And it is this shortcoming of language, its impossible origin that produces the necessity to talk, to *parle*, which is itself derived from Latin *parabola*,[19] thus signifying a junction. It is thus clear why Hegel, in his phenomenology's section on "The Living Work of Art," defines language as "the perfect element in which inwardness is just as external as externality is inward" (Hegel 2008: 439). While his notion of *Begriff* can certainly be defined as a sentence, wherein meaning negates the words, it must to the same extent be grasped as the impetus which secedes language from its natural causality (embedded in the couple world–meaning). The speaking subject is thus not the bearer of meaning or identity, as its essence is only expressed in the act of being touched by language (the big Other). If there is a speculative intervention present in language, it can be found here; it should be understood as a sort of covenant (gr. *diatíthēmi*) with the Other; an arragement or a distribution of the common ground, epitomized by the external being or reality, instilled with the difference between the touchable and untouchable.

As a farewell gesture to the reader, let us resort to a short epilogue worth dwelling on. It is a sort of an autobiographical note left by Teresa of Avila after meeting a bodily manifestation of an angel holding a golden spear. Without warning he plunged the spear into her heart, so deeply that it grabbed hold of her entrails, which he purposelessly pulled out. Teresa described this grotesque scene in a curious manner: "I was utterly consumed by the great love of God." (St. Teresa 1957: 152). While the description is certainly sexual in nature, it also functions as a reminder that God is able to touch by being untouchable. Her pleasurable daze continued until this performance of elation "began to be talked about" (ibid.: 153). Even though these assertions seem implausible or at least a construct of the mind, it is impossible to deny the existence of enjoyment. Something touched her; apparently, God. However, it may very well be that St. Teresa initiated the courtship with God herself through reading the words of the Gospel, which inspired her contemplations on God. And contrary to common sense, the logic of contemplation is precisely the logic of language. What is it then that touched her? Speculatively said, the absent existence of God, inscribed into the community through tireless declarations and testimonials.

Notes

1   *Aufhebung* is a crucial part of the dialectical method and is also known to be almost untranslatable as it encompasses two opposite movements, to abolish and preserve, which is traversed by the third, to "elevate". This speculative meaning as Hegel described it: "What is sublated does not thereby turn into nothing. Nothing is the immediate; something sublated is on the contrary something mediated; it is something non-existent but as a result that has proceeded from a being; it still has in itself, therefore, the determinateness from which it derives" (Hegel 2010: 81). But the easiest way to describe the concept of sublation is to present its application by an example. For Hegel, punishment is not the prerequisite for goodness to emerge. Quite the contrary, punishment serves to cancel the committed crime "not as the production of evil, but as the violation of the right as right" (Hegel 1991: 124–125). Such a violation of abstract right means that punishment functions as *Aufhebung* of crime—it restores the right by absorbing the criminal act as unjust.

2   There is a certain discrepancy present in the gesture of touching, for it needs a second party, a conduit to express itself—a privileged organ of touching, a hand, a

willing hand, in our case, the Hegelian hand that grasps (*ergreifen*) and
conceptualizes (*begreifen*) at once in the notion of *Begriff*. It seems to be the true heir
of the invisible hand of the market, but more importantly it is structured as a cut of
its own continuum, establishing its own parameters of existence. There is also a
Derridaian hand, a hand which grasps and rubs a different kind of material between
its fingers. While the hand is purposely engaging with an object of perception, which
establishes a certain kind of knowledge translatable to the genesis of "I". The question
of the hand thus becomes the question of "humanualism," a human rationale to exert
one's hand in a certain manner, to touch, "they alone can touch, in the strongest and
strictest sense. Human beings touch more and touch better. The hand is properly
human; touching is properly human: it is the same proposition" (Derrida 2005: 152).
The shape of the hand could thus be an ontoteleological figure, a rhetorical figure, or
even a perfect example of a trope that manifests the contours of touch in its general
sense. For instance, a metonymy, a figure of otherness, leading through visibility and
exposition to a surface and further to the psychic realm, while retroactively sewing
this path as always already traversed.

3 Although we have already touched on this theme, a brief remark will benefit the
   clarity of the argument. The German word *Begriff* contains a manifold of meanings:
   firstly, it signifies understanding, comprehending (*begreifen*); secondly, it is used as a
   synonym for a term or word; and thirdly, the most obvious is the use for the notion
   of concept. However, the speculative nature of German language, which Hegel
   skillfully uses throughout his oeuvre, also refers with *Begriff* to the gesture of
   grabbing, grasping, holding and even handling something (*Griff, Greifen*). For a more
   precise elaboration of the concept of *Begriff*, see Mirt Komel's contribution in this
   book (Chapter 1).

4 In the *Lectures on the History of Philosophy* Hegel is even more precise, describing
   Erinnerung as "going-within-oneself, making oneself inward," whereby he deduces
   that we can say "that knowledge of the universal is nothing other than a recollection,
   a going-within-oneself, what shows itself initially in an outward mode, and is
   determined as a manifold, we make into something inward, something universal, by
   virtue of going into ourselves and in this way bringing what is within us to
   consciousness" (Hegel 2009: 188–189).

5 What if the loss or alienation should be celebrated? The spirit of *Aufhebung* resides on
   the premise of reduction, where the sublated or negated object survives the ordeal, but
   not without certain collateral damage: "torn out of its life-world context, reduced to its
   essential feature, all the movement and wealth of its life reduced to a fixated mark. It is
   not that, after the abstraction of Reason does its mortifying job with its fixated
   categories or notional determinations, the speculative 'concrete universality' somehow
   returns us to the fresh greenness of Life: once we pass from empirical reality to its
   notional *Aufhebung*, the immediacy of Life is lost forever" (Žižek 2012: 486).

6 Hegel further elaborates on the ambiguous role of the symbol using the example of
   the lion in his *Lectures on Aesthetics*. He describes the symbol as "an external existent
   given or immediately present to contemplation, which yet is to be understood not
   simply as it confronts us immediately on its own account, but in a wider and more
   universal sense" (Hegel 1988: 304). If we strictly distinguish between meaning and
   expression of the symbol, it is *prima facie* a sign. In general, this quality is exhibited
   in language where sounds coincidentally form a link with ideas expressed thereby.
   Our lion partakes in a similar linguistic parkour.

7 For a more detailed elaboration on the curious nature of naming, see Jela Krečič's
   contribution in this book (Chapter 9).

8 Lacan declared this curious idea during an academic visit to New York, where
   besides insisting "to be allowed to make a private visit to the Metropolitan Opera
   House" (Roudinesco 1997: 376), which his intermediaries resolved by "telling the
   director that Jean-Paul Sartre wanted to visit incognito" (ibid.), and accidentally
   encountering Dalí, he also gave a lecture on the subject of the inner and outer.
   Robert Georgin recounted Lacan's striking responses to the question on thought:
   "We think we think with our brains; personally, I think with my feet. That's the only
   way I really come into contact with anything solid. I do occasionally think with my
   forehead, when I bang into something. But I've seen enough electroencephalograms
   to know there's not the slightest trace of a thought in the brain" (Georgin in
   Roudinesco 1997: 378).

9 The history of the fingerprint in criminal investigation is full of coincidences.
   Regarding its wider use there is a consensus that William Herschel, an English
   bureaucrat, was the first to note the value of fingerprints, not for any investigative
   purposes, but for upholding contractual obligations. It was Henry Faulds who first
   suggested the use of fingerprints in forensic work. He was an English missionary
   who developed a keen interest in ancient pottery. While observing the fine details of
   the latter, he noticed that artists leave a distinctive fingerprint on the bottom of the
   pots, whereby their artworks can be distinguished. Although there were various
   attempts at systematization, especially Galton's, it wasn't until an Argentine detective,
   Juan Vucetich, used fingerprints to solve a case that its usability was also verified in
   practice (cf. Thorwald 1965). Even more astounding is that Mark Twain had this
   exact idea some time before it was applied. In his memoir *Life on the Mississippi*
   (1883), he wrote of a bloody fingerprint as an indicator of identification. Curiously,
   there is another twist, as in all likelihood, Twain's account of the fingerprint was
   inspired by a paper about Japanese pottery published in the journal *Nature*. Its
   author: Henry Faulds.

10 For a more comprehensive interpretation, see Lacan 1998: 103.

11 Mladen Dolar elaborates on the question of grayness in the context of the proper
   color of philosophy, a point which originates from Goethe's *Faust*, where Mephisto

posits the color gray as the color of all theory, a color of non-difference, and opposes it to the color green of (the abundance of difference in) life. In this respect, "gray on gray is the difference of the indifferent, the minimal difference [...] the gray of dawn on the gray of dusk, the difference between two transitions" (Dolar 2015: 889). Malevich thus seems to have missed the proper Hegelian form, since the color white is the absence of color and even minimal difference.

12 In a letter to Robespierre, Saint-Just wrote: "you whom I know, as I know God, only through his miracles." For a broader context of his relationship to Robespierre, see Linton, Maris (2013), *Choosing Terror: Virtue, Friendship and Authenticity in the French Revolution*. Oxford: Oxford UP.

13 http://www.ligonier.org/blog/the-sense-of-touch-in-worship/

14 In this framework ideas are presented as the forms of knowledge (*logos*) which operate as a (timeless) regulatory principle structuring the sensuous phenomena while operating independently of their existence (beauty, justice). An individual can act only through them not according to them. Meanwhile, ideals have a different role in the theater of existence. Their ideal status comes from the universal paradigm according to which there is one (unity) and dyad (diversity), a synthetic unity of the same and the other, which means that ideals essentially also encompass ideas (cf. Plato 1997).

15 "Love is above all a construction that lasts [...], a construction of life that is being made" (Badiou 2012: 29–32).

16 Even if Hegel normally shies away from confronting the tactile implications of beauty as the sensuous expression of free spirit, the structural inference is that both love and beauty are by their nature not to be touched. For an illustration that dares to touch the figure of beauty, see Jela Krečič's contribution in this book (Chapter 9).

17 Suzanne Hommel. Listen to: http://www.radiolacan.com/en/topic/45/1

18 Lacan denotes the subject as $ precisely because of such inherent inability to constitute oneself. The subject emerges exactly at the point where signifying procedure fails as a representational apparatus. Love letters accurately embody such a dissonance in the intention. They work only in those instances when they fail to convey the meaning designated by the addresser. Imagine a perfectly clear love letter; it would surely miss the addressee, for he would not await true feelings to be formulated in a clear manner and would therefore try to find ambiguities in every word. It is such instances that constitute a sign of genuine love, not effective style or clever use of metaphors.

19 The etymological roots of both can be found in Greek parabolé (παραβολή), which does not only signify speech, words and "to make clear by metaphor," but also a comparison, juxtaposition, illustration, and most relevant for the purpose of this article, *(con)junction*.

References

Aristotle (1957), *On the Soul. Parva Naturalia. On Breath*, Cambridge: Harvard UP.

Badiou, A. (2012), *In Praise of Love*, London: Serpent's Tail.

Derrida, J. (2005), *On Touching: Jean-Luc Nancy*, Stanford: Stanford UP.

Dolar, M. (2015), "The Owl of Minerva from Dusk till Dawn, or, Two Shades of Gray" *Philosophy and Society* 26/4: 875–890.

Fichte, J.G. (1991), *The Science of Knowledge*, Cambridge: Cambridge UP.

Hegel, G.W.F. (1977), *The Difference Between Fichte's and Schelling's System of Philosophy* Frühe schriften, Albany: State University of New York Press.

Hegel, G.W.F. (1978), *Philosophy of Subjective Spirit*, Dordrecht; Boston: D. Reidel.

Hegel, G.W.F. (1983), *Jena Lectures on the Philosophy of Spirit (1805–06)*, Detroit: Wayne State UP.

Hegel, G.W.F. (1988), *Aesthetics: Lectures on Fine Art I*, Oxford: Clarendon Press.

Hegel, G.W.F. (1991), *Elements of the Philosophy of Right*, Cambridge: Cambridge UP.

Hegel, G.W.F. (2004), *Philosophy of Nature*, Oxford: Oxford UP.

Hegel, G.W.F. (2007), *Lectures on the Philosophy of Spirit (1827–28)*, Oxford: Oxford UP.

Hegel, G.W.F. (2008), *Phenomenology of Spirit*, Trans. Terry Pinkard.

Hegel, G.W.F. (2009), *Lectures on the History of Philosophy, vol. 3*, Oxford: Clarendon Press.

Hegel, G.W.F. (2010), *The Science of Logic*. Cambridge: Cambridge UP.

Lacan, J. (1998), *Four Fundamental Concepts of Psychoanalysis: The Seminar of Jacques Lacan, Book XI*, New York: W. W. Norton.

Lacan, J. (2015), *Transference: The Seminar of Jacques Lacan, Book VIII*. Cambridge: Polity Press.

Linton, M. (2013), *Choosing Terror: Virtue, Friendship, and Authenticity in the French Revolution*, Oxford: Oxford UP.

Longus (1989), *Pastorals, or the Loves of Chloe and Daphnis*, London: Penguin Books.

Novalis (1997), "Logological Fragments I," *Philosophical Writings*, Albany: State University of New York Press.

Nuzzo, A. (2006), "The Language of Hegel's Speculative Philosophy," in: J.O. Surber (ed.), *Hegel and Language*, Albany: State University of New York Press.

Plato (1997), *Complete Works*, Indianapolis & Cambridge: Hackett.

Roudinesco, E. (1997), *Jacques Lacan*, New York: Columbia UP.

Simoniti, J. (2008), *Resnica kot kreacija*. Ljubljana: Društvo za teoretsko psihoanalizo.

St. Teresa (1957), *The Life of Saint Teresa of Avila*. London; New York: Penguin Books.

Thorwald, J. (1965), *Das Jahrhundert der Detektive*, Zürich: Droemmersche
    Verlagsanstalt.
Žižek, S. (2012), *Less Than Nothing: Hegel and the Shadow of Dialectical Materialism*,
    London: Verso.
Zöller, G. (1998), *Fichte's Transcendental Philosophy. The Original Duplicity of Intelligence
    and Will*, Cambridge: Cambridge UP.

6

The Category of the (Un)Touchable in Haptic Materialism: Touch, Repetition, and Language

Bara Kolenc

Introduction

One can discern two elementary agents of touch, the active and the passive one, *the touching* and *the touched*. It has often been argued that the two are reversible[1], that *the touching* has always already turned into *the touched* and the other way round: as soon as we touch it, it inevitably touches us back. However, despite their inseparability, the two agents of touch *are* and need to be discerned for touch to be conceptually grasped. Even if the dividing line between the active and passive agent of touch seems vague because of the unavoidable reversibility of touch, it can never be totally obliterated: it is impossible that *the touching* would be at the same time also *the touched*. The positions never collide—rather they are in the constant process of exchange. This is precisely what Merleau-Ponty wants to stress with his famous example of self-touching:

> When I touch my right hand with my left, my right hand, as an object, has the strange property of being able to feel too. We have just seen that the two hands are never simultaneously in the relationship of touched and touching to each other. When I press my two hands together, it is not a matter of two sensations felt together as one perceives two objects placed side by side, but of an ambiguous set-up in which both hands can alternate the rôles of 'touching' and being 'touched'.
>
> (Merleau-Ponty 2005: 106)

It is precisely in the crossing and intertwining of the active and the passive object of touch where lies the core idea of Merleau-Ponty's concept of *chiasm*, which forms the key of his mature ontology and his understanding of the relationship between the individual and the world.

From the perspective of language, the idea of touch could be thought on two different levels: the metonymical and the metaphorical (cf. Komel 2009 and Dolar 2008). In his 1956 essay, "Two Aspects of Language and two Types of Aphasic Disturbances," Jakobson described the two axes of language as the two fundamental opposite poles along which language is structured (cf. Jakobson 1987): the metonymic axis, the site of sequential ordering drawing combination between signs, and the metaphoric axis, the site of substitution drawing selection between signs. Jakobson's distinction was consistent with Saussure's rethinking of language as split between paradigmatic relations, which involve the association of substitutable elements *in absentia* (metaphor) and syntagmatic relations, which involve simultaneous or successive combinations *in praesentia* (metonymy). While metaphor substitutes a concept with another, a metonymy selects a related term. Lacan, inspired by Jakobson's work, argued that the unconscious is structured like a language (*l'inconscient est structuré comme un langage*) and that the two dynamic processes of the unconscious discovered by Freud (cf. Freud 1963), displacement and condensation, are equivalent to the linguistic functions of metonymy and metaphor (cf. Lacan 1966).

On the metonymical level, touch is perceived as a direct connection, as proximity without mediation, while on the metaphorical level, it is thought as always already mediated. The metonymical touch touches so much that it becomes one with the touched, while the metaphorical touch does not touch at all—there is always a vast distance between the touching and the touched that prevents the touch proper from ever happening. While the metonymical touch lacks the distance, the metaphorical touch always has it too much. On the metonymical level, nothing can prevent the touching immerse into the touched and to become too much of a touch, so much that the touch as such at once disappears. As soon as the active and the passive agent of touch melt into one single entity, touch is lost. On the metaphorical level, the disposition is just the opposite: nothing can ever shrink the distance between the touching and the touched, nothing can ever connect the separated entities.[2]

We can see that both dimensions of touch, the metonymical and the metaphorical one, come across a certain impasse at some point—what they both essentially miss, is nothing but touch itself. If the two agents of touch are separated, then touch is perceived as something that has not yet happened, relentlessly sticking to the point where it is just about to occur, while if they are perceived as inseparable, the touch is never really there because it has always already happened. In both cases, the touch as such is missed. Touch is therefore a paradoxical category that lingers between two walls of impossibility: the impossibility of distance on the one hand and the impossibility of proximity on the other. In both cases, touch itself is, so to say, condemned to failure—the delicate line between the touching and the touched, defining the elusive moment of touch, is always already missed. You cannot stay on the event horizon: you either pass by or sink into a black hole.

The two walls of impossibility between which touch is ultimately caught install the category of the *(un)touchable* that draws the unconceivable line between the never yet executed and the always already ran over event of touch.[3] Touch as such can only exist in view of its impossibility. This is exactly what Derrida had in mind when questioning touch as *tangential* (cf. Derrida 2005). While metaphorical touch needs yet to bring together the touching and the touched (we can imagine them as a passant in relation to a circle) to establish the event of touch (as a tangent to a circle), the metonymical touch has to, in order to establish touch, work in the opposite direction: it needs to separate the always already related agents of touch (a secant to a circle). We have to keep in mind that neither *metaphor* nor *metonymy* is touch as such—they are functions, setting up the (always impossible) condition of possibility of touch. The presence of touch has to be understood in view of its absence: this is the core idea of Nancy's concept of "touching the limit (*toucher la limite*)" (Nancy 1988: 47). And, as Komel summarizes Derrida's reading of Nancy (cf. Derrida 2005), touch is "defined through the limit, through the asymptotic approaching the point of touch where touch splits into the touchable and the untouchable" (Komel 2009: 25).

The active and the passive agent of touch can be understood as the subject and the object of touch. As touch has always already happened while it has never yet occurred, the object of touch, *the touched*, is something that is at the same time *touchable* and *untouchable*. Moreover, it is touchable only under the condition of its untouchability—and *vice versa*. What can be touched is always already untouchable, but only through its untouchability something can be touched at all. Furthermore, if we perceive touch in itself as the object of touch, as the object of a conceptual grasp, it is touch itself that is at the same time touchable and untouchable: exactly therein lies the conceptual kernel.

Through the category of the *(un)touchable*, touch engages the function of desire. What empowers one's desire is precisely the structural impossibility to grasp its object: what we eventually touch is never that which we desired. But at the same time, this is the only way we can ever touch it, because the inherent impossibility of touch is its very condition of possibility. The category of the *(un)touchable* sets the mechanism of forced choice (cf. Lacan 1966–67): either we touch it in a way that we cannot touch it or we do not touch it at all. And what is structurally (un)touchable within the mechanism of forced choice is not only the elusive object of touch, but also the touch itself as the impossible borderline between distance and proximity.

Here we can remember the Ancient Greek story of Pyramus and Thisbe, masterfully rewritten by Ovid in his *Metamorphoses* (cf. Ovid 2004), the story about lovers who were craving for closeness but were only able to touch each other with their whispering words through a tiny crack in the wall. Once they finally managed to arrange a hidden meeting outside the city walls, the so much desired touch of the other was fatally missed and therefore it tragically turned into a double suicide (an ultimate touch of the self as a radical consequence of the impossible touch of the other). The two loving creatures never managed to enjoy the pleasure of the trembling event of touch: the moment when touch was wishfully expected as something that is just about to happen directly turned into the moment when touch has already passed away (without ever really occurring)—the two corpses lying on each other were suddenly touching too much as one single indistinctive pile of flesh.

Through the structure of the *(un)touchable*, the story of Pyramus and Thisbe embodies an ultimate materialist turn of Plato's fantasy of love, as described in the *Symposium* (cf. Plato 1997), the fantasy of two lost halves finally finding each other and becoming one: the becoming one is the structure of death.

Language and the materiality of touch

Speaking of touch, also in the context of language, we necessarily come across the question of its materiality: is touch unavoidably material or could it be understood as immaterial?

Within Plato's idealism that separated the world of *universals*—ideas as abstract forms, as concepts without sense perception accessible only through intellect (*noumena*)—and the world of *particulars*—concrete physical objects and properties that can be grasped with sense perception (*phaenomena*) (cf. Plato 1997)—the category of *the touchable* and the category of *the untouchable* were strictly delimited. Proximity (i.e. possibility of touch) was set up among perceptible things and among abstract ideas themselves, while an insurmountable distance (i.e. impossibility of touch) between *noumena* and *phaenomena* was kept as the basic presupposition of its dualistic structure of the world, where the transient material existence was merely copying (or participating in) the eternal and immaterial being in itself. Within Plato's dispositive, touch was understood as *sensual* operation, performed towards (and among) factual objects and referred to matter as substance, defined by empirical qualities, and its sensual perception. However, the notion of touch within the realm of abstract concepts was also used by Plato as a metaphorical or allegorical representation of the world of ideas, for example in *Phaedo* within the context of a discussion on the relationship between body and soul: "if one wants to touch the truth of the ideas, one must forfeit the sensory bodily experiences" (Plato 1997: 65a–c)[4]. While the *sensual* touch was understood as material and empirical, the *spiritual* touch was considered abstract and immaterial.

The institution of modern science, historically marked by the Galileian revolution,[5] and Kant's Copernican Revolution (cf. Kant 1986) gave rise to a radical twist of the perspective: the phenomenal world was no longer considered to be separated from the mind processes, quite the opposite—it was now perceived as always already inscribed in the production of concepts. This change of perspective was only possible by bringing forth the new notion of materiality: within the horizon of modern science, matter is no longer substance defined by qualities such as mass, density, weight, shape, structure, but becomes, as Milner puts it, *matter without qualities* (cf. Milner 2002). "Decision for a systematic erosion of all the qualitative and sensory," claims Milner, "can be subsumed under one single notion: matter" (Milner 2003: 166). Albeit without qualities, matter can be measured through its *effects*. And as a direct consequence, the new notion of materiality also brings about a change in the perception of form. There is no pure form—the sphere of concepts is unavoidably perforated by material effects: this is the general disposition of modern science.

In his *Course in General Linguistics*, Saussure emphasizes that the linguistic sign unites, not a name and a thing, but a concept and a sound-image (cf. Saussure 1966). The classical division between a name (i.e. a sign) and its empirical referent is replaced by the division between the abstract and the material aspect of the sign itself: *the signified* and *the signifier*. "Both terms involved in the linguistic sign are psychological," claims Saussure, and "are united in the brain by an associative bond" (Saussure 1966: 65–66). The sound-image is "not the material sound, a purely physical thing, but the psychological imprint of the sound, the impression that it makes on our senses" (Saussure 1966: 65–66). In that manner the sound-image is sensory, but it is not empirical. With Saussure, the notion of materiality refers to the *matter without qualities*: "the sound-image is sensory, and if I happen to call it 'material', it is only in that sense, and by way of opposing it to the other term of the association, the concept, which is generally more abstract" (Saussure 1966: 65–66). Within the realm of modern science, the separating line between conceptual abstraction and materiality therefore persists, but on a different scale. Modern science turns the outer border between ideas (concepts) and matter (empirical things) into an inner division between abstract and material aspects of concepts themselves. For modern science, touch worth examining is no longer touch between abstract concepts and empirical things, but touch between concepts and their inner material aspect. As Milner puts it, the goal of science is no longer to distill the eternal and essential (form) from the transient and variable (matter), but to *mathematize* and to literalize (*littéralise*) the world of *phaenomena* as the material carriers of the ever open, transient and non-whole structure of concepts (cf. Milner 1995). As a consequence of the twist of the perspective and the change of the notion of materiality brought about with modern science, a certain shift in the conceptualization of touch and tactility can be pointed out: with the institution of modern science, the relation between spiritual and sensual touch is replaced by the relation between metonymical and metaphorical touch. This historical thesis, however, only functions as a complement to a structural (i.e. synchronic) reading of mechanisms of touch within language.

Touch and repetition

There is a structural analogy between the category of *the (un)touchable* and the *constructive difference* that is at work within the processes of repetition. This analogy can help us understand the mechanism of touch within the structures of language.

What is essential for the category of touch is that it is performed by two entities that are at once connected and separated. Touch establishes a dual relationship: there is no third party that could ever penetrate this alliance. Touch is set up between two terms of touch—the touching and the touched—as the separating, yet connecting moment between the two. Similarly, the basic scheme of repetition is a relation between two terms of repetition and the difference between them. Repetition does not imply a multiplying singularity but a fundamental duality, a relation between two terms determined by their difference. The notation of the basic scheme of repetition is repeated 1 | repeated 2 (repeated 1 – bar – repeated 2), where bar marks the *constructive difference*: a difference as a connective–separating function (cf. Kolenc 2014).

As a function, constructive difference is defined through a certain ambiguity between integration and differentiation of the two terms between which it arises: at once, it both differentiates and connects the two terms of repetition. It is a cut that yet establishes the relation between the two. It launches the two terms of repetition as absolutely identical and radically different at once. This means that somehow paradoxically the difference between the two terms of repetition (the repeated 1 and the repeated 2, henceforth R1 and R2) is established precisely by the fact that there is no difference between them. It is the very indiscernibility between the two terms of repetition that is the condition of possibility of their difference. Therefore, constructive difference is itself neither positive nor negative, neither present nor absent. Rather, it is a dubious entity, at once an absent presence and a present absence. It is a negation that is itself constructive. As such, constructive difference is the lever of the process of repetition.

Within the realm of touch, constructive difference establishes the category of the (un)touchable: the R1 and R2 touch each other precisely through the impossibility of being in touch with each other, through their difference. From the perspective of touch, constructive difference operates as a bar that establishes the very possibility of touch between the two alienated terms, but at the same time it also builds an unbreakable barricade between them: the possibility of touch between R1 and R2 is conditioned by its very impossibility. This paradox, encapsulated in the category of the *(un)touchable*, is exactly the mechanism that profoundly connects touch with repetition: just as the two terms of repetition, the two agents of touch are never yet connected but are at the same time always already separated. In order for repetition or touch to be established, the two agents should not melt into one, for this would diminish both of them, but they also should not be set as two separated entities, because in this case there would be no conditions for either repetition or touch to ever occur.

Repetition is often considered as a reversible process: as much as R2 repeats R1, to the same extent also R1 repeats R2. But to this point we have to introduce a certain differentiation: despite them being named with the same signifier, the two terms of repetition are two different entities, defined by their difference. Somehow paradoxically, the difference between the two terms of repetition is established precisely by the fact that there is no difference between them—this is the tricky mechanism of constructive difference. The two terms of repetition are not simply interchangeable—the very fact that they are different, yet indiscernible, prevents repetition from being simply thought as a reversible process.

The same goes for touch: in order to conceptually grasp it we have to maintain the difference and, at the same time, connection between the active and the passive agent of touch, *the touching* and *the touched* (i.e. constructive difference). Despite (or, rather, precisely because of) the fact that the same agent (for example a hand) could simultaneously execute two different functions (the function of touching and the function of being touched), they must still be perceived as two different terms.

We have to insist on maintaining this differentiation in order to further elaborate on touch as a function of repetition. This is the fundamental disposition of the category of the (un)touchable.

Saussure: touch and repetition in structural linguistics

In language, claims Saussure, there are only differences. There are no positive elements. Sign is oppositional, relative, and negative—this is a central disposition of structural linguistics (cf. Saussure 1966).

Therefore, language is a system of *values* set through a fundamental paradox:

'On the one hand the concept seems to be the counterpart of the sound-image, and on the other hand the sign itself is in turn the counterpart of the other signs of language'. Which means that, paradoxically, 'language is a system of interdependent terms in which the value of each term results solely from the simultaneous presence of the others.'

(Saussure 1966: 114)

As a system of values, language functions through a double set of relations: through the relations between concepts and sound-images as separated yet connected components of a sign on the one hand, and through the relations of the sign itself towards the other signs of language on the other. The first relation is composed of two chains—the chain of signified and the chain of signifiers: "In an accurate delimitation, the division along the chain of sound-images (a, b, c) will correspond to the division along the chain of concepts (a', b', c')" (Saussure 1966: 104).

When set forth for the purposes of the linguistic science, further argues Saussure, such delimitation however stumbles across a set of unsolvable practical difficulties, and is therefore counterproductive. What he then brings as his answer to this problem is rather surprising: "When a science has no concrete units that are immediately recognizable," he claims, "it is because they are not necessary" (Saussure 1966: 104). His answer is, however, nothing but the twist of perspective in view of a structure: if delimitation causes difficulties, we should not try to get rid of those difficulties, but, on the contrary, see them as crucial characteristics of the object of research. A mistake is not there by mistake.

Hence, linguistic sign needs to be taken as composed of two different entities (signifier and the signified) and in relation to other signs, but only inasmuch as we understand signifier and the signified as the two inseparable components of a sign, on the one hand, and only inasmuch as we see the linguistic sign as appearing within the structure of language, on the other. "Just as the game of chess," says Saussure:

> is entirely in the combination of the different chess pieces, language is characterized as a system based entirely on the opposition of its concrete units. We can neither dispense with becoming acquainted with them nor take a single step without coming back to them; and still, delimiting them is such a delicate problem that we may wonder at first whether they really exist.
>
> (Saussure 1966: 107)

We need to bear in mind all the differentiations that structure language, but as soon as we want to delimit each sub-structure, as a separate system subjected to specialized scientific research, as soon as we want to grasp its concrete units as something existent or perceptible, we lose the very object of linguistics: "Language then has the strange, striking characteristic of not having entities that are perceptible at the outset and yet of not permitting us to doubt that they exist and that their functioning constitutes it" (Saussure 1966: 107). The entities of language are material yet they do not have qualities. They exist solely in their function: through their effects on the structure.

Structural linguistics should therefore, according to Saussure, avoid the division between the chain of sound-images (a, b, c) and the chain of concepts (a', b', c') as two different fields of research. In delimiting substructures of language we can recognize the tendency of linguistics towards totality as the ideal of science. However, if there is anything common to all great materialist positions, claims Milner, it is that they are not aiming for totality—the system as such is necessary non-whole (cf. Milner 1995).

As we have seen earlier, constructive difference that is at work within repetition operates as a bar that establishes the very possibility of touch, between the two alienated terms, but at the same time it also builds an unbreakable barricade between them. It is exactly constructive difference that is at work also within structural linguistics: the impossible event of touch can on the one hand be identified with the bar operating as a cut between signifier and the signified, unifying them into a sign, and, on the other hand, it can also be identified with the bar operating as a connective–separating function between the sign and other signs. As a cut between signifier and the signified, the abstract and the material aspect of the concept, constructive difference is itself neither formal nor material, yet it is both at once. It is a formal difference that cannot get rid of the material effects it produces and the other way round—it is a material difference that affects the very form of the relation between the two, and, subsequently the form of repetition itself.

Within the realm of touch, repetition could therefore be thought in two directions:

1.   as a relation between R1 (signifier–concept) and R2 (signified–sound-image);
2.   as a relation between R1 (sign 1) and R2 (sign 2).

Here, R1 and R2 are functioning as the active and the passive agent of touch, the touching and the touched, while constructive difference is operating through the category of the (un)touchable. The category of the (un)touchable installed by repetition is therefore functioning in two directions in language, which can be topologically presented as a vertical and a horizontal line:

	R1, the touching	*R2, the touched*
R1, the touching	signifier 1 |	signifier 2
R2, the touched	signified 1 |	signified 2

The vertical line is set between the concept (the touching) and the sound-image (the touched).[6] Both entities are, according to Saussure, strictly psychological (not physical), yet they perform the abstract and the material aspect of a sign. As such, they are inseparable (touching too much) yet detached (never yet touching)—they are, as we can say, fundamentally *(un)touched.*

The horizontal line is set between sign 1 (the touching) and sign 2 (the touched). The relation between the two signs in the structure of language is the matrix of the relation of a sign towards all the other signs that form language, i.e. the matrix of the relation of a sign towards the structure. Within this relation, a sign functions as value, which means it could only be defined (and exist) *ad negativum*—not as an identity but as a non-identity, as strictly relational. A sign (any sign in the structure that performs the function of R1—the touching) only exists through its relation to the other sign (any other sign in the structure that performs the function of R2—the touched), which functions as constructive difference. From the perspective of touch, this relation functions through the category of the (un)touchable: a sign is touching the other sign only through the impossibility of touching it, because it is itself existing solely as the (un)touchable value. And the other way round—a sign exists as the (un)touchable value precisely because it can be touching the other sign only through the impossibility of touching it.

The key issue here is that these two lines should not be understood as the axis of metonymy (horizontal line) and the axis of metaphor (vertical line). Rather, we should discern the two axes on each of the two lines. We should find metaphorical and metonymical touch both in relation between the two signs in the structure of language and in relation between the signified and the signifier within each of the signs. Both relations are subjected (and powered by) the category of the (un)touchable: it is precisely the impossible event of touch (which exists only within the dispositive of its very impossibility) that initiates the mechanism of language.

Marx: (un)touchable value

In language, the complex relation between abstract concept and its material counterpart is established through the category of the (un)touchable, which comes to its function through the processes of *repetition*. As a system of pure values, language resembles economical structures, says Saussure: "Here as in political economy we are confronted with the notion of *value*; both sciences are concerned with *a system of equating things of different orders*—labor and wages in one hand and a signified and signifier in the other" (Saussure 1966: 79).

In Marx's formula of capital, we can trace the category of the *(un)touchable* as the very lever of its mechanism. What triggers it all is precisely *the (un)touchable value* which stems from the complex relation between qualitative and quantitative difference in the process of repetition. When asking the question *what kind of repetition* in Marx's theory of the capitalist production, the first thing to say would be the following: *exchange is not repetition*. Why? Because the very first condition of repetition is that its fundamental terms (R1 and R2) are not interchangeable. What Marx actually does in his theory of capital is that in his diachronic decomposition of production processes (from C-C over C-M-C and M-M' to

M-C-M') he gradually turns the logic of exchange into the logic of repetition. And he does this precisely through a separation and yet again a (retroactive) connection of qualitative and quantitative differences. Of course, in Marx's theory of capitalist production there is no such thing as a pure act of exchange. We have always already entered the processes of repetition. In a proper Hegelian manner, the initial form of the direct exchange of commodities (C-M-C) is only a premise, an implication that is itself mythical and comes to its function only retroactively: from the perspective of the explicated formula of capital (M-C-M):

> If we abstract from the material substance of the circulation of commodities, that is, from the exchange of the various use-values, and consider only the economic forms produced by this process of circulation, we find its final result to be money: this final product of the circulation of commodities is the first form in which capital appears.
>
> (Marx 2015: 104)

The first distinction we notice between money that is money only, and money that is turning into capital, is nothing more than just a difference in their form of circulation: C-M-C now turns into M-C-M. But this purely formal twist, however, has substantial consequences. How is this? This is also Marx asking himself: "What distinguishes this form from that of the simple circulation of commodities, is the inverted order of succession of the two antithetical processes, sale and purchase. How can this purely formal distinction between these processes change their character as it were by magic?" (Marx 2015: 111).

So, what is the magic? Marx would answer:

> The independent form, i.e., the money-form, which the value of commodities assumes in the case of simple circulation, serves only one purpose, namely, their exchange, and vanishes in the final result of the movement. On the other hand, in the circulation M-C-M, both the money and the commodity represent only different modes of existence of value itself, the money its general mode, and the commodity its particular, or, so to say, disguised mode. It is constantly changing from one form to the other without thereby becoming lost, and thus assumes an automatically active character.
>
> (Marx 2015: 107)

In circulation M-C-M, value becomes an active factor in the process: "because it is value," says Marx, "it has acquired the occult quality of being able to add value to itself." In its automatic expansion, value produces surplus-value, it "lays golden eggs": "while constantly assuming the form in turn of money and commodities, it at the same time changes in magnitude, differentiates itself by throwing off surplus-value from itself; the original value, in other words, expands spontaneously" (Marx 2015: 107).

The purely formal twist of C-M-C into M-C-M has substantial consequences. This is an indicator that with the developed form of capital, we have entered the logic of repetition where constructive difference operates as a purely formal cut that produces material effects. And with that shift, all the remnants of the logic of exchange have disappeared: "Value therefore now becomes value in process, money in process, and, as such, capital" (Marx 2015: 108). This causal structure forms an open system, the process of limitless expansion:

> The simple circulation of commodities – selling in order to buy – is a means of carrying out a purpose unconnected with circulation, namely, the appropriation of use-values, the satisfaction of wants. The circulation of money as capital is, on the contrary, an end in itself, for the expansion of value takes place only within this constantly renewed movement. The circulation of capital has therefore no limits.
>
> (Marx 2015: 107)

While in the C-M-C formula, the middle term M (money) introduces the category of value in its pure form, which got rid of its empirical materiality, in the M-C-M formula, the process is exactly the opposite: the middle term C (commodity) represents formalized commodity, commodity robbed of its essence—its empirical materiality, which turns into *matter without qualities*, imprinted in the form of money. The M-C-M formula is not launching an abstraction of the qualitative difference into the quantitative difference, but the persistence of the qualitative difference within the quantitative difference, the persistence of a material remainder within the formalized circulation of money. And it is precisely this material remainder that makes production of values an instant production of surplus, which results in the accumulation of capital. The surplus-value, the byproduct of the converted logic of the constructive difference is marked by index '. The allegedly purely formal twist of C-M-C into M-C-M turns out to be always already marked by its inner material effect, producing the scheme M-C-M' on the other end.

Within the twist of the formula of capital, it is the concept of *commodities* that brings about the category of the *(un)touchable*:

> A commodity is a mysterious thing, simply because in it the social character of men's labour appears to them as an objective character stamped upon the product of that labour; because the relation of the producers to the sum total of their own labour is presented to them as a social relation, existing not between

themselves, but between the products of their labour. This is the reason why the products of labour become commodities, social things whose qualities are at the same time perceptible and imperceptible by the senses.

(Marx 2015: 48)

In commodity fetishism that crosses production of capital as its phantasmal compound, it is precisely the *fantasy of touch*, the fantasy of commodities still possessing their material properties, that turns the wheel of capitalist production.[7] This fantasy raises the logic of surplus enjoyment. Within the structure M-C-M', the value as an abstraction of qualitative differences (use-values) into quantitative differences (exchange values) which is not a simple formalization but needs to deal with the unfathomable persistence of the material remainder, triggers an endless tendency towards the unreachable and untouchable object of enjoyment which maintains consumption.

Therefore, the qualities of commodities are, in some unfathomable manner, at the same time perceptible and imperceptible by the senses: they are touchable yet (un)touchable. The fantasy of touch as an absolute proximity, which is nothing but a fantasy of possession of the object of enjoyment, is conditioned by the unsurmountable distance between the empirical and the material (in the sense of matter without qualities) character of commodities. This relation is therefore powered by the category of the (un)touchable as the (im)possible event of touch, which triggers the mechanism of surplus enjoyment: the empirical touch of the product of labor which satisfies men's needs is never the event of touch which men desire—the impossible touch of the object of enjoyment.

Conclusion

In this article, the category of *the (un)touchable* was elaborated on as the core concept of *haptic materialism* that addresses the question of touch, within the structures of language. The mechanism of paradox was shown to be at work at the core of the category of the (un)touchable: the category of the (un)touchable presupposes the concept of touch, which is possible only under the condition of its very impossibility. This was done through a synchronic analysis of the analogy between the processes of repetition, which proved to be central machinery of linguistic (as well as of economic) structures, and the mechanism of touch. The key features of this analogy were argued to be the specific connecting–separating function of the relation between the two agents involved, their irreversibility, and the link between its formal and its material aspect. This synchronic analysis was supported by a supplemental diachronic thesis that with the institution of modern science, the relation between spiritual and sensual touch was replaced by the relation between metonymical and metaphorical touch, bringing about a certain twist in the notion of materiality that gives way to the category of *the (un)touchable*. In the last part, it was shown that it is precisely the category of *the (un)touchable* that is essentially related to the mechanisms of repetition and constructive difference, which lies at the core of both Saussure's concept of sign as the (un)touchable relation between the signifier and the signified and Marx's idea of value as the abstraction of materiality into form—abstraction into the (un)touchable value.

Notes

1   The reversibility of touch, which was already exposed by Aristotle in *De Anima* (cf. Aristotle 1984), was most notably argued by M. Merleau-Ponty in the *Phenomenology of Perception* (cf. Merleau-Ponty 2005). Merleau-Ponty's argument was further elaborated by Nancy in *Corpus* (cf. Nancy 1992) and *Noli me tangere* (Nancy 2003), Derrida in his work *Le toucher: Jean-Luc Nancy* (cf. Derrida 2005) and Lacan in *The Four Fundamental Concepts of Psychoanalysis* (cf. Lacan 1973).

2   For further elaboration see Gregor Moder's contribution in this book (Chapter 4).

3   For further elaboration see Rachel Aumiller's contribution in this book (Chapter 7).

4   For the concise analysis of metaphors of touch in the history of western philosophy from Plato to Hegel see: Komel, M. (2016): "A Touchy Subject: The Tactile Metaphor of Touch" *Družboslovne razprave*, 82: 115–125.

5   The use of the term *modern science* in this article is referring specifically to J.C. Milner's definition of Galileian science in his books *Le Périple Structural* (cf. Milner 2002) and *L'Ouvre Claire* (cf. Milner 1995).

6   It is irrelevant whether we set *the concept* as *the touching* and *the sound-image* as *the touched* or the other way round. Each decision works for conceptualizing the category of *the (un)touchable* within this relation. However, a decision needs to be made for the purposes of this elaboration, because R1 and R2 are not mutually exchangeable.

7   For a further elaboration of the concept of surplus of touch based on surplus value see Mirt Komel's contribution in this book (Chapter 1).

References

Aristotle (1984), *Complete Works*, Princeton: UP.

Derrida, J. (2005), *On Touching: Jean-Luc Nancy*, Stanford: UP.

Dolar, M. (2008), "Touching Ground," *Filozofski vestnik* 29/2: 79–100.

Freud, S. (1963), "Das Unbewußte." In: *Das Unbewußte: Schriften zur Psychoanalyse*, Frankfurt am Main: S. Fischer Verlag.

Jakobson, R. (1987), "Two Aspects of Language and two Types of Aphasic Disturbances." In: *Language in Literature*, Cambridge, Mass. & London: The Belknap Press of Harvard UP.

Kant, I. (1986), *Kritik der reinen Vernunft*, Leipzig: Reclam Verlag.

Kolenc, B. (2014), *Ponavljanje in uprizoritev: Kierkegaard, psihoanaliza, gledališče* [Repetition and Enactment: Kierkegaard, Psychoanalysis, Theatre], Ljubljana: DTP.

Komel, M. (2009), *Poskus nekega dotika*, Ljubljana: Fakulteta za družbene vede.

Komel, M. (2016), "A Touchy Subject: the Tactile Metaphor of Touch," *Družboslovne razprave*, 82: 115–125.

Lacan, J. (1966), "L'instance de la lettre dans l'inconscient ou la raison depuis Freud." In: *Ecrits*, Paris: Seuil.

Lacan, J. (1973), *Le séminaire. Livre XI: Les Quatre Concepts Fondamentaux de la Psychanalyse*, Paris: Seuil.

Marx, K. (2015), *Capital: A Critique of Political Economy*, Moscow: Progress.

Merleau-Ponty, M. (2005), *Phenomenology of Perception*, London and New York: Routledge.

Milner, J.-C. (1995), *L'œuvre claire: Lacan, la science, philosophie*. Paris: Seuil.

Milner, J.-C. (2003), *Strukturalizem: Liki in paradigma* [*Le Périple structural: Figures et paradigme*], Ljubljana: Krtina.

Nancy, J.-L. (1988), *L'expérience de la liberté*, Paris: Galilée.

Nancy, J.-L. (1992), *Corpus*, Paris: Métailié.

Nancy, J.-L. (2003), *Noli me tangere*, Paris: Bayard Editions.

Ovid (2004), *Metamorphoses*, London & New York: Penguin.

Plato (1997), *Complete Works*, Indianapolis & Cambridge: Hackett.

Saussure, F. (1966), *Course in General Linguistics*, New York & Toronto & London: McGraw-Hill.

Tomšič, S. (2015), *The Capitalist Unconscious: Marx and Lacan*, London, New York: Verso.

7

The Lick of the Mother Tongue: Derrida's Fantasies of "the Touch of Language" with Augustine and Marx

Rachel Aumiller

Introduction

Augustine's *Confessions* makes the impossible attempt to return to a time before language. Augustine claims that before we are aware of language, we learn our mother tongue through the touch of the mother. This lesson in language that we often first learn through a gentle touch—the nipple of the mother in the mouth of the infant—is later reinforced by a violent touch—the switch of the schoolmaster. Augustine suggests that any memory of a time before "the touch of language" is purely imaginary. And yet his autobiography is driven (by a death drive) to return to a time before the touch of the mother (tongue).

While Augustine confesses the personal fantasy of returning to an imaginary *time before* the touch of the mother (tongue), Karl Marx articulates the communal fantasy of *a time to come* when we will forget our mother tongue. The fantasy of forgetting the mother tongue is the fantasy of rearticulating ourselves as individuals or a society: the fantasy of self-expression in the creation of a new shared tongue. And yet, as Marx confesses, this fantasy of forgetting the mother tongue that predetermines us is a failed fantasy. We find ourselves bound by the mother tongue, trapped between two imaginary temporalities: the time before and after the touch of language.

Jacques Derrida turns to both Augustine and Marx to repeat the fantasy of escaping the mother (tongue). His lectures on *Spectres de Marx* and his personal autobiography "Circonfession" (or in English, "Circumfession"), both published in the early 1990s, do not explicitly speak to each other (cf. Derrida, 1993; 1991). And yet both works are possessed by the dream of a time before/after the mother tongue: a failed political fantasy confessed also as an unrealized personal obsession. Derrida responds to Marx's analysis of our repeated failure to forget the mother tongue by turning to Augustine's analysis of the mother's touch: we cannot forget the mother tongue because it is licked upon our skin. Even if we could successfully destroy one political (symbolic) system in the creation of the new, the echo of the old is etched into our skin.

The following chapter explores the relationship between the mother tongue and the mother touch by turning to Derrida's relationship to Augustine and Marx. Section one, "Nightmares and fantasies of the mother tongue," explores the relationship between the imagined time "before" and "after" language repeated throughout the history of philosophy: from Augustine's religious ponderings, to Marx's political manifesto, to Derrida's reiterations of both within a psychoanalytic framework. Section two, "Fantasmatic foreskins," argues that the fantasy of escaping the mother tongue is connected to the fantasy of escaping the mother touch. Language first enters us unconsciously through touch. Even when we denounce words that have been attributed to us (our given names), our skin retains the etchings of our first words/touch. The fantasy of being-before-language is often represented through the image of a layer of untouched skin shed at infancy: a layer of skin that possesses our daydreams and haunts our nightmares. I conclude with the suggestion that our repeated failure to escape the touch of language surfaces in the form of barely perceptible interruptions within the language that has been touched upon us.

Nightmares and fantasies of the mother tongue

In *The Eighteenth Brumaire of Louis Bonaparte*, Marx famously compares the dream of the revolution-to-come to the imagined experience of forgetting one's mother tongue (cf. Marx 1979: 106). The series of peasant uprisings erupting in the German states in the 1830s and 1840s—the revolt of the tailors, the pyrotechnics, and potato farmers—seemed to be generating a force that would culminate in a final shattering of all former political articulations. Without clearly knowing what new political articulation would take the place of the old, each small revolt nevertheless attempted to begin a new sentence. Although the young Marx and his revolutionary companions anticipated the emergence a Hegelian self-articulated community, the grand disappointment of 1848 failed to generate a new language.[1] As Marx would later assess the period, what appeared to be a revolutionary breaking point only took the form of newness while ultimately reproducing the content of that which each revolt rebelled against. They sang new words set to an ancient tune.[2]

The proletarian attempts to achieve new political expression failed to rip themselves free from repetition's inertia.[3] Despite being slightly older and perhaps slightly disillusioned, Marx of *The Eighteenth Brumaire* returns to the Young Hegelian dream of a new common language in the erasure of the mother tongue: a revolution-to-come that would not reproduce the contents of that which it aims to destroy. In contrast to the lingering fantasy of a revolution that would "not borrow its poetry from the past but the future" (Marx 1979: 106), the weight of Marx's text looks backward at failure rather than forward toward fantasy, offering an analysis of how proletarian revolutions actually tend to unfold. Rather than erasing the mother tongue, we find ourselves ensnared by it. We try to define ourselves in a single new utterance, but the mother tongue wraps itself around our ankles and pulls us back into itself. Our failed attempts to create a new language that breaks with the content of the old result instead in glitches within the mother tongue, as Marx describes it, instances of scrambled syntax (Marx 1979: 108) or stuttered speech (Marx 1979: 106–107). In such a way, just when the proletarian revolutions seem to gain momentum, to say something new, they interrupt themselves mid-sentence. In contrast to the fantasy of revolution as a decisive breaking point, the actual proletarian revolutions occurred not as a great event, but rather as a series of glitches: events that restarted before they began. Rather than creating a new language, actual proletarian protests and revolts tend to leave us stuttering within our mother tongue. We fail to create something new, but we can no longer smoothly repeat what has already been said. The grand failure to create a new common language leaves us with a series of mini-failures as we fail to articulate our visions of the future through the mother tongue in which we are stuck.[4]

The thought of being deprived of one's first language would seem to belong to the genre of nightmares rather than fantasies: the nightmare of losing one's voice, of being unable to speak while standing (perhaps naked) before an audience, of being unable to call for help when in danger. The experience of losing one's language is the real nightmare of someone who has suffered a stroke or a refugee in a new country where her own linguistic economy counts for nothing. This blurring of fantasy and nightmare is not surprising given Marx's intricate theory of historical genre. We learn that on the world-stage it is often difficult to distinguish freedom from bondage, which often takes the form of a comedy while preserving its tragic contents. Marx's manipulation of genre likewise shows itself in his blurring of the distinction between fantasy and horror in his extended metaphor of forgetting one's first language.[5]

In the late twentieth century, Derrida not only repeats the Marxist fantasy-nightmare of the destruction of the mother tongue as a political metaphor set between tragedy and comedy (with both sides bordering on horror), but expresses it also as a secret confession. His 1993 *Specters of Marx* highlights the linguistic metaphors of *The Eighteenth Brumaire*, focusing on the historical moment of June 1848. A few years earlier, Derrida published his autobiography, "Circumfession", which follows the final days of his mother. In many respects the two texts do not seem related: one takes the form of a political lecture with its focus on Marx; the other takes the form of an introspective analysis of his own estranged relationship to Judaism with references to Augustine. And yet both texts are possessed by the nightmare-fantasy of escaping one's native language: first as the fantasy of a communal dream of revolution, then as a personal dream of redemption.

As I have noted, although *The Eighteenth Brumaire* dreams of a language to come, the weight of the text looks backward toward the failure of history to make a radical cut with its past. When Derrida repeats the vision of a great event to come, he also confesses to its impossibility: a dream that gains in intensity through its deferral. The tension between the stubborn fantasy of an imaginary new language that overwrites the old and the stubbornness of the mother tongue, which does not allow itself to be forgotten, produces a new kind of expression in the form of failed expression: the repetition of our failed protests and revolts, our failure to say anything new, fills us with deep desire and insecurity which causes us to stutter in our native tongue, which we cannot escape but can no longer smoothly articulate ourselves in. We become like a new expatriate who in attempting to speak, think, and dream in a new language begins to speak her own language as if it is a second language. In speaking her mother tongue, she may adopt the accent of those in her new country, speaking disjointedly as she grasps for words that once readily came to her. Before she can master the new language, she begins to relate to her native language as if it were a foreign tongue. In such a way, the failure of revolution can leave a people in worse conditions than before a revolt. Our relationship to the old is disrupted, but there is nothing substantial to grasp onto in its place.

Derrida self-consciously sets himself up for failure in taking on the personal quest to say something that escapes the mother tongue. As he writes in the opening pages of his confessions:

This dream in me, since always, of another language, an entirely crude language, of a half-fluid name too [...] I hear them snigger, poor old man, doesn't look likely, not going to happen tomorrow, you'll never know, super abundance of a flood after which a dike becomes beautiful like the ruin it will always have walled up inside it.

(Derrida 1993: 1.4–6)

The opening imagery of the pent-up levee mirrors the imagery of the barricade in *Specters of Marx*. Derrida illustrates the tensions of June 1848 Paris through the images of the double barricade: while revolutionary chaos swelled up behind the monstrous barricade of Saint Antoine that would later lie in ruin, the barricade du Temple was an inanimate stone-faced obstruction, letting out "not a cry, not a sound, not a breath" (Derrida 1994: 118–119). "Circumfession" redoubles the image of the double barricade in the gaping mouth of the confessor, who is met by the blank stare of the mother who no longer recognizes her son. Derrida describes the experience of his own facial paralysis that distorts his mouth into a gaping sneer. His open mouth alludes to his desire to burst forth in a superabundance of new speech, and yet he can barely let out an inaudible groan, which is met by the mother's silence. In the tradition of a Marxist tragic-comic horror, the text blurs tragedy and comedy, nightmare and fantasy. As Derrida weeps over the deteriorating health of his mother, he fantasizes, to his own horror, about the death of the mother (tongue). "Here I am, since always [...] in alliance with death, with the living death of my mother" (Derrida 1993: 27.137). The impending event of the death of the mother both devastates him and, even in his grief, bizarrely excites him. As Derrida explains, the text will have been successful if he writes a single sentence that escapes the grasp of being translated back into what is known. To write a new sentence is to write the death of the mother.

Derrida's text explicitly connects the dream of a new language to the dream of a time before the mother tongue. The nightmare of the mother tongue—an inheritance that one attempts to disown—is positioned between two fantasies: the fantasy of a time before an inherited tongue and the fantasy of a language to come, which is out of reach. "Circumfession" self-consciously strings together carefully selected—as well as openly contrived—memories; it is a reflection on the self but also a meta-reflection on autobiography, the genre of self-articulation. Derrida's confessed goal of the text is to give birth to himself in the death of the mother. The death of the mother, in whom he has his definition, is also the death of all previous articulations of his self. The fantasy of the mother's death is the fantasy of suicide (Derrida 1993: 7.36–40). In this sense, the text that traces Derrida's "deconversion" away from Judaism also strives to achieve a conversion: the birth of a new self in the death of the mother. In the death of the one who gave him his name (not only his given name, but his secret name given to him as an infant at *Brit Milah*), he attempts to express himself in a new utterance: "I have been seeking myself in a sentence" (Derrida 1993: 2.13). Parallel to his lectures on Marx in which he analyzes the failure of the proletarian revolts to articulate even a single new sentence, Derrida takes on the personal task of attempting to give birth to himself in the construction of a single sentence that escapes being retranslated back into what is already known of himself, his memories, his writing: an unrecognizable utterance that breaks free from repetition's inertia both in form and content.

Fantasmatic foreskins

Derrida's reflection on the death of the mother (tongue) mimics Augustine's *Confessions*, which opens with a speculation on how he first became entrapped by "the bonds of [his] human tongue" (Augustine: I.ix.14). In contrast to Marx who fantasizes about a time after being-in-language as we know it, Augustine's fantasy about being free from the bonds of the mother (tongue) takes the form of a fantasy of a time before being-in-language. According to Augustine, the time before symbolic thought and speech is a time before memory. As he speculates, memories of a time before our speaking-being are likely based on stories our caregivers have told us about ourselves or are based on what we have observed in other infants. Nevertheless, Augustine creates an imagined memory of the moment when language first enters him, displacing his infancy. Since our relationship to our own infancy is fantastical, our infancy neither properly belongs to our memory nor can it be properly forgotten or left behind. The fantasy of a prelinguistic self thus haunts us. As Augustine puts it, "Infancy did not 'depart' for it has no place to go. Yet I was no longer a baby incapable of speech but already a boy with power to talk I discovered only later" (Augustine 1998: I.viii.13). Language first enters us before we are aware of its existence. Its touch is as gentle as a mother's nipple between the lips of an infant. Augustine takes this example beyond metaphor, equating these first moments of skin-to-skin contact between the infant and mother as the child's first lesson in language. As he claims, when the infant takes in nourishment from the mother, it also takes in "the word" of God (Augustine 1998: I.vi.7). Derrida layers this curious passage in the *Confessions* with his own fantasy of the first words of his mother spoken over skin. He recounts a "memory" of his early childhood when he suffered from a fever and was barely conscious. His mother wept and prayed over his body. His earliest "memory" of his mother's touch is a memory of his first word: "Well I'm remembering God this morning, the name [...] as I heard it perhaps the first time, no doubt in my mother's mouth when she was praying, each time she saw me ill [...] I hear her say, 'thanks to God, thank you God,' when the temperature goes down, weeping in pronouncing your name" (Derrida 1993: 23.117–118). Sitting by the bed of his dying mother, Derrida experiences the sensation of the word "God" which his mother touched upon his feverish skin. The bodily memory of the name of God lingers on his skin, even as he confesses to no longer adhere to his mother's faith. After his conversion to Christianity, Augustine still cannot escape the sensational touch of the women from his past who continue to haunt him in his dreams; after Derrida's "cut with Kippur," he cannot shake the touch of the name of God.[5] Both Augustine and Derrida confess to the failure of a radical conversion (or deconversion), in which we forfeit one symbolic system for another. For even when we renounce our given names, our skin reverberates with the touch of our first words.[6] The touch of the mother (tongue) is "the first event to write itself on my body [...] we have to learn to read without seeing" (Derrida 1993: 23.120)[7].

The mother tongue takes us captive by layering itself upon our skin. As Augustine conceived it, language enters us twice: first through a gentle touch, then by force. Augustine continues to imagine what it must have been like to learn his mother tongue by comparing it to his painful experience as a student who was forced to learn Greek. Even as an adult, Augustine remains freshly wounded by the memory of being beaten by his teachers when he, as any child would, wanted to play rather than devote himself to his language studies. In Augustine's mind, language is something that is quite literally beaten into our skin:

> I learnt to articulate my wishes by training my mouth to use these signs. In this way I communicated the signs of my wishes to those around me, and entered more deeply into the storm society of human life [...] it was set before me as my moral duty in life to obey those who admonished me with the purpose that I should succeed in this world, and should excel the arts of using my tongue [...] I did not understand why such knowledge was useful. Yet if ever I was indolent in learning I was beaten. This method was approved by adults and many living long before me.
>
> (Augustine 1998: I.viii.13; I.ix.14)

In a similar vein to Marx, the tyranny of the mother tongue represents for Augustine the reproduction of the status quo, which is driven by the economic agenda of one's society.[8] For Augustine, the mother tongue is not merely a metaphor for the status quo, but the vehicle of the reproduction of societal values. In order for an infant to express its desires, it must learn to translate them into the mother tongue. But the conversion of infant desire into articulated desire also destroys the former as the child must align the form and content of her desire with that of the adults. Augustine's discourse on touch and language highlights two sides of desire: that which is articulated within the symbolic economy of the mother tongue, and the fantasy of a desire that cannot be said. Augustine imagines the events through which the unspoken desire of his infancy was displaced by the words that overwrite him, allowing him to appear as subject. And yet, although he compares this first exchange of unspoken desire for language to his violent experiences of learning languages in school, he also maintains that language has always already been pressed into his skin (inserted directly into his mouth through the skin of his mother). While force shapes our desire by teaching us how to speak, the mother tongue first enters us without our awareness, leaving us without an opportunity to consent or protest, leaving behind no trace or memory of a time before.[9]

The fantasy of a time before language is the fantasy of an untouched layer of skin. The fantasy of being untouched by language requires "the memory" of an actual event in which we identify ourselves as having been cut off from our unspoken desires. The articulation of one's subjectivity is thus constituted by a real cut that symbolizes our original separation from our first skin: a fantastical pre-subjective foreskin untainted by touch and language. Augustine locates the agent of the cut in the symbolic figure of the schoolmaster and the real lick of his switch; Derrida locates the agent of the cut in the figure of his mother and the lick of the mother tongue. He imagines the moment of his own circumcision—a memory mixed with historical legacy—as the first violent touch of the word:

> on the seventh day, when they would put on orange-flower water in Algeria [...] mingling with the blood right on that wound that I have never seen, seen with my own eyes, this perfumed water attenuates the pain which I suppose to be nil and infinite, and I can still feel it, the phantom burning, in my belly, irradiating a diffuse zone around the sex [...] without forgetting all the theories according to which circumcision, another word for peritomy, that cutting of the surround, is instituted by the mother, for her, the cruelty basically being hers, and sometimes the very act of cutting off that sort of ring [...] even the remains would belong

to the mother whom it is said that in the past, in my ancestors' country [...] had to eat the still bloody foreskin, I imagine by first sucking it, my first beloved cannibal, initiator at the sublime gate of fellatio.

(Derrida 1993: 13.65–66)

With the ritual cut of Brit Milah, which is at once a naming ceremony, an alliance is drawn between the mother touch and the mother tongue. Derrida's many references to the mother's mouth, lips, teeth, and tongue suggests that our given names are licked upon our skin. "Circumfession" layers all the ways in which one may be licked (by a switch, by lightning, by a tongue). He chases and is chased by the monster mother tongue as he chases and is chased by the phantom foreskin: "My tongue [...] the one that has always been running after me, turning circles around me, a circumference licking me with a flame and that I try in turn to circumvent, having never loved anything but the impossible" (Derrida 1993: 1.3). Between Augustine and Derrida we find an answer to Marx who questioned the seeming impossibility of escaping language as we know it: the revolutionary goal of shattering the mother tongue fails because our first tongue is licked upon our skin. We cannot forget the mother tongue without shedding our first skin. Or to put this differently, even if we could displace one symbolic order in the creation of a completely new order, our body would still retain the impression of the former. Perhaps this is also what Marx has in mind when he rejects the metaphor of critique as a surgeon's scalpel. Lifting a graft of skin will not kill the cancer. We must completely rip off our first skin (Marx 1975: 177; Derrida 1993: 44.234–235).

Conclusion

"The touch of language" is a metaphor for the grip of language upon our thinking and being. But it is also literal in two senses. In the first sense, the way we are touched or not touched by others is informed by the names we are given. In the second sense, we first grasp the meaning of certain words through a corresponding touch or lack of touch. Symbolic thought is not required to associate "bad" with being struck or "good" with being stroked. Words are soaked into our skin and stored as bodily memory. We are interpellated as subject both by what we are named and by how we are touched or not touched. These haptic and linguistic interpellations cannot be untangled.[10]

The very real grip of language upon our bodies, which shapes our subjectivity, seems to be embedded in a kind of negativity that is expressed through fantasy.

One of these fantasies in Western philosophy is the framing of our speaking-being as embedded between two cuts: one that separates us from a time "before" and another that separates us from a time "after" our determination by the touch of language. Donna Haraway has argued in reference to Marx and post-structuralism that the dream of a common language to come is at once the dream of shared experience "before" our individuation (and alienation) in language: "the myth of an original unity, fullness, bliss and terror, represented by the phallic mother from whom all humans must separate" (Haraway 2000: 292). Our inability to return to a time before or transcend our being-in-language is often represented in the history of Western philosophy through the fantasy of the mother as the gatekeeper. The figure of the mother is developed through the (constructed) memories of our first experiences of touch: an imagined touch in which the caregiver and child cannot be distinguished and the memory of the first violent touch. The first cut from the unity with the mother's skin is often imagined to be at the hands of the mother (or in Derrida's fantasies the mother's lips, tongue, and teeth). With this cut, the blissful skin-to-skin unity of infancy is converted into the dominance of the mother tongue over the body. The fantasy of the first cut is doubled in the fantasy of a second cut. The first severing of our shared skin at the hands of the (m)other is repeated in the fantasy of final cut by our own hands. In some fantasies this second cut takes the form of an individual spiritual conversion or messianic end. Other fantasies of the cut take the form of a world-political conversion in the form of revolution.

The tradition of the conversion narrative stretching from Augustine to Derrida is about the failure to achieve the second cut: testimonies of the failed attempt to repeat and thus recode a first cut from a fantastical origin. The failure to actualize the second final cut can result in small disturbances—a negative glitch—within what has already been articulated for us. Negativity shows itself where the fantastical skin of our materiality pulls at the seams. Marx frames the failed proletariat revolutions as a stutter and scrambled syntax belonging to a historical stage: symptoms of the failed attempt to forget the mother tongue. As discussed above, Marx claims that in order to achieve new expression we cannot draw on the poetry from an imagined past. However, there is also a kind of poetry that emerges from within the mother tongue in both the failure to repeat an imaginary past and the failure to actualize an imaginary future. As Gilles Deleuze notes, it is precisely the stutter within the mother tongue that makes "language trembl[e] from head to toe" (Deleuze 1998: 109). Marx himself similarly states that despite the failures of the revolutions of the nineteenth century "all Europe trembles at the June Earthquake" (Marx 1979: 109).

As Derrida fails to articulate himself in a single new sentence, the poetry in *Circumfession* emerges in passing instances of stuttered or scrambled speech: the scrambling of fantasy and nightmare, the scrambling of the imaginary Monster Mother and Derrida's actual mother Georgette. Speech becomes disoriented in the physical failure of the body as expressed in the example of his mother's body covered in open sores and his own facial paralysis. Derrida weeps over his mother's body, a repetition and inversion of his first memory of "the word" entering him as a child. His mother responds "I have a pain in my mother." The scrambled syntax of mother and son. The scrambled syntax of one articulated subject and another. Our repeated failure to escape the touch of language surfaces in the form of barely perceptible interruptions within the language that has been touched upon us. The symptom of our failure to forget, shatter or return to a time before the touch of the tongue results in tiny ruptures of negativity—a shiver passing over one's skin, a stutter in one's speech—the unconscious resistance of our body from being fully articulated by another.

Notes

1 Although Hegel himself saw the French Revolution as the realization of such a self-articulated community (cf. Hegel 1970: 328–363), Hegel's followers known as the Young Hegelians insisted that Germany must undergo its own revolution in the nineteenth century, instead of romanticizing the events of other countries as its own.

2 In Marx's words, "And just when they seem engaged in revolutionizing themselves and things, in creating something that has never yet existed, precisely in such periods of revolutionary crisis they anxiously conjure up the spirits of the past to their service and borrow from them names, battle-cries and costumes in order to present the new scene of world history in this time-honored disguise and borrowed language ... In a like manner a beginner who has learnt a new language always translates it back into his mother tongue, but he has assimilated the spirit of the new language and can freely express himself in it only when he finds his way in it without recalling the old and forgets his native tongue in the use of the new" (cf. Marx 1979: 103–104).

3 For another perspective on the concept of repetition in its relation to touch and language through a Marxist perspective see the contribution by Bara Kolenc in this book (Chapter 6).

4 Many movements that seek to radically reconstruct a stage of history take Marx's metaphor quite literally. In order to reshape the character of a nation or group, for example, the people must learn to articulate themselves and their desire in a new

tongue (often in the tongue of an oppressor). For this reason a new regime or dictator often introduces a new lexicon: introducing new terms, making old terms obsolete, or recoding words to mean something contrary to their original sense. For a fictional illustration of the way a new regime redefines itself through the creation of a new language in the destruction of a mother tongue we may consider Orwell's Newspeak in *1984* (cf. Orwell 1950).

5   In "Merleau-Ponty and the Touch of Malebranche," Judith Butler similarly characterizes the "touch of god" as a tactile predetermination and compares this to Merleau-Ponty's pre-immersion of the tactile subject in a palpable world (Butler 2004: 181–205).

6   For another perspective on the specific way in which names touch upon us see Jela Krečič's contribution in this book (Chapter 9).

7   For further psychoanalytic perspectives on the way words are etched onto the infant's skins cf. Freud 2001b; Anzieu 2016: 114.

8   For an interpretation of the link between the reproducibility of language and commodity-value in relation to touch see Mirt Komel's contribution in this book (Chapter 1).

9   Derrida connects Augustine's stubborn resistance to learning Greek to his own failure to learn Hebrew. He revisits his memory of being expelled from his Hebrew school for his failure to learn Hebrew. By connecting Greek and Hebrew, Derrida places emphasis on two languages which represent an ideal origin: Greek being the sacred language that gives birth to Western philosophy and Hebrew being the sacred tongue of the Hebrew scriptures. Both languages point to an ideological origin. We might note that Marx too, like many European Jews, had little to no knowledge of Hebrew: Marx, like his father, was raised with a liberal secular education and baptized Lutheran. The philosophers' desire to forget (Marx) or circumvent (Derrida) the mother tongue is haunted by the absence of language "before" their first tongue: not only a time before language but a missing original tongue before the mother tongue.

Although I frame being-in-language (represented through the fantastical figure of the Mother Tongue) as between two fantasies of a time before and after language, there also might be another way to grasp the fantasy of before and after, as the fantasy of being in a language that is other (worldly). A time before language is layered by the fantasy of a missing originary or sacred language. The time after language is also layered with the fantasy of existing fully in a new language that erases the mother tongue (Marx's dream of a new common language after revolution, Derrida's dream of articulating himself in a single new sentence). The ontic experience of learning a second language or having one's writing translated into another language (by another) connects us more deeply to the desire/fear of existing ontologically outside of what has already been articulated or how we have already been articulated as subject. The desire for radical rearticulation is at once the terror of defacement beyond recognition.

10 This use of "interpellation" is used by Louis Pierre Althusser in 1970 to refer to the way we are called up as ideological subjects by the way we respond to our environment. Althusser's sense of being a hailed subject places emphasis on the way we answer to the names we are given. This process can even be as general as turning our heads in response to "Hey you." However, his sense of interpellation includes the way we are unconsciously conditioned by all of the social experience and practice that touches upon us (cf. Althusser 2001).

References

Althusser, L. (2001), *Lenin and Philosophy and Other Essays*, NY: Monthly Review Press.

Anzieu, D. (1974), "Le Moi-Peau," *Nouvelle Revue de Psychanalyse*, vol. 9, 195–203.

Anzieu, D. (2016), *The Skin-Ego*, Naomi Segal (trans.), London: Karnac.

Augustine, of Hippo, Saint (1998), *Confessions*, Henry Chadwick (trans.), Oxford: Oxford UP.

Butler, J. (2004), "Merleau-Ponty and the Touch of Malebranche," In: *The Cambridge Companion to Merleau-Ponty*, Taylor Carman and Mark B. N. Hansen (eds). Cambridge: Cambridge UP.

Deleuze, G. (1998), "He Stuttered," *Gilles Deleuze: Essays Critical and Clinical*, Daniel W. Smith and Michael A. Greco (trans.), New York: Verso.

Derrida, J. (1991), "Circonfession," in *Jacques Derrida* by Geoffrey Bennington and Jacques Derrida. Paris: Seuil.

Derrida, J. (1993), "Circumfession," in *Jacques Derrida* by Geoffrey Bennington (trans), Chicago: University of Chicago Press.

Derrida, J. (1993), *Spectres de Marx: l'état de la dette, le travail du deuil et la nouvelle Internationale*. Editions Galileé.

Derrida, J. (1994) *The Specters of Marx: The State of the Debt, the Work of Mourning and the New International*, Peggy Kamuf (trans.), New York: Routledge.

Freud, S. (2001a), "Note upon the 'mystic writing pad'" S.E., 19, 1923–1925, NY: Vintage, 225–32.

Freud, S. (2001b), "Findings, ideas, problems." S.E., 23, 1937–1939. NY: Vintage, 299–300.

Haraway, D. (2000), "The Cyborg Manifesto: Science, Technology and Socialist-Feminism in the Late Twentieth Century." *The Cybercultures Reader*, New York: Routledge.

Hegel, G. W. F. (1970), *Phänomenologie des Geistes* in Werke vol. 3. Eva Moldenhauer and Karl Markus Michel (eds), Frankfurt: Suhrkamp.

Marx, K. (1975), "Contribution to the Critique of Hegel's Philosophy of Law. Introduction," *Marx Engels Collected Works*, volume 3 1843–1844, NY: International Publishers, 175–187.

Marx, K. (1979), "The Eighteenth Brumaire of Louis Bonaparte," *Marx Engels Collected Works*, volume 11 1851–1853, 99–197. NY: International Publishers, 99–197.

Orwell, George (1950), *1984*, NY: Signet Classics.

8

On the Touch of Swear Words: Swearing and the Lacanian Real

Peter Klepec

Introduction

There are many ways in which words and language touch us, affect us, or, as we tend to say, move us. And there are, of course, many ways to define, understand, or simply explain how, what, and why this happens. It has also been known for a long, long time that certain language, or, to put it simply and yet vaguely, bad language, if directed against us, can be hurtful or injurious. Words hurt, at least some of them do sometimes. Which and when? Or better, what kind of words are those words that hurt and under what conditions do they do that? I am interested here only in some of those words, only in certain types of swear words or swearing, those that are similar to insults or injurious speech (see Butler 1998), but which are, however, slightly different. What interests me here is just a tiny part of what is usually broadly described as swear words or as swearing and what is usually described in English as *swearing at* (at something or somebody). Swearing in the broader sense is usually seen as a vulgar and profane way of expressing strong emotions and affects. As Freud noted, invective and insult replaced direct physical contact through the civilizational process, in an attempt to achieve the same ends by other means. But the aim of swearing is not only to express violence or to say aloud things that one, if civilized, is not supposed to say. Swearing simultaneously tries "to hit the bull's eye," "to hit the Achilles heel" of the other and to show him that neither he nor his supposedly hidden treasure, his *agalma*, is under his control, but on the contrary, it is in the control of the swearer's obscene capricious action. It is this sensitive spot, this Real in Lacan's sense, that swearing aims to touch.

Swearing as such is otherwise quite a complicated phenomenon. Only recently have analyses thereof come to proliferate, after it being considered an undignified or even taboo topic for a long time (Hughes 1998; Jay 2000; McEnery 2006; Hughes 2006; Parkin 2007; Pinker 2007; Sheidlower 2009; Silverton 2011; Mohr 2013; Bergen 2016; Adams 2016; etc.). A notable exception here is Montagu's classic book *The Anatomy of Swearing*, published half a century ago (Montagu 1967). There are many different reasons for this and I will address some of them here only very briefly. Our perception of bad or profane words is surely culturally and historically conditioned and it is also obvious that "the public perception of bad language over the past 400 years has changed" (McEnery, 2006). Swearing is a very special case, but it is only a part of bad language, and there are important differences between bad, obscene, blasphemous, taboo, injurious, and profane language, which we will put aside here. There is a difference between swearing and cursing, and even the praxis of swearing is something that was, in Melissa Mohr's terms, divided in history between the Holy and the Shit. Originally, swearing meant the taking of an oath (see Mohr 2013), and only later did it become synonymous with profane, blasphemous, vulgar, and obscene speech. Two recent milestones in this regard are certainly the two World Wars (see Mohr 2013, 227), and almost everyone agrees today that "there has been a veritable explosion of swearing, and a wholesale violation of decorum in the past half century, especially since the 1960s" (Hughes 2006: xxiv). From today's perspective, it is probably hard to believe that "the very word 'sex' is one that could not be freely uttered, especially in mixed company, until World War I. Nor could there be any direct reference to elimination" (Montagu 1967, 300). So-called four-letter words (such as "fuck, cunt, cock, arse, shit, piss, and fart": Montagu 1967, 303) or George Carlin's list from 1973 ("'Seven Words You Can Never Say on Television': shit, piss, fuck, cunt, cocksucker, motherfucker, tits." Silverton 2009: 11) were and still are deemed obscene and offensive because "they refer to an aspect of life that has long been considered *ob caenum*, that is, filthy" (Montagu 1967: 301). There are some other words not listed above (e.g., nigger), that are considered to be extremely offensive nowadays and there will surely be some others in the future. These things change and in the last fifty years there have been some infamous milestones concerning the public use of such words.

Television (apart from literature, music, and film) has played an important role in this regard: the uttering and frequent use of the f-word by Kenneth Tynan in his BBC interview in 1965 (November 13) is almost universally considered to be such a milestone for the 1960s (see Montagu 1967: 312; Hughes 2006: xxiii; Pinker 2007: 325; Sheidlower 2009: xvi; Silverton 2011: 6); or Steven Jones's (from the Sex Pistols punk band) use of the word "fuck" in his 1976 television appearance; or the statement of (U2's) Bono that: "This is really, really fucking brilliant!" at the 2003 Golden Globes (Silverton 2011: 12). There are, of course, many other prominent instances of such public use of obscene words in recent decades in the Anglo-Saxon world (see Pinker 2007: 325; Sheidlower 2009: i-xxvi; Mohr 2013: 227–252). One should not forget the role played in this process by the 1998 CNN live coverage of the Clinton–Monica Lewinsky case, as DeJean warns us in her *The Reinvention of Obscenity* (DeJean 2002: 1–2). Incidentally or not, it is this coverage that coincides broadly not only with the above-mentioned boom in the public use of swearing, but also with the pornification of our Western societies (starting in the 1960s and 1970s) where something "which should be kept 'out of public view'" (Williams 2004: 3), something considered to be publicly obscene/off-scene, becomes public or simply on-scene. There are many facets to this division; in academia one should mention two poles here: the figure of Slavoj Žižek saying some things aloud which are/were not considered proper or correct in the context of dull Western academia, and the recent politically correct praxis in the form of a "trigger warning."

In the above outline three things are important for us here: first, that there is and always will be what is considered to be obscene for a certain public, and this division between off-scene/on-scene is targeted, as we will see, by swearing. Secondly, this division constantly changes and varies across cultures and through history (see Mohr 2013). To put it differently, some (swear) words simply lose their offensive power (such as "bloody" or "damn," as so extensively analyzed by Montagu) and that is why swearing is "strongly governed by fashion" (Hughes 2006: xix). Despite the fact that swear words seem to be more popular today than ever, despite the fact that they are now prevalent and less taboo in society, there will always be a subtle limit or limitation, call it taboo, civility, good manners, or whatever else. While many researchers nowadays may praise profanity/swearing for its cathartic potential to relieve stress (Parkin 2010; Adams 2016), or simply for being such a good evolutionary means to express strong affects (Jay 2000; Pinker 2007), they seem to forget that this division or taboo has to be operative and constantly recreated. At the moment, it is defined not only in terms of morality/good manners, but also in political terms (through political correctness, the re-traditionalization of contemporary societies, new nationalisms, extremisms, and racisms). So, to cut a long story short, for swearing to be effective, to retain its power, it has to break certain taboos and *to violate*, to offend the public perception of what is publicly acceptable.

Swear words and speaking

We should not forget here that swearing is essentially speaking, a speech act, and to speak means to speak to others, to speak publicly. A swear word is usually spoken aloud, though an unspoken swear word can be imagined as in cartoons, for instance where there are symbols such as #!? written in a cloud above someone's head. When we *swear at* somebody or something we do that aloud and this manner of swearing is always personal. Even if something is not alive or personal, a swear word brings life to it and personalizes it ("Fuck you!" or "Fuck your ...!"). This kind of swearing therefore always involves the other and the Other in the Lacanian sense. Every case of speaking involves such an instance, as an addressee is addressed by every speech act. Whenever we speak we do not only speak to those we are addressing, to others, but also to the instance that Lacan calls the "big Other," which is never identical to any other little other(s). It designates a radical alterity, in some senses also the Other sex as well, and is, as a symbolic instance, not caught in the dialectics of the Imaginary. It "must first of all be considered a locus, the locus in which speech is constituted" (Lacan 1993: 274). This locus, which is beyond one's conscious control, is also what Lacan calls "the other scene," and it is not unimportant, by the way, that for Lacan "the unconscious is the Other's discourse" (Lacan 2006: 10). When talking (to the other) one always talks and speaks to the Other too, or, as Lacan puts it, we always speak *à la cantonade* (meaning: to speak to someone not present (on a stage), to someone behind the curtains; but also to speak to "the good listener", to an analyst, or in this case, to Lacan himself: *à Lacan*: à *la can*-tonade (See Lacan 1998: 208; Lacan 1990: 3).

Why is all this important for us here? Because in *swearing at* we have three participants: the speaker (the Ego, the I), the other, and the Other. In a way, we have here a variant of Lacan's early schema L, consisting of two axes: the axes of the Imaginary and of the Symbolic. The other is on the axis of the Imaginary (with its competitiveness, violence, aggression, and struggle) while the Other is on the Symbolic axis (the impartial third, the locus of speech, the treasure of signifiers, an instance that pacifies the struggle for recognition and in that way stops immediate violence: see Lacan 2006: 40; Fink 2004: 5–10; Feldstein, Fink and Jaanus 1996). For early Lacan the Symbolic is crucial, the Imaginary is the site of blockage and countertransference; one has to avoid being caught in the dialectics of the other, in the following imaginary relation: "If one wants to position the analyst within this schema of the subject's speech, one can say that he is somewhere in O [Other]. At least he should be. If he enters into the coupling of the resistance, which is just what he is taught not to do, then he speaks from *o'* [other] and he will see himself in the subject" (Lacan 1993: 161–162).

Nobody saw this relationship between the other and the Other more clearly than Freud. In a slightly long passage in his *Jokes and their Relation to the Unconscious*, where he addresses the hostile tendencies of jokes, he says the following:

> Since our individual childhood, and, similarly, since the childhood of human civilization, hostile impulses against our fellow men have been subject to the same restrictions, the same progressive repression, as our sexual urges. We have not yet got so far as to be able to love our enemies or to offer our left cheek after being struck on the right. [...] Nevertheless, within our own circle we have made some advances in the control of hostile impulses. As Lichtenberg puts it in drastic terms: 'Where we now say 'Excuse me!' we used to give a box on the ears.' Brutal hostility, forbidden by law, has been replaced by verbal invective; and a better knowledge of the interlinking of human impulses is more and more robbing us – by its consistent *'tout comprendre c'est tout pardonner'* – of the capacity for feeling angry with a fellow man who gets in our way. Though as children we are still endowed with a powerful inherited disposition to hostility, we are later taught by a higher personal civilization that it is an unworthy thing to use abusive language; and even where fighting has in itself remained permissible, the number of things which may not be employed as methods of fighting has extraordinarily increased. Since we have been obliged to renounce the expression of hostility by deeds – held back by the passionless third person, in whose interest it is that personal security shall be preserved – we have, just as in the case of sexual aggressiveness, developed a new technique of invective, which aims at enlisting this third person against our enemy. By making our enemy small, inferior, despicable, or comic, we achieve in a roundabout way the enjoyment of overcoming him – to which the third person, who has made no efforts, bears witness by his laughter.
>
> (Freud 1905: 102–103)

In comparison to a swear word, a joke is something benign and more sophisticated, but both have a similar procedure: the replacement of a direct violent act with more mediate means, i.e. words. As such, there is in both cases a third person present (or the Other in Lacanese), but his role is different in each case: while in jokes one wants to win him over and to enlist him for one's cause, in such a manner annihilating by laughter the energy built up by an aggressive tendency, with swear words he has to be a pure passive witness to the violent obscenity declared. While in a joke he is an arbitrator and the judge of its sophisticated art, in swear word he testifies to its brutal and direct declaration of power. This power is *enacted* by being simply uttered. In other words, swear words actually do what they claim they are doing (the Serbian "*Jebem ti . . .,*" i.e. "I am fucking your . . ." is more telling than the English "Fuck your . . ."; there is a short object that typically follows: "mother!" or the Russian *mat* or Serbian *mamu*). Words are deeds and here we are close to Austin's analysis of performatives where certain words or sentences can (under certain conditions) be deeds themselves. Although Austin did not put the swear word at the center of his research, he does mention it (see Austin 1962: 105, 122, 148) and he came close to it by his main examples of promising or baptizing, which are not far from either the original meaning of swearing (to take an oath) or from its derived meaning (referring to sexual or bodily functions in an obscene way). In swearing, Austin's distinction regarding speech acts between being *felicitous* or *infelicitous* simply does not apply because swearing is always *felicitous*. It suffices that it is uttered and that it is registered by the Other. But what does the Other register? That a taboo has been broken. Remember that two of the oldest and most important interdictions of totemism for Freud are: do not kill a taboo animal and do not have sexual relations or contact with a totemic counterpart of the opposite sex. It seems that swearing manages to do both and that it even escapes punishment for doing so: it breaks and violates the taboo; the forbidden touch is sublimated into words; hostile tendencies are manifested, full satisfaction is nonetheless acquired via language.

To hit the bull's eye

However, things are not so simple. First of all there are many ways of swearing, not only swearing *at* somebody, but ranging from empty blasphemous fillers used rather abundantly, to words that cut and hurt: one can see why for Hegel a word kills a thing and why the proverbial pen is deadlier than the sword. The touch of language might simply be unperceived or it might be lethal.

This range covers what Lacan designated in his *Rome Speech* (1953) as two opposed uses of words being torn between empty speech and full speech. The former is something nonobligatory, passing, meaningless chatter (Heidegger's *Gerede*) devoid of deeper existential meaning,[1] while the latter represents something nearest and dearest to someone. This topic is present in later Lacan; the very first line of *Television* (1973), for instance, presents the following: "I always speak the truth. Not the whole truth, because there's no way to say it all. Saying it all is literally impossible: words inevitably fail. Yet it is through this very impossibility that the truth holds onto the Real" (Lacan 1990: 3). The last sentence is worth quoting in the French original: "*C'est même par cette impossible que la vérité tient au réel*" (Lacan 2001: 509). Lacan does not claim that the truth is impossible, but that through its very impossibility it holds onto the Real. This point, that the impossible *can and does happen* (sometimes), is of crucial importance for psychoanalysis: "The cure is a demand that originates in the voice of the sufferer, of someone who suffers from his body or his thought. The astonishing thing is that there be a response, and that throughout time medicine, using words, has hit the bull's-eye" (Lacan 1990: 7). To hit the bull's eye is also the aim of a swear word. Lacan's original French phrase "*faire mouche par des mots*" is described by the *Robert* dictionary as "to hit the black point in the middle of a target." But how does one know that the swear word did indeed hit the target? From the reaction of the person targeted or sworn at. This reaction testifies to the fact that a certain point connected with him *was touched* in an *obscene* or improper way—keep in mind that another English translation for "*faire mouche*" proposes the verb *to score* with all its possible meanings, including the obscene ones.

Swearing is a violation of what is appropriate. It is an aggression, violence; it might entail the definite cessation of relations with the other, the end of communication and contacts. It aims at silencing the other, it wants to shock him, to stop a conversation by literally taking the breath from the other. But this could be achieved by other means—by simply insulting the other ("Idiot!"), ordering him to shut up ("Shut up!" in French: "Ta gueule!" in German: "Halt dein Maul!") or by directly threatening him ("or else . . ."). Why include an obscenity, why add obscene details to this order, threat, or insult? This addition is crucial. While swearing is similar to insulting in defining, smudging, or soiling the other, it adds something crucial to all that: the *attitude* of the swearer towards the insulted, the sworn at. This attitude represents the relationship between the active and the passive: the obscenity of swearing is first of all the obscenity of power. Even more: the swearer reasserts and identifies himself with the *active* principle that has been identified since Aristotle with the male principle predominant in our contemporary cultures: it is I who *can do* this, I *am* the master, I can do whatever I *want*. It is not unimportant in this regard that swearing represents a *violation* of good manners. Even more so, the swearing is a protest, demonstrating open disrespect and opposition to the good rules of society; in a way it is against all authority. It makes a hole in the Other in the Lacanian sense of the word *and* at the same time devalues, degrades, and humiliates the other with reference to (sexual or obscene) activity. There are no taboos or rules for the swearer, nothing sacred or holy for the

Ego of the swearer; swearing is frequently, but not always, spoken in the first person singular. Not surprisingly, a swear word expresses an extreme infantile relationship towards the world. It is this narcissism of the swearing Ego that makes a difference when one compares swearing and cursing. Why? They both express powerful affects, they both use strong language, but swearing intentionally *directly* insults or injures the other, while cursing does that *indirectly* via the Other—in cursing one expresses a wish that the other be hurt by external forces or the Other. In principle, this happens *in absentia,* but it can also be expressed in front of someone—*be cursed, damn you, be damned.* On the other hand, swearing happens *in praesentia* and in this way serves not only to express one's supremacy and narcissism, but also to release strong affects and emotions. Austin already emphasized this (Austin 1962: 105), and half a century later this seems to be the dominant view (see, for instance, Pinker 2007; Parkin 2007; Adams 2016). From a Lacanian point of view, we would only add that swearing—as with every speaking and talking—is also enjoyment: "In other words—for the moment, I am not fucking, I am talking to you. Well! I can have exactly the same satisfaction as if I were fucking" (Lacan 1998: 165–166). In other words: "Where it speaks, it enjoys" (Lacan 1999: 115). But if this is so, if swearing is enjoyment, as such it is bound to all of the paradoxes of enjoyment including the obscene superego injunction to enjoy, which as Freud knew is a mission impossible. Or better, one cannot *not* enjoy; we always enjoy, though, one can always do/enjoy better, more, there is never enough.

Here we have a proper paradox of swearing: it fulfills its function by being spoken, it asserts the power of the speaker, however, it always searches for a point that would bring a surplus, last but not least, a surplus of enjoyment. This can only happen by bridging the gap between words and flesh, by touching the Real, by supplementing the signifier.[2] How exactly?

To touch the real

It seems that we are again back at the beginning. We began with a provisional definition of swearing as a speech act with a purpose. We said that a swear word is never neutral and that it is always loaded with strong affects, aggression, violence, and violation. It is something purely verbal, but never only that. Words are never just words, and if anywhere, this is clear in swearing. A word can be stronger than a thousand blows with a sword, it might be more real than reality itself. In fact, its own obscene activity is referred to as a *fait accompli,* as something real or something that will inevitably happen. A swear word has an explosive power, but this power depends on many factors, perhaps the most important being the reaction of the other. What exactly is targeted here? There are actually two levels of swearing; while one level is verbal, the level of enunciation, the other is *not beyond* it, but paradoxically in it—without being identical to it. What do we mean by that?

In a way, there is only one level, the level of words. There are only signifiers, *except that* there is something at their limit, at their margin, at their edge, and this point is targeted by a swear word. There is no guarantee that it will succeed or that the same procedure will have the same results in the future. As if the swear word tries to constantly find new, more appropriate ways and new words to swear with—in that way it testifies to the violent side of language (see Lecercle 1990; Žižek 2008). Take the example of an infamous Serbian swear: "Let an elephant fuck your pregnant sister on your mother's grave while your father is forced to look at all this from a wheelchair, *and so on.*" As if a shorter version of this ("Sister!" or "Mother!") would not suffice (unless you are Zinedine Zidane playing the last minutes of the World Cup final on July 9, 2006) and as if the activity has to be done by some humiliating animal (or something big, and therefore supposedly hurtful in the above example). What this example shows is that swear words always search for juicy obscene stuff that can be added—in order to fulfill the mission, i.e. to touch a sensitive point in the other. Swearing as such in principle keeps looking for such words which by definition lack (Lacan: *les mots y manquent*). That is why in Serbian swearing one frequently adds—instead of "*and so on*"—another inclusive: "everything on the list" or "all alive and dead."

But instead of being a manifestation of omnipotence, this swearing testifies to impotence and the difficulty in "nailing things down." The trouble is that the real "power" here is *not* on the side of the swearer: if the other does not react, the mission of swearing is not complete. Here, swearing testifies to the well-known fact that there is no master of language, or as Heidegger put it, *die Sprache spricht*, the language speaks. The speaker or sender of the message is not the master because "the sender receives from the receiver his own message in an inverted form" (Lacan 2006: 30). It is the receiver who decides whether something is perceived as an insult or a swear word—even if it was not meant to be one. What is interesting is that this conundrum is even recognized in certain Serbian swearing when one swears at the sun: "*Jebem ti sunce!*" ("I fuck your sun!"). Why the sun in the first place? Perhaps the reason is that the sun is so clearly out of everyone's reach—one cannot touch it, for sure. That is impossible. And yet by swearing at it this seems to be possible and this is the ultimate point of swearing in general: it touches what one is forbidden/unable to touch and what is impossible to touch (cf. Derrida 2005). One surely asserts one's supreme power by swearing, so to speak. But why swear at the sun, and not at the galaxy, at the universe, at outer space, or at aliens? Because one stays, so to speak, inside our solar system, one is in that way faithful to the logic of our narcissism and one denies the claim that "the I is not the master in his own house," as Freud put it (enlisting in the same line as himself Copernicus and Darwin). In principle, there would be no problem for the swearer to swear at the universe ("Fuck your infinite universe!", why not?), however, one more frequently swears at the sun or at the world because that is part of what Lacan called the logic of the whole and what Koyré named the closed world (in his *From the Closed World to the Open Universe*): every rule, every whole, has an exception to it and the one swearing wants to be that exception. And because there is only one true master, one is inevitably driven into what Hegel has described as the struggle for recognition between master and slave or lord and bondsman and what Lacan subsequently conceptualized as the Imaginary. The point of a swear word is to show the other that he is not the master, that nothing related to him—his fame, glory, status, right up to the sun and the moon and all things in between—is under his control, but that of the swearer. The point is then to reach and to touch the point where this other whimpers, to hit his dearest part—to hit the Real: "Insult is the modus that Lacan signals for touching the Real" (Miller 1985: 40).

By means of language, by swear words, one not only touches that sensitive point, one "hits the bull's eye," "hits the Achilles heel" of the other, but one also shows that this point in particular is under the control of the swearer, left to his mercy, to his obscene doing.

To touch what?

That is why the purpose of the swear word is not the same as the purpose of the insult (to hurt, to injure): it is simultaneously less and more. Sometimes it might not even be perceived as such (as hurtful), and sometimes it might be perceived as a direct act of aggression where things are irreversible, one cannot undo what has been said. For some linguists (Guiraud), swearing equals physical contact, a wound similar to a physical wound, and it seems that this is the case for Judith Butler too: "The notion that speech wounds appears to rely on this inseparable and incongruous relation between body and speech, but also, consequently, between speech and its effects. If the speaker addresses his other body to the one addressed, then it is not merely the body of the speaker that comes into play: it is the body of the addressee as well" (Butler 1997).

However, are there really only bodies and words? The pain in our body caused by words is certainly there, but is there something else also involved? Is the target and the touched only our body or something even more real than our body? Hegel—who else?—in his Jena period (1805–1806), worked intensively on the question of what happens when there is a verbal insult, a slander, or defamation. A verbal *Schimpfwort* (the same German expression, by the way, as in Freud's citation above, translated as "invective") or a verbal injury, *Verbalinjurie*, makes the other in the sphere of the universal something unworthy, null, *Nichtiges*, something negated and sublated, *Aufgehobenes* (Hegel 1987: 215). Hegel's point is simple—not only physical reality is affected by invective, insult, or swearing, but also another, perhaps even more important, reality, the sphere of the universal. This is a well-known idea from Hegel that is subsequently developed in his *Elements of the Philosophy of Right* (1821) concerning the necessity of punishment for a crime, and Hegel even goes so far as to defend capital punishment for major crimes by relying on the principle of *lex tallionis* ("an eye for an eye"). But what would be a similar measure in the case of an insult or invective? Quoting Lichtenberg in his *Phenomenology of Spirit* (1807): "You certainly act like an honest man, but I see from your face that you are forcing yourself to do so and are a rogue at heart," Hegel himself adds: "without a doubt, every honest fellow to the end of time, when thus addressed, will retort with a box on the ear" (Hegel 1977: 193). Quoting the same reaction in Lichtenberg's case as Freud ("a box on the ear"), Hegel actually testifies that there is a problem with an insult or invective (and we would add swearing here too): what is actually hit by it? What kind of wound does it cause? One is clearly at the level of a body, but the other one is doubled, so to speak: it is symbolic and at the level of the sphere of the universal, as Hegel clearly saw, and at the same time made of rather special stuff.[3] In a way, a swear word, without going into too much detail, has a double mission similar to the drive: "When you entrust someone with a mission, the aim is not what he brings back, but the itinerary he must take. The aim is the way taken. The French word *but* may be translated by another word in English, *goal*. In archery, the goal is not the *but* either, it is not the bird you shoot, it is having scored a hit and thereby attained your *but*" (Lacan 1998: 179).

So the aim of a swearing is the itinerary it takes, the form of violation it takes in relation to the public, this third person or the Other that also testifies that "a hit has been scored," so to speak. However, this subsequent "score" is only hit if the other recognizes it as such. This wound is not only physical or symbolic, universal, but also something else, which Lacan called *objet petit a*, a supposed hidden treasure in the other. I try to hit something *en toi plus que toi*: "I love you, but, because inexplicably I love in you something more than you—the objet petit a—I mutilate you" (Lacan 1998: 263). This hidden treasure in the other is not only the object of love, but of hate too—that is why Lacan in his *Seminar XX* joins the two expressions into one: *hainamoration*, "hateloving" (Lacan 1999: 90). Another name for this hidden treasure is the Greek term *agalma* analyzed by Lacan in "Seminar VIII." It is this object, *agalma*, which in Plato's *Symposium* Alcibiades accuses Socrates of having inside himself as a hidden treasure (cf. Plato 1997). In the tenth lecture of "Seminar VIII" Lacan even presents the etymology and uses of the word *agalma*, in Ancient Greece (used, by the way, also for the content of the Trojan Horse, but otherwise for something celebrated, adorned, something to take pride in, to rejoice at, meaning also a statue, a figure, a treasure). It is this treasure, this pride and joy of mine, which is targeted by a swear word. Swearing defames, degrades this *agalma*, tries to annul it, to smudge it, to turn it into junk, to shit, to *paleo*. It is not surprising, then, that "for more than two thousand years, swearing has alternated between the twin poles of oaths and obscenities, between the Holy and the Shit" (Mohr 2013: 7). However, the point of swearing is not to alternate between, but *to identify the two poles*: what is holy to someone is actually shit. The highest and the lowest coincide as in speculative judgment ("spirit is a bone"), as Hegel knew very well:

> The *depth* which Spirit brings forth from within – but only as far as its picture-thinking consciousness where it lets it remain – and the *ignorance* of this consciousness about what it really is saying, are the same conjunction of the high and the low which, in the living being, Nature naively expresses when it combines the organ of its highest fulfilment, the organ of generation, with the organ of urination.
>
> (Hegel 1977, 210)

Is there a way out? Is there a way out of swearing's obscenity other than a violent acting out? Perhaps the only way out is a paradoxical one—the only answer to an instance of swearing is perhaps just more swearing: How the fuck do I know? Fuck it! This violent side, the taboo-breaking side of swear words, is simply hard to handle non-violently. A swear word does the impossible and gets away with it. It supposedly manifests the supremacy of the swearer and provides him with the satisfaction that he has not only broken the taboo (killed and done with the forbidden object whatever obscene things he pleases), but that he has done that by purely verbal, linguistic, means. In that way, the forbidden touch is not only sublimated into words but is celebrated as more real than reality itself since it manifests to the other/Other that the supposedly hidden treasure in the other, his *agalma*, is under the swearer's control: what is to you holy *is* actually nothing but shit. The message of a swear word is therefore: I *can touch* this hidden treasure of yours, *whenever I like*, and *I can do* with it *whatever I want*!

Notes

1 Nowhere is this more explicit than in the following story: "A young soldier comes home to his family after World War II. His grandmother asks him how his time was in the army. The truth is that he has seen many men, friends, and enemies die horrible deaths, and he returns with a heavy heart. He does not want to burden his family, though, so he says, "The boys sure were funny, Grandma—they had so many great jokes." "Tell us one, tell us one," his family begs. He says, "Oh, I can't do that. You see, the boys also used an awful lot of bad language." His family really wants to hear a joke, though, so someone suggests that he just say "blank" whenever he comes to a bad word. He agrees, and tells a joke: "Blank blank blank blankity blank. Blank blank blank blank, blankity blanking blank blank. Blanking blankity blanking blank, blank blank blank blank fuck" (Mohr 2013: 227).

2 For a further elaboration of the surplus of enjoyment in relation to touch as the crossroad between the Lacanian *objet a* and the anthropological concept of *mana*, see Karmen Šterk's contribution in this book (Chapter 3).

3 For a further elaboration of touching in relation to language in the context of Hegel's discussion of the universal, see Goran Vranešević's contribution in this book (Chapter 5).

References

Adams, Michael (2016), *In Praise of Profanity*, Oxford: Oxford UP.

Austin, J. L. (1962), *How to Do Things with Words*, Oxford: Oxford UP.

Bergen, Benjamin K. (2016), *What the F. What Swearing Reveals about Our Language, Our Brains and about Ourselves*, New York: Basic Books.

Butler, Judith (1997), *Excitable Speech. A Politics of the Performative*, London & New York: Routledge.

DeJean, Joan (2002), *The Reinvention of Obscenity. Sex, Lies, and Tabloids in Early Modern France*, Chicago: Chicago UP.

Derrida, Jacques (2005), *On Touching: Jean-Luc Nancy*, Stanford: Stanford UP.

Freud, Sigmund (1905), *Jokes and their Relation to the Unconscious*, in: The Standard Edition of the Complete Psychological Works of Sigmund Freud (2001), London: Vintage Books.

Hegel, G. W. F. (1977), *The Phenomenology of Spirit*, trans. A. V. Miller, Oxford: Oxford UP.

Hegel, G. W. F. (1987), *Jenaer Systementwürfe III., Naturphilosophie und Philosophie des Geistes*, Hamburg: Felix Meiner Verlag.

Hughes, Geoffrey (1998), *Swearing. A Social History of Oaths, Profanity and Foul Language in English*, Oxford: Blackwell.

Hughes, Geoffrey (2006), *An Encyclopedia of Swearing*, New York: M. E. Sharpe.

Feldstein, Richard, Fink, Bruce & Jaanus, Maire (eds.) (1996), *Reading Seminars I and II. Lacan's Return to Freud*, New York: State University of New York Press.

Fink, Bruce (2004), *Lacan to the Letter. Reading Ecrits Closely,* Minneapolis: University of Minnesota Press.

Jay, Timothy (2000), *Why We Curse. A Neuro-Psycho-Social Theory of Speech*, Philadelphia/Amsterdam: John Benjamins.

Lacan, Jacques (1990), *Television. A Challenge to the Psychoanalytic Establishment*, trans. by Denis Hollier, Rosalind Krauss, & Anette Michelson, New York: W.W. Norton.

Lacan (1993), *The Seminar, Book III. The Psychoses*, ed. by Jacques-Alain Miller, trans. by Russell Grigg, New York: W.W. Norton.

Lacan (1998), *The Seminar, Book XI. The Four Fundamental Concepts of Psycho-Analysis*, ed. by Jacques-Alain Miller, trans. by Alan Sheridan, New York: W.W. Norton.

Lacan (1999), *The Seminar, Book XX. Encore: On Feminine Sexuality, the Limits of Love and Knowledge*, ed. by Jacques-Alain Miller, trans. by Bruce Fink, New York: W.W. Norton.

Lacan (2001), *Autres écrits*, Paris: Seuil.

Lacan (2006), *Ecrits. The First Complete Edition in English*, trans. by Bruce Fink, New York: W.W. Norton.

Lecercle, Jean-Jacques (1990), *The Violence of Language*, London & New York: Routledge.

McEnery, Tony (2006), *Swearing in English. Bad Language, Purity and Power from 1586 to the Present*, London & New York: Routledge.

Miller, Jacques-Alain (1985), "H_2O", in: *Actes de l'ÉCF*, no. 8, Paris, pp. 22–26.

Mohr, Melissa (2013), *Holy Shit. A Brief History of Swearing*, Oxford: Oxford UP.

Montagu, Ashley (1967), *The Anatomy of Swearing*, Philadelphia: University of Pennsylvania Press.

Parkin, John C. (2007), *Fuck It. The Ultimate Spiritual Way*, New York: Hay House.

Pinker, Steven (2007), *The Stuff of Thought. Language as a Window into Human Nature*, London: Penguin.

Plato (1997), *Complete Works*, ed. by Cooper, John M. & Hutchinson, D. S., Indianapolis: Hackett.

Sheidlower, Jesse (2009), *The F-Word*, Oxford: Oxford UP.

Silverton, Peter (2011), *Filthy English. The How, Why, When and What of Everyday Swearing*, London: Portobello.

Williams, Linda (2004), "Porn Studies: Proliferating Pornographies. On/Scene: An Introduction", in: *Porn Studies*, ed. by L. Williams, Durham & London: Duke UP, pp. 1–23.

Žižek, Slavoj (2008), *Violence*, London: Polity Press.

9

Proper Names: Being in Touch with the Real

Jela Krečič

Introduction

We hear that, sometimes, words can hurt more than actual physical beating. In our culture everyday spontaneous ideology presupposes that words can touch and affect us much more powerfully than the "real" touch of fists. The aim of this paper is to examine this common notion. Does it hold only on a metaphorical level, or is it more grounded? How can words touch, how can language gain tactility? Plato's *Cratylus* reveals several problems with names and naming. The following text is centered around Jacques Lacan's investigation of the relationship between the Symbolic and the Real. This framework offers a conceptualization of the touch with special regard to proper names, their effects on their bearers and their touches.

The difficulties with naming

Plato's *Cratylus* (cf. Plato 1997) is an early serious philosophical attempt to bring some insight to the question of naming. We use names in order to describe the world around us, in order to get closer to its truth, but we usually take them for granted. The moment we try to examine what their nature and status is, it turns out that names are not innocent; they are not natural or neutral. This is, at least, one of the points we can draw from Plato's *Cratylus*.

In this dialog Plato tries to establish an intrinsic link between names and the things they name: according to him the name should reflect the essence of the thing named. The closer a name is to the essence of the thing named the truer the name is, and the less the name grasps this essence the more false it is.[1]

He examines particular words (397b) and finds a certain justification for them in their etymology, which affirms a special connection between names and their bearers. Incidentally, Plato finds that the same is true for proper names. He discusses the names "Hector" and "Agamemnon" in exactly the same way he discusses "gods," "truth," etc.[2] A proper name reflects the essence of the person it names. However, the problem with this analysis is that the semantic value of the name is supported by the semantic value of another name.[3]

Plato's second endeavor is to establish that a name has a mimetic dimension. Words are like pictures and letters are like colors, the difference being that words are imitating things with sounds. As there are pictures that are more or less true to the things they depict, the same goes for things they name. There is no perfect picture and no perfectly correct name, since nothing can replace the things themselves (432b).

It seems that Plato is constantly torn between an attempt to establish a privileged link between names and things by likeliness, and on the other hand keeping names (like pictures) forever separated from the higher ontological entities (bearers of names on the one hand and the Ideas on the other).[4]

Names are too close to the thing itself and pose a danger to legitimate bearers of the name, so Plato presents yet another solution. He proposes direct access to things without having to depend on names. If we were to capture the essence without the intermediary of a name, we would hold a basis for examining the correctness of names. Here we are dealing with fundamental philosophical fantasy: gaining direct access to the thing itself as if the realm of names is preventing us from accurately grasping the thing. The problem names supposedly pose, is that they seem to be the only tool with which we can think, understand, and gain knowledge about the realm of things, but, on the other hand, this tool— because it is an intermediary—is exactly what is preventing us from ever reaching a full and complete knowledge.[5]

This structure of names can be seen in an analogy with the structure of a touch as it is perceived already in Ancient Greece. Touch is a tool to get as close as possible to things and bodies alike, but at the same time it poses the final barrier to direct contact with them. Touch is always in the way of the thing as language is always in the way of directly apprehending things.[6]

The realm of the signifier

According to Plato the world of names is chaotic, not only because they imply an endless etymological chain of referencing and not only because of its presumed mimetic function. Even if we take into consideration only the sphere of names themselves, we encounter an inherent ambiguity in them. One can hardly pin down meanings or make sure that names make univocal sense without the threat of evoking other meanings and misunderstandings, etc. So Plato discovered a dimension of language that cannot be simply handled by means of language—a dimension that is elusive and cannot be integrated into the order of sense.

Psychoanalysis, especially that practiced by Jacques Lacan, focuses on exactly this realm of language, always prone to double entandre, wordplays, homonymity, and punning. For Lacan this dimension of language demands an investigation into the linguistic structure; he claims that on the level of language—the symbolic—something does not quite add up. His endeavor throughout his opus is to establish why it does not work or what exactly does not work. Crucial shifts in Lacan's thoughts, which revolve around the examination of the Symbolic and the Real, will guide us toward a more elaborated notion of touch and toward an understanding of how a proper name—this special signifier—can touch.

In the early phase, Lacan's focus was on the symbolic (the linguistic structure, also known as "the signifier" or "the law"), as a field of meaning and sense, but in which there is a certain lack that makes it incomplete. This is the field that enables all intersubjective relationships including psychoanalytic practice: symptoms are considered formations of the signifier that can be approached, analyzed, and transformed by the signifier itself. In this early phase there was no elaborated notion of the real. Lacan introduces this concept in the *Seminar VII: Ethics of Psychoanalysis*, where he conceives the Symbolic as a field of social order; however this field of prevailing social rules is based on the exclusion of another dimension, that of the Real or *das Ding* (the Thing).[7] More precisely, social order is based on lists of prohibitions, while the domain of the Real is not reigned by the signifier, there is no law that governs it—it is a massive, unsymbolized entity that represents the abyss of the symbolic and of the subject of the symbolic. To illustrate the Thing, Lacan refers to Sophocles' *Antigone*: in her demand that her traitorous brother be buried according to the established customs, Antigone is prepared to abolish the law—enforced by the King Creon, her uncle—and die for her cause. Her death is not one: the moment she violates the prohibition (of the burial of her brother), she is excluded from the Symbolic Order and trapped between the two deaths: the symbolic death and the real death, i.e., she is still (biologically) alive while already dead (for the community). Lacan conceives this "in-between" as the source of Antigone's sublime beauty which he meaningfully defined by employing a tactile metaphor as "a beauty that mustn't be touched" (Lacan 1992: 239).

Why is the beautiful dangerous, dangerous to the extent that it should not be touched? Antigone's beauty is sublime, and, for Lacan, the sublime object is an ordinary object which comes to occupy the place of the impossible/prohibited Thing, "elevated to the dignity of the Thing," as he puts it (ibid.: 112). This is why, while we can touch ordinary objects, it is prohibited to touch sublime objects. To put it another way, sublime beauty forms the link between the Imaginary and the Real, it characterizes an imaginary object which finds itself occupying the place of the Real.

So does touch belong to the Real or to the Imaginary? It can be understood exactly as an "in-between," between the two heterogenous domains. More precisely, in this case, touch is the reason the Imaginary (the beautiful) functions only as a screen that provides pleasure to the subject (the recipient of an art work). In touch, its imaginary object is in a vicinity of the Real, amortizing it, but at the same time evoking it. The touch can thus be perceived as an (invisible) mark of this vicinity of the two domains; a mark that, again, keeps them close and apart at the same time.[8]

In this phase, as we can see, touch is conceived as a structure—firmly connected to prohibition—that enables a relationship between Imaginary and the Real, while there is no place for the Symbolic in it. Why? Lacan's further analysis of Sophocles' *Antigone* might provide us with an answer.

As already said, a subject gets a life in the Symbolic at the expense of a life in the Real, as shown by Antigone, who is, after being excluded from the Symbolic, a dead subject even when her body is still alive. Lacan conceives of the Real from the perspective of the Symbolic, as a negative category, as an immanent limit of the Symbolic. When we force the Symbolic to its limit, we approach the abyss of the Real that threatens to swallow us. Insofar as what Lacan calls *jouissance* (excessive "enjoyment" as opposed to mere "pleasure") is such a Real which eludes symbolization, his thesis is that enjoyment "is prohibited to whoever speaks, as such" (Lacan 2006: 696). Enjoyment can only be evoked as missing, as an abyss that threatens to engulf us; there can be no connection between the Symbolic and the Real; thus the only way to approach the Real is through the imaginary: sublime beauty.

In Freud's *Totem and Taboo* we find a passage that helps us further develop the connection between touching and prohibition. Moreover, this elaboration also shows how—along the lines of Lacan's reading of *Antigone*—the Symbolic and the Real intersect through the forbidden touch. Freud deals with the prohibition of names in some so-called primitive cultures, where it is a *taboo* to pronounce the name of the deceased. There are different manifestations of this prohibition in different geographical areas, but the avoidance of the name of the deceased is as a rule kept with extraordinary severity, and the penalty for not following it is very strict. The name of the deceased is considered extremely dangerous. Why? "Calling a dead person by name can also be traced back to contact with him, so that we can turn our attention to the more inclusive problem of why this contact is visited with such a severe taboo" (Freud 1985: 76).

Contact is in this sense equivalent to touch: by pronouncing a deceased's name, we somehow get in touch with him or her, i.e., we enter the obscure domain of the dead, more precisely, of the "undead" the domain where the dead continue to live (ibid.). Death is perceived as something most horrible and the deceased are perceived as demons, haunting the living (for the period of grieving). It takes only the proper name of the deceased, an uttered word, to summon the demon which then becomes active and dangerous. However, when the so-called primitive mind attributes the power of touch to the name, a power to affect the living, it is not simply wrong; it rather touches something which concerns us all, namely, the symbolic efficiency of proper names. How, exactly?

Crucial here is the link between the prohibition of the name of a deceased and the process of mourning.[9] Prohibition is intrinsically linked to the touch: entering the Symbolic Order occurs at the expense of the Thing and it is as if, in the case of death, the entire person of the deceased moves into this prohibited zone. Names become forbidden when their bearer dies since the dead are perceived as instances of the Thing, of the impossible/real Thing, which must remain separated from the living, from those who dwell in the symbolic. The function of the process of mourning is precisely to resymbolize the deceased, to reintegrate him or her into our symbolic universe, which is behind the belief that the dead haunt us during mourning, until the settling of the symbolic accounts of the dead is accomplished.[10]

Through the process of mourning, a proper name thus undergoes a deep transformation: at birth and during a person's lifetime, it grants him or her Symbolic status, a place in the community, but with his or her death this order is perturbed. It is as if the dead body touches us much more directly than a living person to whom we can relate through the safety net of symbolization. The function of mourning is to lay the deceased to rest, to acquire a proper (symbolic) distance from him or her, so that he or she will no longer touch us directly as a non-symbolized Real. The paradox is thus that the true function of mourning is not to keep the deceased close to us but, on the contrary, to locate them at a safe distance, so that our lives can go on unperturbed by the deceased. From the domain of the Real the name of the deceased threatens to literally touch and destroy the Symbolic, so the aim of mourning is to get out of touch with the deceased.

As we have seen, according to early Lacan's teaching there is a tendency in human society to keep the Real as far away as possible from the Symbolic. With *Seminar XI: Four Fundamental Concepts of Psychoanalysis* (cf. Lacan 1998) his perception of the relationship between the Symbolic and the Real radically shifts according to the following logic: if *jouissance* is something excluded from the field of the symbolic, it means that it forms a void of enjoyment in the the symbolic—but as a void it is also inscribed in that field. It cannot be simply outside it, attainable through a radical act of transgression as Antigone was. Consequently, Lacan replaces the concept of the Thing, the impossible/real core of enjoyment, with a much more modest agency *objet petit a* or "object small a." So Lacan's endeavor in Seminar XI is to conceptualize such an object, itself an obstacle that disturbs the functioning of the Symbolic Order. He finds the reason for this inherent *impasse* in the drive.

More precisely, according to Lacan, the chain of signifiers colonizes the body, but not completely—it leaves some remains since the signifying process does not have a smooth outcome. It leaves some bodily zones unoccupied by the signifier. These leftovers of the symbolization which generate *jouissance* (through those parts that function as openings of the body: mouth, anus, vagina etc.) are the domain of drives. In other words—drive belongs to a part of the body that has not fallen under the rule of the signifier. It is the result of a signifying operation but, as a partial drive, it is attached to bodily parts that cannot be integrated into the field of meaning or the intersubjective relationship. What disturbs the symbolic structure is the existence of these erogenous zones occupied by drive and enjoyment. Drive therefore introduces a totally different logic to the signifier: it is a permanent force, and it knows "no day or night, no spring, no autumn no rise and fall" (ibid.: 165). So, not only does it not follow the logic of the signifier, it does not even function according to biological needs.[11]

So how can we conceive of a touch in this new context? Freud's findings in *Totem and Taboo* provide us with a possible elaboration. He claims that in very early childhood the subject shows a strong desire to touch, and this inclination is soon met with the prohibition of a particular kind of touching. Here Freud inserts an interesting footnote: "Both the desire and prohibition relate to the child's touching his own genitals" (Freud 1985: 82, cf. Dolar 2008). While Dolar only hints that "particular kind of touch" is related to a child's sexuality (Dolar 2008: 92), the interesting part of his observation is that it—again—connects touching and prohibition: touching sexualizes a certain part of the body, but what constitutes a (sexual) drive is exactly its prohibition. Drive (connected to touching) is not abolished by prohibition, prohibition merely represses it, banishes it to the unconscious where it persists forever: "Both the prohibition and the drive persist: the drive because it has only been repressed and abolished, and the prohibition because, if it ceased, the drive would force its way through into consciousness and into actual operation" (Freud 1985: 83).

The symbolic prohibition that comes from the Other (parents) and the drive revolves around touching which thus creates a knot of human experience out of the collision of two heterogeneous domains, signifiers and drive. As Mladen Dolar points out in his text *Touching Ground*, the problem lies in the fact that prohibition can never work if it is simply imposed from the outside (from the parental authority), but rather "the prohibition itself has to take the form of touching, it cannot be sustained by mere word, it has to be a word sustained by touch, the word touching flesh, imposed by parental touch, this first language imposed on the infant, the mother's touch being his first mother tongue" (Dolar 2008: 93).[12]

What complicates matters even further is that touch is primarily introduced by the Other. When, in his *Three Essays*, Freud analyzes the nurture of children, he comes to a paradoxical conclusion: it is as traumatic for children to get too much parental care (including the touching of the genitals while washing the child) as to get too little of it. (cf. Freud 2001). One might say that, when one is raising a child, there is always either too much touching or too little touching, and this, along with parental prohibitions, is exactly what forms an enigma for a child. This enigma can be formulated as: "What does the Other want (from me)?"[13] The child tries to understand the Other's actions, but he cannot grasp the enigma before he or she is fully integrated in the symbolic. However, when a meaning or an explanation of the Other's enigmatic behavior is supposed to be provided, it is always too late. In other words, the enigma is deeply entangled in the formation of a child, in his/her entering a language, the signifying chain is always already marked by this enigmatic core and can therefore never provide an adequate understanding of it, it remains forever stained by this initial knot that binds drive and the signifier. The primordial (prohibited) touch stands at the crossroads of two different realms: the realm of the symbolic—that is forever marked by the exclusion of touch (drive)—and the real (drive, primal touch)— that cannot be integrated into the field of meaning and understanding.

The prohibition of a touch does not make touching impossible, it just excludes any direct or unmediated touch: once the prohibition (of touching) is introduced, a subject will always touch with all the symbolic baggage that makes him a subject. Touching thus becomes a knot connecting and separating the Symbolic and the Real (drive). It is the limit, the gap itself that separates the two. One could also say that Lacanian theory of touch abolishes a preconception of a touch as belonging to a mere sensual experience: for Lacan, the materiality of touching is already the materiality of the symbolic or the signifier.[14]

He fully draws this consequence in his late *Book XX: Encore* where Lacan (cf. Lacan 1998) yet again revises his understanding of the Symbolic and the Real. One of the famous slogans of this seminar is: "Where it speaks, it enjoys and it knows nothing" (Lacan 1998: 104).

This somewhat mysterious line is connected to another radical shift of his notion of how language and enjoyment (belonging to the real) are related: he conceives language itself as an apparatus of enjoyment: "I will say that the signifier is situated at the level of enjoying substance (*substance jouissante*)" (ibid., 24). While in Seminar XI the Symbolic and the Real are interwoven so that drive's enjoyment causes the gaps in the signifying order, in *Encore* the heterogeneous registers of the Symbolic and the Real are brought together, united in one and the same apparatus: the symbolic is no longer just a structure that enables meaning, it is also a vehicle for enjoyment.

There is an enjoyment of babbling and Lacan's term for this aspect of language is *lalangue*: meaningless exercises of speech, slips of tongue, enabled by homophony and similarity of sounds, etc. (ibid.: 139). The structure of the signifying chain is organized by the differentiality of signifier, but there is a dimension of language that cannot be submitted to these signifying laws since it is organized around coincidences and of sonic likenesses.[15] An example of this playfulness of language is the very term employed by Lacan, *lalangue* itself, which combines the determiner "the" (French "la") with the French word language ("langue")—the standard English translation is *a language*.[16] While this new word includes the term language, it also mobilizes other dimensions: Lacan points out that poetry and especially modern literature are based on this ability of language.[17]

The signifying chain produces meaning, but with it also produces something more, a surplus enjoyment which cannot be reduced to the level of sense. The enjoyment of the signifier does not serve the production of meaning—it serves nothing, according to a known Lacanian definition of it. The unconscious formations are signs of its enjoyment, so we are a long way from Lacan's early stages when these same formations were the proof of unconscious following certain linguistic laws. In *Encore* language and speech are no longer only functions of recognition of the Other, they do not enable intersubjective relationship—rather they function as an apparatus of enjoyment.

So it could be also said that enjoyment, placed in the signifying chain, becomes the new realm of touching. As we have already seen, touch is a paradoxical entity, a kind of gap that combines and separates the two heterogeneous fields of the Symbolic and the Real, which basically means that one always touches through one's symbolic frame, a frame that is itself distorted by the circular movement of drives. When these fields share the same structure, that of *lalangue*, touch is taking place at the level of the signifier itself, or, better yet, at the level of *lalangue* where we can observe how words (or parts of them) are colonizing other words or echoing in other words.

In short, inside the dimension of *lalangue*, touch no longer concerns the relationship between words and bodies since words are directly touching each other. In this case, touch is located in the tiny gap that separates signifier from its enjoyment: drive can at any time take over the signifying function for its enjoyment and touch is the almost imperceptible and elusive line of separation between the two. As we had seen, Plato acknowledged this dimension of the language, but did not provide a conceptualization for it—for him the real remains separated from words, while Lacan introduces the concept of real, which is already inscribed in the realm of names, meaning that our lives, our status as a subject can be much more affected by the real of words than the real of bodies.

Proper name

We have seen that proper names—at least the prohibited ones—can produce real effects, that they do touch the subject and have wider social impacts. We can elaborate this thesis further if we try to approach the proper name from another angle—if we examine what curious kind of signifier it is.

It seems that a proper name is a signifier that refers to a singular entity (subject) whose specificity consists of a unique combination of properties and features.[18] This, at least, is the claim of the descriptivist theory developed by Gottlob Frege and Bertrand Russell (cf. Russell 1905): a name has a meaning, a semantic value of some definite description. The semantic value of "Aristotle" is "Plato's student," "the teacher of Alexander the Great," "the author of *Poetics*," "the founder of the peripatetic school of philosophy," etc. Descriptivists take the meaning of a name to be such a collection of descriptions, and the referent of the name is the word which satisfies these descriptions.

In *Naming and Necessity*, Saul Kripke (cf. Kripke 1980) rejects this theory and claims that proper names are "rigid designators." A rigid designator is a signifier which refers to the same thing in *all possible worlds* in which that thing exists. This, in short, means that names are not equal to the description of what they denote; they do not refer to a cluster of features. The cluster of descriptions denoted by a name may be true, but that is not necessary. "Aristotle," for example, was in fact "the teacher of Alexander" and many more things, but this is not a necessary truth. There is no necessary link between the fact that Aristotle existed and any descriptions of him. It is not necessary that Aristotle studied with Plato or that he should have become Alexander's teacher—it was possible for him to do another set of things altogether and not the ones he is known for.[19]

So while descriptivism considers proper names abbreviated descriptions, Kripke tries to establish the identity of a certain object beyond or despite all of its contingent properties. This puts Kripke in the vicinity of Plato's search for the true name, which would designate the eternal and necessary essence of a thing or a person. But what Kripke effectively discovers is a tautological dimension of language itself. A rigid designator aims at exactly this: the only ground of a reference that is constant and consistent in all possible worlds is the name itself—bearers of a name are named that way because we name them that way. But does this mean that there is nothing in the bearer that can justify her name? Are proper names just arbitrary? Kripke's implicit Platonism is justified, but with a (performative) twist: a name points to a certain "essence," to a certain surplus in its bearer that cannot be reduced to the name or to the signifier, but it also cannot be reduced to some properties or features of the bearer.

The effect of naming is that it points at something in its bearer that is more than the bearer herself, it points at a certain X that cannot be grasped by the signifier, to use Lacanian terminology. How can one understand this mysterious X? What is the status of naming? Lacanian theory seems to appropriately complement Kripke's notion of a rigid designator: the appearance of essence or identity beyond proper names is an illusion of the signifying process. It provides an illusion of the fullness, of completeness of a certain designator, which in fact covers a void in the bearer. Lacan's name for this X is *objet petit a*, the object cause of desire, and the paradox of it is that, while it seems to hint at a mysterious "essence" deeper than all the bearer's properties and features, it does not preexist the act of naming, but it is rather its effect. Naming cuts a void, a hole in its bearer.

Psychoanalytic conception of proper names can be seen as belonging to a field where descriptivist and anti-descriptivist theories intersect. Whenever we speak of a person, we can denote her by a set of descriptions and features: but no matter how thorough we might be, no amount of signifiers seems to grasp the essence of her. The link with desire is obvious here: when I love a woman or man, the cause of my love cannot be reduced to his/her positive properties that can be described, it is a mysterious "I don't know what" that eludes all description.[20]

Lacan argues similarly in one of his unpublished and unedited seminars, *Crucial Problems of Psychoanalysis* (cf. Lacan 2011). The properties of a proper name (and its bearer) belong to the field of signifier: we can describe a person with an endless series of signifiers—however, it seems that the "essence" of the bearer of the proper name is displaced in this chain and cannot fully exhaust the referent it is signifying. A "displacement" or a "jump," as Lacan calls it, is thus connected to proper names; we may find an endless chain of descriptions that denote a person, but something—the essence—will always elude the signifying chain (ibid: 57).

A proper name seems to denote a singularity, it is irreplaceable, argues Lacan. However, its irreplaceability means that it denotes a lack: a proper name covers this lack: "It is designed to fill the holes, to be a shutter, to close it down, to give it a false appearance of suture" (ibid.: 59). A name at first hand seems to grasp the depth of its bearer, it seems to capture its most inner essence, the elusive and mysterious X, but the effect of completeness only covers a void, quilts the impossibility of ever adequately filling it.

Until now we have followed the imaginary and symbolic dimension of a proper name, and we have seen how, at those levels, we touch the dimension of the real: the void linked to the name's bearer belongs to the real, it is a void that disturbs the field of symbolic meaning.

In this sense, a proper name is a signifier, but at the same time it forms a link to the real, to *objet petit a*. It is a paradoxical structure since it enables its bearer to function in the symbolic, to participate in the society, but at the same time it connects the bearer to the dimension of real.

For a better understanding of the name as belonging to the domain of the real and its connection to touch one must turn to another example, originating in the field of art. In 2007 three Slovene artists—Emil Hrvatin, Davide Grassi and Žiga Kariž—changed their names to Janez Janša.[21] Through the years their name started to produce unexpected effects that the artists had no control over.

The new name was relatively unknown and created confusion in their private lives and in relationship to their previous work, done under a different name. Since the three artists worked in a relatively small Slovene scene, their new individual projects also became indiscernible. In regard to their artistic career, a name-change was a symbolic suicide, while confusing real authorship, market prices, copyright issues etc.[22]

As far as the projects the three artists created together go, they in a somewhat "duchampian" gesture exposed their name as an art object, which also opened up a variety of questions and consequences.[23]

Putting a name (its several aspects) on display again surrendered their subjectivities to the realm of a name and its effects. It is the name that gets the spotlight of the show, while the artists could be prosecuted for the neglect of their legal documents. Artists themselves as artists become a curious version of *homo sacer*, excrements of their own name. Self-inflicted obliteration resulted in exposing the artistic subject as a mere leftover of his name.

All the Janša's activities bring us again to the ontological dimension of a name, which has haunted philosophy for centuries. Once turned into a piece of art, a name begins to produce various effects on a subject and on the Symbolic Order. The effect of completeness of its bearers is in this case lost. Or, better yet, the three artists, sharing the same name, get lost in the (same) name. The name starts to destabilize the symbolic universe, the universe of meaning, understanding and interpretation—it becomes the real it was supposed to name. The name is the real bearer constantly disrupting subjectivity of its authors, but also artistic and political discourses. A name itself becomes a bearer, waiting to be accepted into the symbolic field. This sheds another light on Plato's elaboration of names and their bearers: in the case of Janšas, the name Janez Janša becomes the real bearer that constantly disrupts the Symbolic Order and yet awaits its acceptance in it.

Therein resides the final (and rather sad) lesson of the Janšas' experiment: touching (in the sense of bodily contact) does not really matter, our lives can be much more traumatically affected by the real of words which cannot be integrated into our meaningful Symbolic Order. What ultimately resists symbolization are not bodies but words themselves, the first being our proper names.

Conclusion

Plato is the first philosopher who found names and naming problematic, since they bring us closer to things, they name, but at the same time prevent us from really grasping them. The main contribution of Jacques Lacan's analysis is that he conceptualized the inherent barrier, the impasse, always pertaining to names and naming. More precisely, he found the Real, which signifiers were presumably unable to properly grasp, does not lie as an unreachable instance somewhere outside the language, but that the Real—as an obstacle or as unsymbolized *jouissance*—is entangled with the symbolic. Moreover, the signifiers themselves can function as the body of the Real (the Drive).

The concept of touch, conceived in such a psychoanalytic framework, is exactly the limit through which heterogeneous domains of the Symbolic and the Real intersect. In Lacan's late work his thesis even radicalizes as the signifier itself and is established as the structure where words touch each other and can form a body of enjoyment.

That means that our commonly accepted notion of the touch must be revised. We always touch already embedded in linguistic structure as entangled with the Real (obstacle, i.e. *jouissance*). Moreover, we can be touched by words in a very literal sense: words use us (as subjects) to touch each other and consequently also to touch us.

This is perhaps most true for proper names, special signifiers, pertaining to persons; the forbidden names of the deceased haunt the descendants with the power of a dangerous touch. The name of the loved one—on the other hand—may be close to his or her most inner being, so we pronounce it very carefully or rather do not even utter it. On some rare (artistic) occasions a name can take over someone's life and dictate the terms of their living. Thus names and proper names are not failed attempts to grasp the real, as Plato argued, they can hurt or affect us as much as a great many fists.

Notes

1 For a more detailed reading of *Cratylus* cf. Dolar (2014).
2 Through etymology he finds that the word Hector is connected to the words master and ruler (393a–394a), while the word Agamemnon is linked to Greek words "worthy of admiration because of his persistence" (395a).
3 The same goes for parts of names and their meaning and even for syllables and letters, which themselves must be justified in the same way. However, in the end we can only legitimize them by introducing another semantic entity. In a very interesting passage for example he thoroughly analyzes the letter "r" (*rho*). One must emphasize that Plato conceives of word-building along the lines of his conception of geometry. As atoms build material forms, so do letters and sounds (*stoicheia*) build words (*logoi*). A dimension of tactility is crucial in word-building, since the connection of sounds, (their) touching, builds the words in the same way the touching of atoms builds forms.
4 Reading Plato's passages one cannot but think of his dialogues *Republic* and *Sophist* where the pictures and sophist's speech make it impossible to distinguish between the original (idea) and the false imitation (mimesis) or between philosophical discourse and sophist's seductive speech. So replicas, mimesis, and sophistry create a

confusion, an ontological mess. Throughout his work his problem is that he cannot successfully divide these worlds: pictures from their models and sophistry from philosophy. The problem of sophistry was well elaborated, for example, by Barbara Cassin (1995).

5   This fantasy haunted philosophers for centuries and can be articulated with Thomas Acquinas' famous formula for accurate knowledge *Adaequatio rei et intellectus*.

6   The full extent of this thought will be developed further on, where I will corroborate this thought through a psychoanalytical approach. Here let me point to a text "A Touchy Subject" by Mirt Komel, where he provides a similar reading of *Cratylus*: "At the end of *Cratylus* Plato somehow repeats the point from *Phaedo* in stating that ultimately there 'must be possible to learn about the things that are independently of names.' (439b–c) Translating this Platonic problem into touch we have three possible outcomes: words touch things through meaning (Cratylus); words touch each other through sensory sound (Hermogenes); the meaning of things is touched upon without words or sense, i.e. metaphysically (Phaedo)" (Komel 2016: 122).

7   I am using capital letters for the Symbolic and the Real here because of the way Lacan conceptualizes the two dimensions in his *Ethics*. They are considered as "absolute" categories, which are absolutely divided, while in his other works the conception of the two dimensions is revised, as I will elaborate later on.

8   Here we can discern Lacan's own understanding of art. In opposition to Plato, Lacan suggests that art is not only a reflection, a more or less accurate mimesis, but that the beautiful, the imaginary dimension of art is intrinsically linked to the real. For further elaboration on structure of touch see Moder in this volume (Chapter 4).

9   For a beautifully elaborated take on the problem of mourning as a distinctively modern phenomena, see Comay 2010.

10 This is exactly the problem of Antigone (who is not allowed to perform the proper rituals with her brother's corpse) as well as of Hamlet (haunted by his father's ghost because he was not laid to rest properly).

11 For a thorough articulation of the relation between drive and signifier see Zupančič 2017.

12 For a detailed elaboration of the relationship between the mother's touch and language see Rachel Aumiller's contribution in this book (Chapter 7).

13 For a further elaboration of the concept of enigmatic Other, cf. Laplanche 1999.

14 For a further elaboration of the concept of materiality through touch and language see Bara Kolenc's contribution in this book (Chapter 6).

15 For a further analysis of the relation between Lacanian *lalangue* and linguistic phonetics see the contribution by Tomi Bartole in this book (Chapter 2).

16 The phrase and the musical title *La La Land* (2016) also uses this characteristic of language: echoing the first two "la-s" also in the "land."

17 It is probably no wonder that Lacan in this seminar takes into account James Joyce's *Ulysses*, and especially his *Finnegans Wake* (ibid.: 37).

18 According to Webster's dictionary, proper name is a word or group of words (such as "Noah Webster," "Kentucky," or "U.S. Congress") that is the name of a particular person, place, or thing, and that usually begins with a capital letter. In this text I will concentrate on proper names pertaining to persons, since there is a certain dialectics involved in bearing a name: a person has a special relationship to his or her name, and he or she can bear consequences of a family name, which does not apply to places and things.

19 Moreover, this also goes for at least some generic notions. Kripke's example is gold: a certain object was at a certain time in history named gold, and, at that time, certain features were attributed to this object; however, with increasing knowledge, this cluster of descriptions of gold changed and is now classified by a number of scientific tools. Kripke even supposes that a further scientific development could amount to an insight that all the properties attributed to gold were wrong, but the word "gold" would continue to denote the object that was called gold. And if an object was found containing all the features that were so far attributed to gold, this object would not be called "gold" (Kripke 1980: 116–119).

20 In the TV series *Sex and the City*, the main character's ill-fated partner is throughout the six seasons referred to as Mr. Big—we (the viewers) do not find out his name until the very last part. Why is he not named like every other man in the series? The obvious answer is that with the exclusion of his name the heroine Carrie can keep her fatal love in the realm of a fantasy. By not allowing anyone to pronounce his (real) name, she is sustaining the mysterious X that is the object-cause of her desire, as if the abolishment of his name keeps her in direct touch with his most inner treasure, his *je ne sais quoi*. As "natives" ascribe power to the names of the deceased, people in love seem to do the same with the names of their loved ones—the difference being that in case of love a name serves as an imaginary screen, covering the dangerous the Thing in the loved one.

21 At first their gesture was perceived as a provocation, since the Slovene prime minister at the time was a rightist nationalist leader called Janez Janša. For further examination of their work see my own contribution on this topic, Krečič 2017.

22 One might add that the name change also attributed to some real-life inconvenience. When they were traveling together, airlines' systems only registered one Janez Janša, since it recognized the other Janšas as one and the same person.

23 For example, in the exhibition *Name-Readymade* in Graz in 2008 they exhibited their legal documents—documents that were still legally binding. In several street-actions they inscribed their new name in the landscape or streets (with stones or umbrellas etc.). At another exhibition, *Signature*, they exhibited paintings of their signatures.

References

Comay, R. (2010), *Mourning Sickness*, Stanford: Stanford UP.

Dolar, M. (2008), "Touching Ground," *Filozofski vestnik* 29/2: 79–100.

Dolar, M. (2014), *What Is in A Name?*, Ljubljana: Aksioma–Institute for Contemporary Art.

Freud, S. (1985), *Totem and Taboo*, in *Freud Library, vol. 13: Origins of Religion*, Harmondsworth: Penguin.

Freud, S. (2001), *Complete Psychological Works Of Sigmund Freud, Vol 7*: "Three Essays on Sexuality," London: Random House.

Komel, M. (2016), "A Touchy Subject: the Tactile Metaphor of Touch," *Družboslovne razprave* 32/82: 115–125.

Kripke, S. (1980), *Naming and Necessity*, Cambridge: Harvard UP.

Lacan, J. (1998), *Four Fundamental Concepts of Psychoanalysis: The Seminar of Jacques Lacan, Book XI,* New York: W. W. Norton.

Lacan, J. (1992), *Ethics of Psychoanalysis*, London: Routledge.

Lacan, J. (1998), *Book XX: Encore 1972–1973*, New York, London: W.W. Norton.

Lacan, J. (2006), *Ecrits*, London: W.W. Norton.

Lacan, J. (2011), *The Seminar of Jacques Lacan: Crucial Problems of Psychoanalysis 1964–1965* (trans. Cormac Gallagher from unedited French manuscripts). Available online: http://esource.dbs.ie/bitstream/handle/10788/161/Book-12-Crucial-problems-for-psychoanalysis.pdf?sequence=1 (accessed May 26, 2017).

Laplance, J. (1999), *Essays on Otherness*, London: Routledge.

Plato (1997), *Complete Works*, Indianapolis & Cambridge: Hackett.

Russell, B. (1905), "On the Denoting," *Mind* 14: 479–493.

Zupančič, A. (2017) *What is Sex?*, Cambridge: MIT.

10

Ethics of Touch: *Doctor Who*'s Untouchable Touch

Eva Vrtačič

Introduction

"For every action, there is an equal and opposite reaction," says Newton's third law, meaning that every interaction is characterized by a pair of forces acting on the two interacting objects. Touch, both in terms of physics and philosophy, is then by definition dual, even dialogical: one touches and is (with equal force) touched back at the same time. Merleau-Ponty gives a beautiful example of another peculiarity of touch, namely, its asymmetric reciprocity: touching the tip of a finger with another finger, it is impossible to direct attention to both of them, consciousness resides in only one of them, making it the touching one, and the other one the touched. As self-evident and unworthy of further reflection as these claims might sound, let us consider this question: what will, both in terms of physics and philosophy, change, if/when emerging digital technologies that traditionally mediated the gaze, start convincingly mediating touch?

We are not academically equipped to contemplate the physics part of the puzzle, but rather, very curious to ponder on the philosophical part. While doing so, we will utilize Haraway's method *cat's cradle* (1994, 1997), named after a game in which players create increasingly complex patterns by manipulating an elastic band. By adopting an open-ended methodological principle that presupposes epistemological equality of every source, we will be able to place our thought in the intersections of theory, fiction, technology, fictional science, and science fiction. This choice is founded in our background in anthropology, which perceives all these sources as much as products of culture as they are its creators.

Touching nothing: having the last touch

Until now, the topic of touching without being touched back has only been explored in science fiction with super powers like telekinesis.[1] However, in the emerging market of digital sex suits, we can already see prototypes that are built on this premise. They are designed for the neurotic, germ-phobic, narcissistic individual, who is afraid of being touched back. Individuals, who can be physically located in different parts of the world and connected through the internet, engage in sexual contact by interacting with controllers that adjust the other person's gadgets, settings, and features. Technologically mediated sex plays on the fantasy of touching without being touched back, on the desire to control the other's pleasure and experience, while maintaining control over one's own body at the same time.

However, as the prototypes of these sex suits demonstrate, such one-way touching is, literally, empty. What technology can do is stimulate the receiver's body according to (remote) user input. The user who controls them wears a special glove with sensors that read the force with which one, for example, squeezes their fingers, and the same force is then applied to the receiver's body suit. For the receiver, the experience can be quite compelling. On the other side, however, we are left with nothing, or rather, with an empty touch, as technology cannot yet simulate the resistance to touching that is normally provided by the other object. The user who controls the digital glove does not feel like they are touching anything but thin air.[2] The emptiness of such experience goes to prove that it is not our touch, but rather, the other's reaction to it, the reverse touch, that enables us to really experience otherness. With emancipation of touch from its mirror image, the other ceases to exist and the only otherness one can still encounter is—their own. The other thus exists merely as a mirror, providing us with the illusion of being identical with ourselves; but when removed from the equation altogether, it becomes clear there is no other but myself.

Touching without allowing oneself to be touched back appears to free touch from the logic and structure of dialog, converting it into monological form. This seems appropriate in the contemporary context where everybody is determined to have the proverbial last word. The last touch, just as the last word, allows one to frame their attempt at touching (upon) something as sensible, as pertaining to reality. In fact, "reality is understood as being-in-touch-with-something-real" (Elo 2016: 272). As the other does not talk back and/or touch back, it therefore does not exist, it is not alive. If the other is dead and does not exist, then I, who am defined by differentiating myself from the other, live and exist. The postmodern subject thus finds it easier to contemplate the idea of being alone in the world, than the fact of being unimportant among millions of others. When we are faced with the otherness of the other—when they do talk back, touch back, etc.—we are in fact face-to-face[3] with the utter unimportance and complete otherness of ourselves: dialogical nature of conversation and touching serves one merely with mirror images of oneself. In dialog, one throws words at the other, receiving back words that are thrown at them. One does not talk to the other, rather, they both talk at the other. The other only appears to talk back; from their perspective, the situation is the same as our own: they talk at the other.

This is even more apparent in dialogical touching where the dimension of time is omitted. Everything happens in a single moment: there is no lag and no need to wait for the response. The mirror image of one's touch spawns at exactly the moment of touching the other. When two people touch, they both simultaneously touch the other and are touched by the other themselves. Nevertheless, even if "touching is contact with the touched, there remains something inaccessible and withdrawing, something even untouchable inherent to the touched. This withdrawal lends to the contact an affective tension: the touched becomes the touching. In other words, touching is over-determined by otherness as strangeness, and it turns out to manifest traits of a 'foreign-sense', with respective ethical significance" (Elo 2016: 274).

Such mirror images of language and touch reveal that the other can merely familiarize one with their own selves rather than with the (imaginary) other. The other exists merely through and for this very touch, dissipating back into ultimate alienation and otherness immediately as the bonds of communication are severed. Attempts at remotely touching the other reveal this beautifully: digital haptic technology does not have a problem with developing smart suits that can simulate the feeling of being touched. Instead, science has yet to find a way to provide for the feeling of being touched back. Experiencing this position of always having the last touch, of reaching out to the other without the other automatically returning whatever is thrown at them with exactly the same force, however, leaves one in a position of autistic isolation.[4] Or does it?

The touch of the Doctor

In the BBC sci-fi series *Doctor Who*, the alien protagonist owns a special "sonic screwdriver" that works by manipulating the air with different frequencies, transmitting the Doctor's touch to any object the screwdriver is pointing to. The sonic screwdriver is both a remote controller and an interface; it is the medium that enables the Doctor to touch things without being touched back. If one can clearly feel the force of a screw when using a normal screwdriver to loosen it, the sonic screwdriver does not follow the same (Newton's) law as it mediates touch only one-way: not unlike superheroes with telekinetic powers, the Doctor can loosen the screw without the phenomenological experience of unscrewing.

The Doctor is a positive character, by whom many, especially his fellow human companions, are touched. However, as he goes around saving the world time and time again, he maintains his alien position by not allowing himself to be touched back. Although he carefully cultivates and preserves his position of otherness, he is loved and respected by humans. In this aspect, the series makes a compelling argument for the reciprocity of touch not being a necessity when encountering and dealing with otherness. Perhaps, and this extends well beyond science fiction into our everyday experience with otherness, the productive strategy in approaching otherness is neither proclaiming it dead, barbaric, or violent (so that we can position ourselves as alive, civilized, or peaceful) nor attempting to domesticate it (so that is becomes us), but rather, facing and celebrating the fact that it cannot or should ever be domesticated.

Let us now explore the idea of otherness put forward by writers of the series *Doctor Who*,[5] in which the Doctor is a human-looking alien, protecting the earth and traveling through time and space with his human companions. The Doctor is unarmed, carrying only a high-tech tool that can manipulate objects remotely: a sonic screwdriver. With its help, the Doctor is capable of touching and manipulating objects without being touched back by them, which is what keeps him (an) alien and enables him to maintain the position of otherness. Despite the fact that he is not prepared to give up his otherness, he is still able to show compassion to humankind and he repeatedly risks his own life to save humanity. This goes to prove that otherness does not require domestication in order for it to coexist alongside "normal life"—it merely requires acknowledgment of existence and acceptance.[6] The Doctor does not allow himself to be touched (back) in the physical sense, and only rarely finds individual human beings worthy. Rather, he is touched by humanity—in different senses of the word's meaning—and seen as a *little touched* by it as well.

The Doctor appreciates human beings collectively; living for as long as he has lived,[7] he has seen it all—there is no singular story of life, love, sacrifice, or courage that could really move him; instead, it is their "eternal return" (Nietzsche 2006) that fascinates him.[8] To the ever-repeating, endless human drama, he responds by employing humanity in the second sense of the word—being humane, benevolent. He can forgive individual crimes, bad decisions and acts of unreason—as they might mean the end of the world for the ones involved[9] (Derrida: 2001), for the Doctor they are but a piece in the mosaic of life. As he keeps saving the world with the use of a sonic screwdriver and words (actually, to be honest, mainly words[10]), he allows himself to be touched by humanity in the context that invokes his one and only unchangeable feature—his name. We never do learn his actual name; it is said that it is unpronounceable by humans, and it should not be spoken anyway,[11] but humans have come to know him as The Doctor.

Touch as differentiation from others and formation of the self

One of the main modalities of touch, according to Cranny-Francis (2003: 26), is what she calls differentiation.[12] According to her, "touch identifies the difference between self and other, even as it establishes some kind of connectivity between the two." Touch is employed when we want to learn about others, categorize them within a cultural matrix of meaning and understand them. As we touch other people or objects, however, we do more than learn about them: "we create ourselves, as that which is not the other but yet in constant relationship with others and the world" (ibid.). Here, the author refers to Nancy's idea of "being singular plural",[13] claiming that the self is not isolated, but rather, "negotiated through relationships with others and the world" (ibid.). As we differentiate ourselves from others by touching them, this inevitably also "signifies the formation of the self" (ibid.).

When interacting with the world by the use of his sonic screwdriver, Doctor Who refuses to be differentiated from the objects he interacts with, thus refusing any "formation of the self" (ibid.). That is indeed characteristic of a man who goes merely by his calling and whose name cannot be spoken. Perhaps it could be argued that his fondness for swapping touch with sonic manipulation originates in his disconnection from his own physicality[14]—the Doctor is not just an alien, but a Time Lord, a creature capable of physical regeneration; a manifestation of eternal return of his own.[15] Throughout his life he has had different faces, voices, and skins, sexual identities, and, consequently, different personalities, quirks, and tastes. For example, in his recent incarnations portrayed by David Tennant (tenth) and Matt Smith (eleventh) the Doctor did allow himself to be physically touched, especially by his—by the people who touched him on another level. However, with the twelfth Doctor, portrayed by Peter Capaldi, we were yet again faced with the fact that the Doctor is not human. Capaldi himself describes his character as "more alien than he's [the Doctor] been in a while" (web5). We were confronted with the Doctor's cold and distanced demeanor immediately as he entered the series in his twelfth regeneration, and it was in the very first episode, titled "Deep Breath" (2014), that his distrust of touch was already apparent.

Towards the end of the episode, Clara, struggling to recognize the Doctor in his new body and character, receives a phone call from the eleventh Doctor, who reassures her it is indeed still him, and begs her to help him. The twelfth Doctor emerges from the Tardis, realizes who [sic!] is calling her, and, after she hangs up, reminds her he is not in the telephone, but rather, here. He begs her: "Please, just see me!" Clara walks over, takes a good look at him, smiles, and thanks him for the phone call. Then she embraces him, but he tries to shake off the hug, responding nervously and in apparent discomfort: "I don't think that I'm a hugging person now." In the next episode, "Listen" (2014), he exclaims that he is "against hugging!" and as he finally gives in, in the last episode of the season, "Death in Heaven" (2014), returning Clara's hug, it does not come without a warning: "Never trust a hug. It's just a way to hide your face."

The Doctor's refusal to be touched could be interpreted as a way of being able to stay an alien, of maintaining the position of otherness, not only in relation to the world around him, but also to himself. For him, to allow himself to be touched back would mean to be constituted, in terms that the show uses, "as a fixed point in time," something that is, albeit fleeting, still stable, identifiable, filled with meaning, and referring to both his own past and future. However, being a Time Lord, capable of travel through time and space, back and forth, reinventing both history and the future, creating fixed points in time is something one might want to avoid. His whole existence is open for constant manipulation; his decisions are never final, consequences never inevitable. It appears as if any kind of identity, including the ones ascribed to him by others, are nothing but a burden, a set of expectations to live by,[16] something that might cloud his judgment in the only moment that actually counts, the only one that touches upon the Real, the one that is not yet and at the same time not anymore available for interpretation, theorization, and articulation. The moment that is beyond the rules of the Symbolic Order,[17] the one that language can only meditate in terms of what might be and what might have been, but can never catch it when it actually is—the moment called now.

At some point,[18] the Doctor even goes as far as attempting to remove himself from the collective memory of the universe. For a person who has lived as long and has helped so many, an attempt at anonymous life means disconnecting oneself from their deeds. And as he indeed temporarily manages to delete himself from history, removing the doer from the deeds, the universe forgets he ever existed; for we are not constructed by what we see, think, say, or even touch, but rather, by the acknowledgment of others that they have indeed been touched by us; by our thoughts, words, or our touches. If Doctor Who can guard himself from the touches of (lesser) minds that he befriends for brief periods of time with humor, cynicism, and just plain linguistic dominance, it is physical interaction with the world and people around him that he finds himself bewildered by. And he seems equally distrustful of his own body (that is especially apparent after regenerations) and of others' bodies.

By refusing to differentiate himself from the world around him, he also refuses to be positioned as a self-reflexive embodied subject. Instead, he always remains on the threshold—he is between the past and the future, locked in a permanent now that lacks borders between yesterday and tomorrow, fusing them together in a non-linear open-ended narrative. Nevertheless, let us not forget that, with the help of a machine called the Time And Relative Dimensions In Space, TARDIS, he does not only travel through time, but also through space. Thus, not only he is not constrained by temporal borders, physical ones do not interpellate him either. And it is precisely the problem of the border[19] that marks the contemporary human relationship with technology.

Not unlike Doctor Who and his sonic screwdriver, we use technology as a mediator between others and ourselves. However, as our gadgets become ever smaller and smarter, users' perception of the interface fades, dissipating the border between oneself and technology. The interaction with technology is thus more and more "naturalized," robbing the contemporary subjects of their own positioning in the world. Instead, they are consumed by the discourses that create the technology in the first place (ibid.). Doctor Who until recently kept his sonic screwdriver in line with seamful UX design: "in opposition to the prevailing aesthetic and practice of seamlessness" (ibid.) seamfulness can be seen "as empowering to users" (ibid.), enabling them to "adapt devices to local conditions". (ibid.). As Doctor Who regenerates, so does his faithful companion, the sonic screwdriver, getting ever more advanced and flashy.

However, it was with the twelfth Doctor that the screwdriver's look was markedly changed: instead of a pointed device that resembles an actual screwdriver, the Doctor now displays a preference for wearable technology, opting for sunglasses[20] instead. Some might ascribe this fact merely to the twelfth Doctor's fondness for rock 'n' roll and interpret it as a fashion choice to match his electric guitar, whereas others might go into Freudian interpretations of why a lens replaced a phallic object. Either way, the fact remains that the interface of the screwdriver changed dramatically for the first time in Doctor Who's history. The sonic device has been removed from his jacket's inner pocket and put on his face, covering his eyes, and creating an additional filter—now not only does he manipulate the world in a technologically mediated manner, but he also experiences it through a technological lens.

The border between the Doctor and technology is becoming increasingly blurred. At the same time, the maintaining of the border between himself and the world enables him to stay an alien; not by differentiating him from others, but rather, by not differentiating him, by making him unidentifiable, open-ended, fluid, and thus enabling him to renounce any kind of self-identity—and fit in any given Symbolic Order. By not allowing himself to be domesticated by the other's touching gaze, he is able to act like a "good man," yet remaining an alien to, primarily, himself. His identity is a mere potentiality, or, as he says in *The Almost People* (2011), "I am and always will be—the optimist. The hoper of far-flung hopes. The dreamer of improbable dreams."

It must be noted, however, that the use of the sonic screwdriver is not the Doctor's only way of tackling physicality: his attitude to body language[21] does change between one regeneration and another, but it would be unfair to claim that technology is his preferred mode of tactile communication in every single situation. He is not opposed to touching *per se* and he even gives in to hugging, kissing, and the like when the social occasion demands him to, but his first interaction with a new object or a living form is normally marked by scanning it with the sonic screwdriver. Thus, he uses the screwdriver to make sense of the world around him, objectifying its substance in scannable variables and attempting to manipulate it according to his needs. Being a time and space traveler has inevitably also made him an anthropologist: he must be aware of the fact that touch is "*seme*ful in that it is full of meanings—physical, emotional, intellectual, spiritual—and those meanings are socially and culturally specific. Far from being a simple, muscular action or response, touch locates us in the world, connects us to each other, and enables us to operate effectively as embodied individuals and as social subjects" (Cranny-Francis 2003: 35). By choosing to withhold his touch when interacting with the world, he avoids more than just himself and his own embodied subjectivity; he also avoids a possible cultural misunderstanding fueled by the misuse of touch in an unknown context.

By doing so, he allows the others' perception of touch to stay "natural or 'common sense'" (Cranny-Francis 2003: 36). By limiting his participation in everyday human shenanigans, the Doctor behaves like an anthropologist, trying to blend in and fully comprehend the cultural dynamics of the natives, rather than imposing his own cultural logic on them in a colonial manner.

The Doctor as an anthropologist

As he travels through time and space, should he behave according to the custom of his own people—or even according to human "common sense"—he would very quickly find himself in the middle of a cultural misunderstanding. Thus, it is probably fair to say that he has no other choice but to adopt the anthropological persona. He encounters different cultures all the time and matching his bodily behavior to any of their varied and contradictory standards would inevitably put him at odds with others. By touching via technology rather than his own body, he can avoid the attribution of socially constructed meanings and interpretations of physical touch, which is easier both for him and for the ones he encounters. By refusing to touch them with his own body, flaring his sonic screwdriver towards them instead, he does not disrupt the "normal" order of their cultural logic of touch. This logic constructs touch "simply as a physical action or sensory response" (Cranny-Francis 2003: 35), where the semeful aspects of touch might be incorporated in the tactile encounter itself, but are "not discernible or recognizable for the meanings that it [the touch], specifically, brings to the encounter" (ibid.).

By insisting on his own culturally specific modality of touch, he would make manifest the latent symbolic order that seems natural and common sense to others. It is only by destabilizing "the obviousness or naturalness of touch" (ibid.: 35) that it is possible to "locate how touch affects our everyday experience," (ibid.) "explore the biopolitics of touch" (ibid.) and expose the "technologies of the self" (Foucault in Martin et al., eds.: 1988). Instead of forcing others to deal with the otherness of his ways, he instead chooses not to touch, or, better, to touch with a technological prosthesis that allows him to categorize and understand others, yet refuses them the same privilege.

In order to construct meaningful relations to others, Fanon proposes "an effort at disalienation" (Fanon 1967: 231): "to scrutinize the self ... to touch the other, to feel the other, to explain the other to myself." The Doctor is notoriously secretive about himself, his experience, relationships, etc. He gradually opens up to his companions, allowing them a bit closer—both in terms of physical and emotional closeness—but it is only River Song, his wife, who gets to know his name.

Perhaps his main tragedy is the fact that he has chosen to protect a planet inhabited by a life form with a much shorter lifespan than his own. Although he looks perfectly human, the Doctor in fact has two hearts, an infinitely potent brain, is capable of regeneration and is hundreds of years old. While his influence on the people he invites to travel through time and space with him is life defining, to him, a Time Lord who has seen the beginning and the end of the universe, all those friendships, as close as they can get, only represent a fleeting moment in time. He recognizes the universal need not to be alone and has seen the harm that centuries of isolation can do to a person,[22] but does not have any meaningful relationships that would last long enough for him to be fundamentally influenced by them—with the exception of River Song, of course, who is half Time Lord herself, but that story has its own tragic dimension.[23] The relationships he creates with people are so short compared to his lifespan that he can reinvent himself with every new companion; rather than building lifetime relationships, he is merely repeating the honeymoon phase of friendship over and over again, rarely stopping to notice that he is permanently influencing his human companions' lives while their whole existence, to him, is a mere moment in time.

It would be unfair to say that the Doctor is not profoundly touched by some of the relationships he forms with his human companions; it is just that he has learned the inevitability of their end, which is marked by human mortality. As he moves from one physical body to the other and from one companion to the other, the only thing that remains stable is not his personality, his look, nor his relationships with others. Rather, it is the name that he has become known for— the Doctor, the one who aids those in need.

To do so, he does not use weapons, but, rather, tools. The sonic screwdriver enables him to scan (living matter and objects) and manipulate (objects) without having to form any kind of relationship first. It invades boundaries without having to ask for permission first, it objectifies the other, reducing it to data that can be collected, analyzed, and, perhaps, manipulated. It translates the phenomenal experience of touch into language, making it a suitable *weapon* for a hero who saves the world on a daily basis, not by the force of touch, but rather, by the touch of compassionate words. He is a hero whose ethics demand him to lie, cheat, and deceive, but always with the humankind's best interest in mind, and a hero who can talk his way out of almost any kind of a crisis. But for the Doctor physical force usually comes before diplomacy, his version of resorting to physical force being the sonic screwdriver and its technologically mediated touch, which, as the Doctor explains in the episode "Doomsday" (2006) "Doesn't kill, doesn't wound, doesn't maim. But I'll tell you what it does do: It is very, very good at opening doors."[24]

According to Merleau-Ponty (2012), our body is our perception of the world, but in the case of Doctor Who that is only partially true. Indeed, his personality changes with every new incarnation, for example in the change from eleventh to twelfth he goes from a flamboyant and witty young man to a grumpy old cynic, who suddenly sports a Scottish accent and an electric guitar. His tastes change: with new bodies, he enjoys different foods, different forms of entertainment, different clothes, etc. Even his relationships with those close to him adopt a different dynamic. However, his basic attitude towards the world remains unchanged, as he is bound to it in ways beyond the physical.

He remains the Doctor, focused on the ethical promise to serve and protect, to uphold humanity and to prevent destruction. It is as if he can see beyond his individual and changeable perception of the world, precisely because it changes together with his bodies. Interestingly, for Merleau-Ponty (1964: xv), "primacy of perception" does not mean reducing reflection to sensations, but, rather:

> the experience of perception is our presence at the moment when things, truths, values are constituted for us; that perception is a nascent *logos*; that it teaches us, outside all dogmatism, the true conditions of objectivity itself; that it summons us to the tasks of knowledge and action. It is not a question of reducing human knowledge to sensation, but of assisting at the birth of this knowledge, to make it as sensible as the sensible, to recover the consciousness of rationality.
>
> (Ibid.)

By perception, however, things are objectified and mortified, frozen in the moment. The eye cannot see the dynamics of the world, and the perception of movement is merely that—a perception. Not unlike the camera, the brain takes pictures of the living world, it freezes the world frame by frame (or touch by touch) and plays them back to us edited, enhanced, and filtered to our culturally prescribed likings. What we perceive as movement or any other phenomenal sensations are in fact just static impressions: seeing leaves in a different position than they were moments ago does not mean we can see the wind, perceiving our body differently than we did a moment ago does not mean we can actually feel the touch.

This point is illustrated beautifully in the Doctor Who series' depiction of Weeping Angels,[25] among the scariest recurring characters in the series. When one is looking at them, they are merely statues, but when one does not look, or when one merely blinks, they are freed from their symbolic mortification, free to move and attack their prey—by touching them. Unlike other predators in the series, they do not kill. Instead, they attack by utilizing time paradoxes: by touching them, they send their victims to a point in the past before they were born, feeding off the potential energy of a life that the victims would live in the present. As explained in the episode "The Time of Angels" (2010) by the Doctor, the Weeping Angels do not simply stop moving when one is looking: "In the sight of any living being, the Angels literally cease to exist. They're just stone: the ultimate defense mechanism." The Doctor describes them as the loneliest creatures in the universe as they are incapable of any interaction. Should they look in each other's eyes—or even in their own, like the one in the episode "The Time of the Doctor" (2013)—they would be left quantum locked, becoming stone. Just like Schrödinger's cat, they are an entity that only exists if one attempts to observe them, and not entirely unlike the other who only exists if they can attempt to touch us back, either by sense or sensibility.

Living up to one's name: touched by language

In the episode "A Good Man Goes to War" (2011), it is revealed that the etymology of the English word "doctor" in fact originates from the Doctor himself.[26] It is a name that he chose for himself and with it, he took an oath, which he repeats in "Day of the Doctor" (2013): "Never cruel nor cowardly. Never give up. Never give in." Thus, first there was the Doctor, a self-given name that was basically a promise, and then came the word—doctor. When people are very scared and in need of help, they call on him, and he never fails to answer,[27] for he is touched by—language.[28] Both touch and language can be performative. Fischer-Lichte (2008: 60) interprets touch as "the invasion of real into fiction." Discussing Abramović's performance *The Lips of Thomas* she claims that the gaze is primarily an aesthetic decision, whereas touch[29] is an ethical choice (ibid.: 64). Refusing to be touched physically, while touching others, the Doctor readily accepts the touch of language, reaffirming the ethically binding promise that is—his name.

In this sense, it is interesting that one of the basic prerequisites of being a doctor,[30] is precisely the one of physical distance between doctors and patients. When a doctor does touch a patient, that touch is full of scientific, not human meaning. The doctor's touch adheres to a completely different signification structure, and is not considered a proper human touch.

Conclusion

Is it necessary to take a stance about which of the pair (touch–language) is superior to the other? As long as there is something that we can feel convinced by, that we can believe in, something other than ourselves, be it an idea, a feeling or an experience, then we have reason to turn to others. Moreover, when we do, Doctor Who teaches us that we should always do so with compassion. It should be compassion, rather than the illusion of understanding or even agreeing, that drives us to touch others on any level. For what makes us human is not the ability to recognize, understand, or feel—it is, rather, the mere desire to do so.

Notes

1 There are numerous fictional characters who can manipulate physical objects without touching them—they can be found in (comic) books (from Roald Dahl's Matilda to Marvel's Doctor Strange), films (from Neo from the *Matrix* to Yoda of the *Star Wars* franchise) and TV series (from several *Heroes* characters to Eleven from *Stranger Things*).

2 Indeed, there are attempts to technologically "reproduce touch and to engage the user with 'force feedback'" (Paterson 2006: 691), especially in video gaming and VR. The first "virtual handshake" happened back in 2002 (ibid.), yet, fifteen years later, it is safe to say that when we do encounter a thoroughly convincing digital experience, it is due to tricking the body into feeling (for example, with Oculus Rift) rather than due to phenomenal feeling *per se*. The untranslatable nature of touch is a problem that goes beyond engineering and computer science, because—as Parisi (2014: 228) puts it—"the project of incorporating complex touch feedback into computing entails not just a transformation of spatiotemporal field accessed by touch, but a wholesale redefinition and rearticulation of touch as a category of human experience."

3 See Levinas (1985) for a discussion of people's responsibility to one another in face-to-face encounters. Ethically, the human face calls the subject into "giving and serving" (ibid.: 119) the Other.

4 To continue developing the touch–language parallel, let us list three communication phenomena associated with autism: "pronoun reversal (using the pronoun *you* when the pronoun *I* is intended, and vice versa), echolalia (repeating what someone has said), and a reduced or even reversed production-comprehension lag (a reduction or reversal of the well-established finding that speakers produce less sophisticated language than they can comprehend)" (Gernsbacher, Morson, Grace 2016: 413). Eerily enough, these appear to touch on the same mirror logic mentioned above.

5   Although the program has been running since 1963 (web1), we will only focus on the series since its revival in 2005, especially Series 5 (broadcast in 2010) and onwards, when Steven Moffat (who contributed to the program since 1995, increasingly so after 2005) became head writer and executive producer, and Matt Smith was introduced as the eleventh Doctor. The series began as a children's program and many credit Moffat for its most dramatic changes: taking a darker turn, becoming intellectually more challenging, and aimed at older audiences. Moffat wrote and produced a large portion of the episodes featuring the eleventh and twelfth Doctors, the latter portrayed by Peter Capaldi, and decided to leave the show together with Capaldi. The last episode he wrote and produced has not yet aired at the time of writing of this chapter, but it is known that Moffat left the last part, when the thirteenth Doctor (portrayed by Jodie Whittaker) was introduced, to Chris Chibnall to write and produce (web2). Chibnall was head writer and co-producer of *Torchwood*, a science fiction drama spin-off from Doctor Who. Since 2007, he has also been writing for Doctor Who (web3).

6   This idea was put forward by scholars associated with postcolonialism, who argued that "subaltern peoples" (Gramsci 2001) should be empowered to speak for themselves and produce their own cultural discourses rather than having to identify with those produced for them by colonialists.

7   It is impossible to say how old the Doctor is, but the sixth incarnation of the Doctor claimed he was 900, the twelfth Doctor claimed he had lived for 2,000 years, and Jodie Whittaker, the first woman ever to play the Doctor, currently represents the thirteenth incarnation.

8   Nietzsche speaks of eternal return in terms of a hypothetical question rather than scientific fact. He finds the idea paralyzing, seeing it as a burden, but he comes to terms with it, even embraces it, with the idea of *amor fati*: "My formula for greatness in a human being is *amor fati*: that one wants nothing to be other than it is, not in the future, not in the past, not in all eternity. Not merely to endure that which happens of necessity, still less to dissemble it – all idealism is untruthfulness in the face of necessity – but to *love* it . . ." (2004: 77–78). This is a note worth returning to as we bring up the Doctor's ability to regenerate, which allows the character to (eternally) return, portrayed by new actors. The Doctor's attitude toward his previous selves (with whom, being a time traveller, he often interacts), indeed appears to be that of *amor fati*.

9   Derrida's book *The Work of Mourning* is a collection of essays, eulogies, and funeral orations in honor of his contemporaries who passed away, such as Levinas, Althusser, Lyotard, Deleuze, Barthes, Foucault, etc. In French, the book was published under the title *Chaque fois unique, la fin du monde* (Each time unique, the end of the world). The book is a performative work of mourning as well as an exploration of the ethics of melancholia. Each chapter begins with a short biographical sketch of its

protagonist, speaking both of and to the dead, and attesting to both singularity of each friendship and uniqueness of every existence: "It is a world that is for us the whole world, the only world, and it sinks into an abyss from which no memory – even if we keep the memory, and we will keep it – can save it" (2001: 115). Or, in the words of the Doctor: "You know that in 900 years in time and space I've never met anyone who wasn't important before."

10 It would seem that when his words fail him, touch interferes—as in a romantic situation in which a lover is confronted with the beloved one and her words fail to convey meaning, so she offers a kiss instead. However, with the Doctor it appears to be the other way around. He usually tries to solve things the easy way, but as usually that does not work, he is often forced to resort to the mightiest weapon of them all—the word. There are numerous episodes, in which after lots of running, jumping, and fighting, the sonic screwdriver is put away in his pocket, and the crescendo comes in a great speech rather than explosions and action.

11 In the episode "The Time of the Doctor" (2013) it is revealed that his name is the answer to the question "Doctor who?" transmitted by Time Lords, whom he had saved from obliteration by trapping them in a pocket universe. Should he speak his name and answer the question, the Time Lords would return, which would inevitably start a new disastrous war in the universe.

12 For a more detailed exploration of touch as a differentiating and connecting element in Saussurian structural linguistics, see the contribution in this book by Mirt Komel (Chapter 1).

13 Nancy, in *Being Singular Plural* (2000) wonders how it is possible to speak of a plurality of a *we* without making that we a singular entity. He argues that, as "I" does not come before "We", there is no existence without co-existence.

14 As discussed before, the Doctor works best when disconnected from others. As he renounces touch in his dealings with ordinary objects, swapping it for sonic manipulation, he finds himself in an awkward position, where it is language that touches him more than touch itself. If the romantic lover from the Chapter 10 endnote 12 feels as if her object might deny her touch, she might, embarrassed, try to win them over in a safer manner, with words (perhaps reciting a poem or a beautiful quote). The Doctor, too, will resort to words when all else fails, but not because language would offer him more distance and safety—on the contrary, to him, it is (the mediated) touch that is cold, impersonal, and safe, yet lacking meaning, for him language conveys meaning, carries risks and embarrassments, and intimacy. He is, after all, the very last speaker of the language once spoken by the most advanced civilization one can imagine, the lost language of the Time Lords. As he exclaims in the episode "The Time of Angels" (2010), "There were days, there were many days, where these words could burn stars, raise up empires, and topple gods."

15 For a discussion of who exactly it is that gets regenerated—the same person or
   not—see Episode 1 of *Doctor Who & Philosophy* (2010), especially the chapters by
   Stokes and Johnson.

16 There is an obvious analogy between this Doctor's characteristic and the
   postmodern subject, who appears equally afraid of any (self-)definition, and,
   consequently, (self-)restriction. For more on this, see, for example, works by Salecl
   (2004, 2011).

17 In Lacanian psychoanalysis, the Symbolic is interpreted as the arbitrary system of
   meanings (language) into which we divide our world, a system of differential
   relations that preexists us, and is the only environment wherein we can expect the
   birth of a subject. The Real is what resists Symbolization, has no representation in
   the signifier, it is a realm of object a, which is the reminder of the process of
   subjectivisation through the Symbolic, which can never be complete. The Real
   represents a crack in the symbolic networking. The Imaginary is an internalized
   image of ideal; it is a perspective of Symbolic *qua* whole, without gaps and cracks,
   and the subject *qua* whole without the residue, which could not be translated into
   language (Žižek 2005).

18 This is an important sub-plot in Series 7 (2013), and there is also a supplemental
   episode, released as a home video, and written by Moffat, *The Inforarium* (2013),
   which details his attempt to erase himself from every database in the universe (web6).

19 For a detailed analysis of border in relation to the problem of touch and language,
   see Gregor Moder's contribution in this book (Chapter 4).

20 Sonic sunglasses are first featured in the episode "The Magician's Apprentice" (2015),
   a year after Google Glass became publicly available (web7).

21 The question of body-language, addressing the issue of mother's tongue and her
   touch, is tackled in detail by Rachel Aumiller's contribution in this book (Chapter 7).

22 See 2015 episodes "The Girl Who Died" and "The Woman Who Lived." In the first
   one, the Doctor saves a dying girl called Ashildr. By doing so, he grants her
   immortality and leaves her with another piece of technology that made her
   immortal so that she would be able to share her life with someone. In the next
   episode, we meet her 800 years later. She has not shared immortality with anyone
   else and has lived so long that she has forgotten not only the people she once knew
   and things that happened during this time, but also her own life—and her name. She
   now calls herself Me and has, of course, crossed over to the dark side. Throughout
   the episode, it is the Doctor who reminds her of what it means to be human and as
   they part, she decides that she will spend her life looking after his human
   companions as he abandons them.

23 River Song is the Doctor's wife and a fellow time and space traveler. However, as they
   meet in various points of time, it is revealed that their timelines are not
   synchronized. In fact, they are moving in opposite directions: when they first meet

(from the audience's perspective), it is the first time for the Doctor and apparently the last time for River Song.

24 Although the sonic screwdriver is almost like a magic wand, it has one defining shortcoming, that is, it does not appear to be effective on wood. It is explained on multiple occasions that the screwdriver could in fact be able to manipulate wood, but as every piece of wood is slightly different and because of the specific resonance of wood, the necessary calculations for finding the right frequency would take centuries. The only time the sonic screwdriver probably would have worked on wood was in the episode "The Day of the Doctor" (2013), where a younger incarnation of the Doctor started the calculation that took centuries to complete on the sonic screwdriver—but just as the eleventh Doctor, whose version of the screwdriver finished the calculation, was about to attempt to open the wooden door with it, his companion Clara burst in to the room, revealing that the door had in fact been open all along.

25 For a discussion of Weeping Angels in relation to perception, see Smithka (2010). Weeping Angels as the ultimate horror are discussed by Saint and French (2010).

26 River Song, the Doctor's wife, explains: "When you began, all those years ago, sailing off to see the universe, did you ever think you'd become this? The man who can turn an army around at the mention of his name? Doctor: the word for healer and wise man throughout the universe. We get that word from you, you know" (ibid.).

27 Even the Doctor's technologically advanced spaceship that is engineered to blend in to the environment by assuming an image of everyday objects characteristic of the place where it lands proves that—it malfunctioned during his time travel to 1960s London when it assumed the image of a police box. Police boxes were used by constables to keep in contact with police stations until the late 1960s and early 1970s when walkie-talkies were introduced the public began to gain universal access to telephones, and the 999 emergency number was introduced.

28 For a detailed analysis of the relation between name and touch see Jela Krečič's contribution in this book (Chapter 9).

29 For Fischer-Lichte (ibid.), touch is a feature of bodily copresence, characteristic of performance art. For a discussion of presence and copresence through haptic technologies, see Paterson (2006).

30 Of a profession that, in the universe of Doctor Who, got its name from the Doctor himself.

References

Cranny-Francis, A. (2003): *Technology and Touch*. NY: Palgrave Macmillan.

Derrida, J. (2001): *The Work of Mourning*. Chicago, London: Chicago UP.

Elo, M. (2016) "The New Technological Environment of Photography and Shifting Conditions of Embodiment." In: Kuc, Kamila and Joanna Zylinska (eds.) (2016): *Photomeditations: A Reader.* London: Open Humanities Press. pp.: 268–282.

Fanon, F. (1967): *Black Skin, White Masks.* New York: Grove Pres.

Fischer-Lichte, E. (2008): *The Transformative Power of Performance: A New Aesthetics.* London: Routledge.

Foucault, M. (1988): "Technologies of the Self." In: Martin, Luther H., Huck Gutman, P.H. Hutton (eds.): *Technologies of the Self: A Seminar with Michel Foucault.* London: Tavistock Publications.

Gernsbacher M., E.M. Morson, E.J. Grace (2016): Language and Speech in Autism. *Annual Review of Linguistics* vol. 2, : 413–425.

Gramsci, Antonio (2001): *Selections from the Prison Notebooks.* London: The Electric Book Company.

Haraway, Donna (1994): "A Game of Cat's Cradle: Science Studies, Feminist Theory, Cultural Studies." *Configurations* 2(1): 59–71.

Haraway, D. (1997): *Feminism and Technoscience.* New York, London: Routledge.

Levinas, E. (1985): *Ethics and Infinity: Conversations with Philippe Nemo.* Pittsburgh: Duquesne UP.

Merleau-Ponty, M. (1964): *The Primacy of Perception.* Northwestern UP.

Merleau-Ponty, M. (2012): *Phenomenology of Perception.* London, NY: Routledge.

Nancy, J.-L. (2000): *Being Singular Plural.* Stanford, California: Stanford UP.

Nietzsche, F. (2004): *Ecce Homo.* London: Penguin Books.

Nietzsche, F. (2006): *Thus Spoke Zarathustra.* Cambridge, New York: Cambridge UP.

Paterson, M. (2006): *Feel the Presence: Technologies of Touch and Distance.* Environment and Planning D: *Society and Space* 24 : 691–708.

Saint, M. and P.A. French (2010): "The Horror of the Weeping Angels." In: Courtland, L. and Smithka, P.: *Doctor Who and Philosophy.* Chicago and La Salle: Open Court.

Salecl, R. (2004): *On Anxiety.* London, New York: Routledge.

Salecl, R. (2011): *The Tyranny of Choice.* London: Profile Books.

Smithka, P. (2010): "To Be Is *Not* to Be Perceived?" In: Courtland, L. and Smithka, P.: *Doctor Who and Philosophy.* Chicago and La Salle: Open Court.

Stokes, P. (2010): "Just as I Was Getting to Know Me." In: Courtland, L. and Smithka, P.: *Doctor Who and Philosophy.* Chicago and La Salle: Open Court.

Žižek, S. (2005): *Interrogating the Real.* New York, London: Continuum.

Webpages

web1: https://en.wikipedia.org/wiki/Doctor_Who
web2: https://en.wikipedia.org/wiki/Steven_Moffat
web3: https://en.wikipedia.org/wiki/Chris_Chibnall

web4: https://en.oxforddictionaries.com/definition/humanity

web5: Peter Capaldi reveals his Doctor Who is "more alien than he's been for a while. Mirror." Available at: http://www.mirror.co.uk/tv/tv-news/peter-capaldi-reveals-doctor-who-3932096, (accessed on Oct. 8, 2017)

web6: https://en.wikipedia.org/wiki/Doctor_Who_(series_7)

web7: https://en.wikipedia.org/wiki/Google_Glass

11

Haptic Contagion: The Scream Mutating Touch and Language

Zack Sievers

Introduction

A mood, a yawn, laughter, screams can become contagious. In this contribution I take a transdisciplinary approach to developing a concept of contagion which acts as a dynamic threshold for the production of anomalies. The production of anomalies can initiate mutations in and of ontology—ontology, here, concerns what we consider to be natural organizations of relation, process, and generation; mutation concerns the indeterminate potential of these organizations to emerge otherwise than by ontological prediction and predetermination. The end of this contribution will conceptualize screaming in terms of haptic contagion in order to demonstrate that the scream can produce anomalies in touch and language.

Contagion

In order to broaden the concept of contagion beyond epidemiological constraints, I develop contagion as a social-tactile topology and then apply to it the work of thinkers who encounter and conceive contagion in the context of ontology oriented by "a sense of belonging to mutant matter" (Parisi 2007: 44). The process ontology of complex emergence and mutation, on this view, conceptualizes contagion as the spread and production of anomalies within and throughout living, mutant matter, which Luciana Parisi describes as "a metastable dynamics of change across thresholds,"(ibid.: 48) and which Gilles Deleuze and Felix Guattari describe as changes in nature that pass and cut at the farthest lines and enveloping edges of humanity, nature, intensity, and affect (Deleuze and Guattari 1987: 244–5). As a prefatory note, we must try to think of ontology in terms of thresholds and passages in continuous, virulent variation, a vast and volatile becoming by and through portals, intervals, vibrations, and modulations. Ontology, as mutant matter, can generate novel, porous, and variable contact interfaces as it continuously produces more fomites out of more and more fomites—a mutant ontology of human and social contact, conceived through touch and language, here, is viewed as an intense expanse of contagious carriers emerging not so much linearly or in terms of equivalence and/or distinction (analogy, resemblance, representation) but instead by mutual contagions.[1]

Virulence, in contemporary epidemiology, attempts to measure a contagion's power to produce infection (Shah 2016: 219). Virulently, contagions overcome human bodily defenses in the ways they involve, deform, and produce novel capacities for spreading and intensifying their powers to become untameably infectious (ibid.: 72, 208). Contagion, in epidemiology, describes an infectious disease that spreads through direct and indirect contact (ibid.: 219). The pathogens incubate their contagious powers according to a variety of factors, for example, strains of cholera will fluctuate in virulence according to the surfaces they can attach to and colonize, but also according to the physical and chemical characteristics of the environments within which they move (Colwell 1996: 2026–7). The environmental dimensions influencing the virulence of a contagion such as cholera include the quality of water supplies, the architecture of municipal sanitation infrastructures, the severity of seasonal floods, and fluctuations in ocean currents, the temperatures of land, and the sea's surface. These powers of contagion, then, are powers of contingency, virulence, and tactility: the touch, its proximity and degree of contact with strains of contagion, the way it moves and spreads, but also the complex yet momentary variations of tactility, can more or less empower the spread of infection.

While we garner an impression of the extent to which the concept of contagion is permeated with intentions to measure, control, and experiment with the spread of infection, concepts of contagion do not necessarily confine their affects to epidemiology, where contagion seems to get reduced to being conceived as a threatening, negative externality (production of and by "disease") that must be controlled and excluded at all costs. For example, Dixon and Jones generate what they term "tactile topologies" to articulate contagions at play in the "irruptive immanent materialisms of viral life" (Dixon and Jones III 2015: 223), as shown, for instance, in the 2011 film *Contagion*. They argue that *Contagion* does not merely represent or resemble contagion but rather "provides us with a corpus of touch: on bodies human and non-human, and on the spaces these create, occupy and traverse" (ibid.: 230). Here, contagion shows us the risk and horror of infection as well as how humans and the spaces within which they live mutually modify each other by connecting in tactile ways. The epidemic thematized in the film forces us to rethink cinematography as well as both bodily and social boundaries, particularly with its "viral-eye" focus on fomites, the objects and surfaces—windows, doorknobs, public water fountains, hotel beds, restaurant glassware—which become infectious agents when touched or breathed upon. Dixon and Jones argue that the film provokes audiences both to rethink anthropocentric assumptions about touch and space, and to reject the ontological tendency (Dixon and Jones locate this bias in existential phenomenology) to narrowly place topological objects *in* space, *for* human observation (ibid.: 231).

What is important to retain now is that bodily-social thresholds of contagion are to be conceived as tactile topologies, as networks engendered by but also teeming with spreads of contagion which continue to channel contagions in the ways they can produce and facilitate touch. If the social body is linguistic, it can channel and transmit communications across tactile mediums; touch, say, through the choice to retweet a meme, can spread concepts and ideas just as virulently as cholera spreads through a city water-treatment infrastructure. In their article *Complex Contagions: A Decade In Review*, Douglas Guilbeault, Joshua Becker, and Damon Centola chronicle theoretical and empirical studies of complex contagions across a variety of social domains including health, innovation, social media, and politics. The authors study the effects contagions have on the structures of network topologies, specifically their mutation variability in contact with several contagions at once, their topological potency to accelerate or decelerate, simplify or complexify, cascade and/or percolate contagious processes. They also study variations in network threshold dynamics, which they consider in terms of the flux of group membership, peer pressure, and the variability and malleability of sociological willingness to adopt and/or terminate new behaviors, beliefs, and attitudes. With attention to network structure and its dynamic thresholds, the authors distinguish complex contagions, contagions whereby the spread of behaviors, beliefs, and attitudes requires repeated contact with multiple sources of activation, from simple contagions, contagions whereby a single, activated source can be sufficient for transmission (Guilbeault, Becker, and Centola 2018: 4). The social, here, is rationally and linguistically conceived: any social network's thresholds can mutate in contact with human and bot (digital, algorithmic) activities that function according to axioms and thresholds of logic, choice, and agency. For example, Twitter bots can influence a political election through the ways they engineer disseminations of propaganda (Guilbeault and Woolley 2016). Contagions modulate these thresholds, sometimes engineering novel social behaviors by spreading language across tactile topologies, carnal and digital alike.

If we broaden our notions of contagion beyond their containment by systems of analysis, resemblance, and representation, we come across the problem of nonlinguistic contagions—contagions that neither necessarily translate nor necessarily reproduce either the architecture of the systems (logic, axiom, choice, agency) through which they emerge or the conditions we can locate for their emergence as intelligible and meaningful. Nonlinguistic contagions require a rethinking of ontology, particularly as it concerns generation, process, and relation. These kinds of contagions emerge in Luciana Parisi's work on contagions in contexts of biotechnology, specifically bacterial sex, the continuous modification and transmission of genetic make-up amidst active generation and infection, and algorithmic computation, specifically the aesthetic operation of algorithms which escape formal-logical and axiomatic registers of computation and thus become random, unprecedented, and irreducible to the laws of the systems they emerged from (incomputable objects). The many anomalies produced by these contagions, for Parisi, prove that the architecture of digital computation is neither closed nor predetermined, nor predictable, but is instead incomplete and semiopen to variable and contingent probabilities. Parisi conceptualizes this contagious space as a Whiteheadian mereotopology which seeks to describe the relationships of parts and wholes as being semiopen to each other, "discrete and separable on the one hand and as undivided and continuous on the other . . . there is no gap between parts, and neither are there *infinitesimal* points constituting continuous trajectories (or topological surfaces)" (Parisi 2013: xi). The semiopen character of algorithmic mereotopology describes the generation of contagious architectures wherein and throughout which "infinite amounts of data irreversibly enter and determine the function of algorithmic procedures" (ibid.: xii). The algorithm can produce the proliferation of increasingly random data, incomputable spatiotemporalities, and novel spatiotemporal actualities—all through the unpredictable immanence of randomness in programming, which Parisi terms contagion. In other words, the language of the program never completely predetermines the program to necessarily produce and/or reproduce language; the language of the program is an interminate potential that can outstrip itself completely through contagions.

This emergence that escapes the parameters of its own production is also touched upon by Parisi in her study of bacterial sex. Here, Parisi shows that ontological presuppositions anchored in species-based approaches to generation and evolution (Darwinism's focus on natural and sex selection as the sources of evolutionary fitness and innovation, Neo-Darwinism's reliance on notions of inert matter, natural selection, sexual filiation, and predetermination) are ill-equipped to think through the turbulence and unpredictability of mutual material-mutation and transgenesis, i.e. the fact that unprecedented mutations emerge in ways that do not resemble in any way any of the parts out of which they were generated (ibid.: 39). The barriers[2] between parts and wholes, in these cases, become irreversibly scrambled, irreducible to predeterminable designs of nature. Parisi thinks these transitions in terms of turbulence and transduction, whereby "the viral modification of molecules entering other molecules implies the mutual modification of their genetic pool composing a new molecular body, rather than the inheritance of the pool through filiative reproduction or constant self-replication" (ibid.: 42). Parisi argues, through Deleuze and Guattari's concept of "machinic phylum," that each modification entails the modification of all of the parts of newer compositions (transgenesis), and that the machinic relations across this phylum "privilege neither the organism nor the environment, internal nor external force, time nor space, nature nor culture. What comes first is neither the one nor the other. What comes first is the mutant relation: mutual feedbacks of contagion" (Parisi 2006: 42). These feedbacks privilege neither predetermination nor predictability because they produce anomalies at ontological levels of organization, process, relation, and generation.

Shifting ontological primacy from the maintenace of predictable, contained relations to mutual feedbacks of contagion attends to the primacy of unpredictable, asymmetrical relations, something we might describe in terms of heterogeneous implication and becoming. Deleuze's theory of differential relations supplements the contagious tactile ontology I have outlined so far in the sense that, following Zourabichvili:

> Deleuze's most profound insight is perhaps this: that difference is also communication and contagion between heterogeneities; in other words, that a divergence never arises without reciprocal contamination of points of view.
> (Zourabichvili 2004: 99 [Cited by de Castro 2009: 112])

Difference conceived as processes or machines of contamination and divergence suggests an ontology wherein touch can be laced with communication, wherein the moment when touch differs or separates from itself is conceivable by the contagious spread of tactility. In the thresholds of this communicative, contagious difference, Deleuze and Guattari are interested in contagion insofar as it produces anomalies—in our case, with attention to the haptic and screaming, these anomalies will come to bear upon the occurrence of ontological mutations within as well as throughout touch and language.

For Deleuze and Guattari, contagion escapes human natural history (Deleuze and Guattari 1987: 234). What is at stake in the becomings of plateau ten of *A Thousand Plateaus,* where contagion surfaces, is to experiment with escaping from natural history and human reproduction through becoming-intense and becoming-animal. These becomings express a cautious yet volatile experimentation with variation, contagion, and production. Experimentation, for Deleuze and Guattari, escapes history[3] insofar as its becoming varies itself and its goals continuously and, at moments or thresholds, produces anomaly (Deleuze and Guattari 1987: 292). In this vein, and similar to Parisi, Deleuze and Guattari express contagion as production that escapes filiation, predetermined genetic structure, sexual reproduction, and nature (and by doing so, becomes cosmic, machinic).[4] The escape, or the production of the anomaly by contagion, is characterized as "unnatural participation": contagion escapes human natural history through unnatural participations, whereby nature and natural differentiations between, for example, species or individuals, mutate. Contagion generates novel multiplicities that do not reproduce the natural differentiations immanent to their geneses or structures—contagion does not simply reproduce what it transmits, nor does it transmit anything other than itself, nor does it reproduce nothing.[5] These anomalous productions, or unnatural participations, vary or begin human nature over again otherwise than it was, is, or can predictably be.

The anomalous, for Deleuze and Guattari, is never simply an exceptional individual. Neither does it produce or arise from a single origin (simple contagion). There is never an occurrence of single contagion that can be traced to a single beginning point of contact because the contagion and its beginning are always already multiple and variable. Differently from what we consider abnormal, or that which refers to what goes against or outside norms we are capable of conceiving, the anomalous describes the space or edge of the enveloping line or farthest dimension of contagion, a position or set of positions that is neither an individual nor a species, beyond which the natures of the pacts and forces involved in becoming-animal and becoming-intense mutate.[6]

How might we think the topology of the space of the anomaly, a mutant event passing at and through the edges of contagion? To confine it simply to one or several variations of synthesis and/or catalysis, or to make the anomaly and/or contagion simple catalysts, appears reductive at this point insofar as we wish to account for the complex production of and producing by the novel itself. Here I invoke the concept of maceration, not to become a singular or simple explanation for what happens at the edges of contagion, but rather to introduce a way to further complicate the process and relation-based ontologies and tactile topologies we have at play, in accounting for the emergence of anomaly. It is my intention that maceration will provide a tactile topology implying mutual mutation through contact.

Through maceration, bones and skin can soften and break down from solids to fluids to nearly absolute dissolutions through the intensifications of too much contact with chewing teeth and/or moisture (saliva, or any other body of water); maceration can grind and blend shit or ice into smaller and smaller pieces, can shift shape, catalyze and mutate matter for processes of digestive exchange and passage; the grape's tannins can be leeched from their skins, stems, and seeds to produce the color of wine—the brief contact macerating the skins of grapes can produce novel viscosities and colors through modulations of pressure and contact; bones exude a glossy pallor when immersed and contained in acids that macerate their lingering flesh; hydrochloric acids macerate geological materials, revealing the visibility of fossils; we mash roses into ointments and perfumes, liquefy and unctuate roots into aromatic purees by maceration; the stomach, by hydrochloric acid, macerates eaten food; the mouth macerates words, such as "catalyze" and "synthesize," in the moment of speaking them through the lips, throat, vocal chords, tongue, saliva, and glands. A paradox seems to emerge here: contagion and its anomalous macerations can touch too close, too much, too fast, so fast that their touch eclipses the limit of the edge as well as the passage through it.

A first kiss can, by contagion, spread through, invade, or infect as much of the lips, teeth, tongues, gums as "it" can according to virulence and turbulence of the contact, and in so doing, produce these organs and their organizations irrecognizable, absolutely heterogeneous, from their previous unkissedness. Brand-new lips, teeth, gums, tongues, saliva. Brand-new cutting edges, and thereby brand-new touch, brand-new spit, a new spray of words.

Contagion is not trapped in the middle of the lips of the first kiss. It is not simply a middle voice, a between, a margin, a border, an intercalation inserted or grown into the between interstitially. Contagion is neither a limit nor an origin. Neither is it simply beyond limits and origins. Rather, following Parisi, Deleuze, and Guattari, the middle of the kiss, the lips, spit and tongues half-open and half-closed, touching and not touching (the breath breathing through the first kiss directly as well as indirectly), defines relations vastly internal as well as external to their contact, and thereby becomes a portal or interval for mutual, mutant generation of the new. The contagions of touch occurring through the lips branding each other in excess of each other, anew, produce incomputable tactilities vastly internal and external to their direct and indirect contact. Thus the topology specific to maceration's contagious tactility would never be able to confine itself to the space or the time between two terms. It would instead concern proliferating and incubating the anomalous spatiotemporalities of contagion spreading, transmitting, and spawning novel tactilities across, throughout, and beyond the organs directly and indirectly involved in, for example, two mouths kissing.

Haptic

What can a tactile body do? For haptic contagion, no body cannot become tactile. The haptic spreads mutations of touch. What can a body do becoming-tactile anew? An orifice? A membrane? The body becomes contagious tactility through touching too close, so much, too much.[7] But the body, too, can become tactile without directly touching or being touched. Touch can generate the infectious spread of novel tactilities without touching any body, or for that matter, anybody.

What haptic means here is to initiate as well as become tactile-variation. The haptic expresses an invasion of the tactile, possibly volatile, which blurs or smears depth and optical distance; the haptic macerates distinguishable subjects and objects and their natural differentiations of space, in this case the distance or proximity of contact, and time, in this case the moment or duration of direct, indirect, and perhaps even the failure of contact. Recall that, for Parisi, the mereotopology of contagion at the farthest thresholds of algorithmic processes and bacterial sex produces novel spatiotemporalities. Dixon's and Jones III's tactile topologies are keen on describing the haptic as that which lacks overarching spatial (Euclidean) metrics for orienting relationality (Dixon and Jones III 2015: 226). We must remember that a lack of metrics does not simply negate the production of topological borders and spatiotemporal variations.[8] What haptic contagions produce are textural and intensive spatialities that escape computation by optical metrics. These spaces are incomputable by an ontology that holds permanent, predetermined divisions both internal and external to touch, particularly as touch relates to vision.[9]

Let us focus on the example of an eye becoming-tactile, an example which embodies the power of the haptic to mutate traditional spatiotemporal distinctions between senses.[10] That the haptic can invade the seeing eye and impose a tactile function upon it means that variations of touch can produce anomalies out of, but also through, the natural differentiations which relate and relay organizations of sense, for example, the thresholds which separate and connect eyes to and from skin. The thresholds that precede natural differentiation, the spatio-temporalities that escape human natural history, can be breached as well as produced by contagion just as much as by the haptic. The haptic, in this sense, already embodies and resonantes with contagion: it invades, it produces anomalies, it mutates ontological organizations regarding the traditional ways that we predetermine differences between senses. In surpassing its optical thresholds the haptic eye becomes a new ductility, an anomalous, porous elasticity, a scrub or a graze whose look cannot visually distinguish itself from soaking, drying, sliding—eyes that scrape, dive, and splash rather than observe.

It can happen that the eye becoming skin affects a horror—perhaps ejection from the stable delineations between vision and touch can occur according to horror at the extremely ambiguous limits preceding haptic contagion between senses.

We might speculate that the eye turned tactile sees/feels noise where it tries to maintain its traditional distinctions between touch and vision. The extremities may give way to unprecedented textures and intensities that macerate what was once distinct and contained. Perceived as a lack, such an experience calls up images of athletes losing their contact lenses behind their eyes during competitive play. Trying to fish out the lens, the face of the athlete will sometimes pucker and writhe until their finger suddenly emerges with the lens on its tip. Reliable distinctions between touch and vision in their recognizable constancy may return to the athlete out of this gap in time and space where their fingers and their tremulous touch communicated with and to some extent became the scope of their visibility. This haptic moment of horror ebbed but subsided. A return to preferred natural differentiations—the eye separate from the finger separate from the contact lens, then the eye merging back with the lens imperceptibly—somehow emerged again out of the scrambling of these differentiations.

In their writing on contagion, Deleuze and Guattari invoke Lovecraft's "nameless horror" of the outsider passing at the edge, a horror "teeming, seething, swelling, foaming, spreading like an infectious disease" (Deleuze and Guattari 1987: 245) to describe becoming contagious. The outsider mistakes, perhaps due to the nepenthe in his veins, a "cold and unyielding surface of polished glass" for the rotting, outstretched paw of a monster (Lovecraft 2005: 13–4). This is a haptic horror par excellence—the touch varies itself unpredictably, unfolds as unfathomable contact. Just before touching this monster through the glass, Lovecraft's outsider trembles at the thought of what might be lurking near him unseen. In the same moment, he crosses the sill upon entering a large room "when there descended upon the whole company a sudden and unheralded fear of hideous intensity, distorting every face and evoking the most horrible screams from every throat" (Lovecraft 2005: 12). The outsider trembles, listening to the screams tear out of these mouths and vanish into echoes, as members of this company become "delirious fugitives"; the outsider stands shocked, dazed, alone yet trembling and riddled by the contagious force of these screams. These screams contagiously spread the haptic and the grotesque, a nameless horror that expresses a tactile topology of "hideous intensity," contagious across the fingertips mutating virulently with the screams, fur, and glass.

The eye and the voice mutating tactile through touch are examples of haptic contagions of touch and language. In both cases, organs that we naturally separate from each other (eyes distinct from voice distinct from skin) are invaded/contaminated by touch and their natural differentiations are scrambled. In the scrambling there can be a recoil to return to the prior state of differentiation; this recoil may never reach a return to organization. But there is a problem, here, with casting these haptic, contagious events in terms of horror and the grotesque alone. The transdisciplinary approach I've taken so far to conceptualizing contagion is meant to challenge the history of contagion being conceived as the horrifying and grotesque loss of the human, contagion as only a negative, violent externality. The scream of haptic contagion shows that the human voice, akin to bacteria, or the algorithm, is itself already contagious; this voice—including its linguistic and tactile capacities—is a power of and by contagion. In the following section I will show screaming to be a power that can generate as well as mutate our social-linguistic relations to touch and language.

Scream

How can the scream, if it is already or can become haptic and contagious, inform us concerning the question of touch as it relates to language? Where and what is a scream? Following Lacanian psychoanalytic logic, Mladen Dolar, in his text *A Voice and Nothing More,* locates the scream as "the most salient inarticulate presymbolic manifestation of the voice" (Dolar 2006: 27). The voice, for Dolar, is the middle ground where body and language touch and do not touch each other; it bears a relation of body to language that can be exceeded as well as negated by the scream. Lacanian psychoanalysis focuses on the retroactive transformation or development of the scream into an appeal—the development of the physiological body into language and speech—because Lacan assumes that the scream is predetermined to manifest in the purview of speech, and because the first function of speech is to enunciate an address to the other for the purpose of eliciting an answer. In this sense, the scream is predetermined by imperatives to become linguistic; but as presymbolic, the scream reveals a threshold for entering into the symbolic orders of language, and thereby, into a social, public, and sexual world.[11] On Dolar's account, as the source of the voice, all screaming calls for a reply:

> The scream, unaffected as it is by phonological constraints, is nevertheless speech in its minimal function: an address and an enunciation. It is the bearer of an enunciation to which no discernible statement can be ascribed, it represents the pure process of enunciation before the infant is capable of any statement.
>
> (Ibid., 28)

Here, the scream screams through the infant purely without statement, yet it somehow still bears the tract of enunciation and address. The voice is carried to enunciation through the scream "by an interpretation of the unfathomable other with which it tries to cope" (ibid.: 28). The other becomes recognizable, latently, as the co-producer of this scream, interpreted as a scream moving simultaneously with the scream itself and with the scream as interpretation of the other. Lacan demonstrates this retroactive transformation, as Dolar notes, by playing with the pun *cri pur*, pure scream, turning it into *cri pour*, a scream for. The scream tends to direct itself toward speech, yet it appears precisely where speech fails or becomes inaccessible.

This "elusive mythical scream," or "primal scream"—the first scream—sets in motion interpretations concerning the transformative developments of human physiology into meaning, of body into the social worlds of language, and vice versa, through the unstructured-structuring source of the voice (scream). Dolar pushes the elusiveness of the scream, the non-structured voice that miraculously starts to represent structure as such, the signifier in general" (ibid.: 29), when he analyzes Munch's painting *The Scream*. Here, Dolar is interested in viewing a representation of the scream coming out of the mouth or another bodily aperture without hearing it (ibid.: 68). One could analyze the distorted landscape around Munch's screamer as the effect of the scream spreading through nature, but also as a force sucking natural backgrounds into its orifices, contracting them instead of expanding through them (ibid.: 69). In either case, for Dolar:

The painted scream is by definition mute, stuck in the throat; the black opening
is without the voice which would mollify it, fill it, endow it with sense, hence its
resonance is all the greater. Not only are we unable to hear the scream, it is also
the homunculus, the strange screaming creature, the alien, who cannot hear us;
he/she/it has no ears, he/she/it cannot reach anybody by the scream, nor can he/
she/it be reached.

(Ibid.: 69)

Negating the sound of the scream can increase the intensity of the scream
insofar as it makes the scream more and more unreachable. In compounding
this untouchability, Dolar depicts the scream in Munch's painting as "a source of
voice to which no voice can be assigned, but which for that very reason represents
the voice all the more" (ibid.: 69). Munch's screamer gets closer to representing
the voice through the scream the closer it can raze off the efficacy of the scream's
sonorous appeal to touching the screamer and the scream's/screamers' witnesses.
Closing in on the scream in this way appears to radicalize Dolar's earlier insights
concerning Lacan: the more severed the scream is from the enunciation and
appeal, the more it intensifies alterity that escapes interpretation of the scream as
interpretation of the other, the more the scream returns to its primal or elusive
mythical status as unstructured source of the voice and relation to the other, the
body, and language.

These double movements between interpreting the scream and interpreting the
other that plunge into abysses and nadirs of alterity, mouth, and voice resonate
with Merleau-Ponty's treatment of vociferation in *The Visible and the Invisible*. Yet
Merleau-Ponty trains his focus on the sound of the scream rather than the
muteness of the painted scream representing the voiceless source of the voice. For
Merleau-Ponty, vociferation expresses a reversibility of inside and outside, an
incomparable singularity that is simultaneously social contagion of sound:

Among my movements there are some that go nowhere—that do not even go
find in the other body their resemblance or their archetype: these are the facial
movements, many gestures, and especially those strange movements of the
throat and mouth that form the cry and the voice. Those movements end in
sounds and I hear them … I hear my own vibration from within; as Malraux
said, I hear myself with my throat. In this, as he also has said, I am incomparable;
my voice is bound to the mass of my own life as is the voice of no one else. But if
I am close enough to the other who speaks to hear his breath and feel his
effervescence and his fatigue, I almost witness, in him as in myself, the awesome
birth of vociferation.

(Merleau-Ponty 1968: 144)

Although he does not mention contagion here, Merleau-Ponty's example of screaming emphasizes the contagious aspect of the sound of vociferation. Differently than Dolar's attention to the muteness of the painted scream, here, an excess of sound transmits the contagion of vociferation across witnesses. This explosion of sound throughout the proximities of screamer and witnesses shows the reversibility of their throats and breaths. My most idiosyncratic feature—me incomparably hearing and feeling myself crying with my throat, my body in the process of losing/forming my voice—explodes in my vicinity through sonorous movement that goes nowhere. Is this movement that "goes nowhere" one that escapes language? It is clear that my scream is social as well as anonymous, transmissible as well as singular, yet it produces a movement incomputable by resemblance and archetype. It is through this strange discord or escape from resemblance and archetype that the other and I almost witness not each other but "the awesome birth of vociferation." The incomparability and contagion of my voice or the other's imposes upon me an imperative to almost witness this awesome birth. This birth does not so much "call" or "appeal" to the vociferation as "enunciation" or "appeal" because the movement of the voice, as Merleau-Ponty says, "goes nowhere"—it is not necessarily directed toward speech as we can know it from resemblance or archetype. Vociferation speaks anomalously. In the proximity between screamer and witness there emerges instead a contagion of effervescence and breath—hearing the cry of a voice that goes nowhere drags me into a proximity of the other wherein and throughout our bodies no longer resemble one another nor follow nor find the same archetypes for movement, enunciation, touch, or language.

Reminiscent of the earlier discussion of Parisi, Deleuze, and Guattari conveying what passes at the edges or is produced at the farthest extremity of a system (Chaitan's Omega), what is at stake in both Dolar's and Merleau-Ponty's descriptions of screaming is an interpretation of how screams can emerge at the ontological thresholds of systems; in Dolar's, the scream emerges as the voice at the farthest thresholds preceding and sourcing it, the body, and language in Merleau-Ponty's, it emerges as sonorous contagion at the farthest thresholds of resemblance and archetype in movement. In both cases we witness screaming producing as well as mutating the thresholds of touch and language. Furthermore, the contagion of vociferation that I read into Merleau-Ponty echoes his remarks on how children enter speech, although his emphasis shifts from the sound of the scream to the emergence of visible composition. For Merleau-Ponty, speech enters into language and develops linguistically through audio-visually witnessing oppositions emerging in and through itself. Perceiving discord for the first time, splitting of and off from oneself, children enter speaking language by way of an imperative similar to the haptic variation "imposing" tactility upon the optical habits of the eye: the child is snapped up by the whirlwind of spoken language and thereby swayed over to the speaking world.[12] We can speculate that, following this turbulent entry into speech, the scream, for Merleau-Ponty, would have to emerge visibly composed on a phonemic scale for the awesome birth of vociferation to register as speech. Like a whirlwind, this emerging audio-visual intelligibility—the form of a scream emerging out of nascent oppositions, say, between body, voice, language, and speech—would drag or direct the scream into speech. The history of this whirlwind, the "whole of spoken language surrounding the child," for Merleau-Ponty, evinces unimpeachable circumstances that continuously mutate the capacity to appeal as well as enunciate, for example, "the contagion of other tongues, invasions" (Merleau-Ponty 1973: 24). Thus, if we supplement Dolar with Merleau-Ponty, we have an account of screaming and contagion producing—at the most primal thresholds of body, language, self, and other—the conditions for entering, modulating, and escaping social-linguistic worlds.

Screaming haptic contagions

Both Dolar and Merleau-Ponty describe the scream at play in the generation and modification of the ontological foundations of the social body and language. Deleuze's insights on screaming resonate with Merleau-Ponty as well as Dolar insofar as all three locate a generative power of the scream. In Dolar, the painted, mute scream produced the best representation of a voice impossibly caught between body and language; in Merleau-Ponty, proximity to the sound of the scream produced witnesses of the awesome birth of vociferation. In both of these cases, the visibility of the scream played a role in allowing the scream to emerge pre-linguistically.

Like Dolar, Deleuze approaches screaming through studying the art of painting. In his study of the painter Francis Bacon, Deleuze argues that Bacon's painted screams produce nervous intensities affected by and affecting invisible forces being exerted upon the mouth and face, forces which escape form through their deforming precision (Deleuze 2003: 50). We might recall the outsider's horror, here, amidst the horrible screaming and distortion of faces of bystanders, at the thought of what lurks and remains unseen. This "hideous intensity" echoes the precision of deformation in Bacon's paintings, and for Deleuze, it can deform the organized natural postures of bodies by exerting imperceptible forces upon them. Bacon's screams mark zones where invisible, imperceptible forces are in the process of striking the body. Thus, what is imperceptible somehow strikes, makes contact with the body, and the scream marks this zone of intense albeit grotesque tactility passing at the thresholds of perceptibility. These zones are to be thought of as utterly nervous, following Antonin Artaud and Gaston Bachelard, and Francis Bacon himself, as meat and head rather than bone and face. As in Artaud, the scream, for Deleuze, generates a power to dissolve or macerate contained bodily forms (Dixon 2011: 439).

Deleuze is careful to remark that Bacon is "nervously optimistic"; Bacon, too, goes so far as to reproach himself for painting too much horror and moves more and more toward painting screams without horror (Deleuze 2003: 52). Nervous optimism, here, describes a confrontation between visible (organized, cerebral) bodies and nervous powers of the invisible. The body, like a wrestler, can actively struggle through this confrontation and can affirm the possibility of triumphing in an act of vital faith "which was beyond its reach as long as these powers remained invisible, hidden in a spectacle that sapped our strength and diverted us" (Ibid.). If and when the wrestler confronting these powers screams, the scream does not simply negate their bodily organizations. The scream gives life to the haptic struggle of a visible body in touch with contagious, invisible forces. The scream, too, produces an indominable and insistent presence whereby new life and direct powers are given to the body wrestling with invisible forces.

The screams in Bacon's paintings act as anomalies that macerate the organizations which typically contain a body, and thereby produce the body's organizations anew; for Deleuze the screams proliferate and propagate temporary, novel polyvalent orifices and indeterminate organs through the scream's unprecedented deformations. This "body-without-organs" of the screamer, characterized as a virtual space or diagram of intensity and affect, conjures up an image of there being everywhere multiplying an interminable, incessant, and invisible presence acting or touching (striking) directly on the nervous system. For Deleuze, this nervous touch is transmitted not by Bacon's representation of the scream, but by the affect of Bacon's haptic process of painting, particularly its capacity to liberate the eyes and other bodily organs from predetermined organization:

Painting ... *it does not treat the eye as a fixed organ* ... it also liberates the eye from its adherence to the organism, from its character as a fixed and qualified organ: the eye becomes virtually the polyvalent indeterminate organ that sees the body without organs ... as pure presence. Painting gives us eyes all over: in the ear, in the stomach, in the lungs (the painting breathes ...).

(Deleuze 2003: 45)

This rampant, unbridled proliferation of "eyes all over" produces the liberation of the eye from its adherence to histories of bodily organism: eyes escape vision and venture tactility. We must add that these escapes, in Bacon's case, can be considered haptic. The eyes that pop up in novel places, these new eyes, become tactile in excess of the optical.

Bacon painted a handful of screaming popes. In these paintings the scream is not first an appeal to another unfathomable screamer, nor is it a contagion that drags and plunges the screamer into the speaking world. For Bacon and Deleuze, the screams do not manifest a movement backward or forward in the development of human voice or speech, for example, a regression from human back to a prior or primal state of brute nature, infancy, or animality. Rather, the screams produce bodies anew as howling *meat*, "the [states] of the [bodies] in which flesh and bone confront each other locally rather than being composed structurally" (ibid.: 20–1). In other words, there occurs, through Bacon's screamers, a maceration (in this case, local confrontation rather than adherence to preceding and predeterminable structural composition) of the thresholds of the nervous, organized body. The scream that produces this "becoming-meat" generates a nervous, haptic threshold through which the entire body escapes.[13] Deleuze conceives the production of this anomaly as the acquisition of powers of nonlocalization. Akin to the variation of optical (metric, archetypal spatiotemporality) into haptic, this anomaly is not cast as a force which simply negates the orders and locales that were thought to ontologically predetermine it. The bone becoming meat, the mouth becoming "severed artery" or "jacket sleeve," acquires a power of escaping its sensory and spatial predeterminations anomalously: the nonlocalized movement goes nowhere that it has gone before, goes nowhere it could imagine prior to or during the moment of screaming. In this escape it produces new nerves, meat, orifices.

Bacon's screams mutate the bodily organizations of his screamers and their viewers in the ways they produce haptic contagion. Haptic contagion occurs at the cutting edges of the scream-breath: it carries the contagious spread of tactility through the thresholds we mistake to be between senses. I noted earlier that the haptic invades bodily organizations. It is this sense of tactile invasion in which Bacon's screamers act as fomites of and for haptic contagion: the scream itself not only mutates the face and the voice of the screamer anomalously; it also acts as a carrier and a threshold for the production of more—too much— haptic contagion. When screaming becomes a fomite for haptic contagion in the thresholds of social networks, such as Lovecraft's screamers, organizations of social and linguistic behaviors can mutate the ways we know our own face as well as the faces of others. The mouth that speaks words mutates just as unpredictably as the eyes turning to skin, fur, and/or glass. Any speech organ can mutate. These transgeneses can produce anomalies: they give birth to unprecedented bodily organizations, unpredictable social-linguistic orders, novel network dynamics, and tactile topologies, all incomputable and unrecognizable according to the contexts from and through which they emerged.

Why does Bacon, famously, endeavor to paint the scream more than the horror? Deleuze interprets Bacon as endeavoring to unleash forces of the future and establish unprecedented relationships between the tactile visibility of the scream (the open meat or bodily aperture) and the invisible forces that strike the body of the screamer imperceptibly, and thereby to bestow or infect the body with powers of the future (Deleuze 2003: 51–2). I assume these powers of the future are powers of experimentation: the contagious, experimental thought has the power to escape history, and thus the power of the future is never necessarily bridled to prediction and/or determination by the past.[14] We might add that these forces and powers of the future are powers of the scream and haptic contagion: they are powers of touch and language that can produce as well as be produced by anomalies. Akin to the brand-new mouths that emerge from the first kiss, these powers of the future are powers that renovate the organizations of bodies anomalously in the ways they touch and are touched, the ways they speak and are spoken to.

There are many variations of screaming haptic contagions that macerate and cut across touch and language. The actor and the musician learn to modulate their screams according to drama, context, tempo. We scream the name of our lover or friend over the murmur of a crowd; we scream for help, in the throes of pain, frustration, and oppression; we scream in excitement and jubilation at concerts and sporting events; we scream during labor and childbirth; we scream across the lines of a political protest, hurling polarizing insults and slogans. The screams that touch across these social contexts can divide as well as unite communities. They mutate the ontological organizations of these communities. The qualities of the scream produce and modulate the nature of the messages communicated. While we normally associate screaming with horror and pain, screaming can also occur at the farthest, deepest thresholds of pleasure, a contagion that is as lustful as it is voluptuous, the haptic contagious power of a voice dynamically plunging and dragging through caresses, the scream sometimes erupting silently, as gnarled as it is loosened, thrown by excesses teeming and rippling across the surfaces. The surfer screams as they first enter and carve through the barrel of a towering wave. The skydiver howls as they exit the threshold of the plane mid-air. And of course other anomalies can occur: screams that escape the natural differentiations between pleasure and pain, ecstasy and anguish. These screams produce thresholds where voices can escape human intention and affection altogether, where touch and language can verge the thresholds of utter absurdity and alienation otherwise than horror.

Notes

1 There are many resonances between the approaches to process ontology and complex emergence grounded in mutation and contagion (mentioned above) and chaos theory, particularly on the topics of nonlinearity, indeterminacy, predetermination, and turbulence.

2 In several instances, Parisi invokes transgenesis as a variation of symbiosis wherein and through which is produced "the emergence of an unprecedented mutation that does not resemble any of the parts out of which it was generated" (Parisi 2007: 39). For Parisi, these mutations confound notions of barrier that presuppose ontologically permanence concerning generative asymmetries between parts and wholes. The Weismann barrier, for example, is characterized by Parisi as a barrier which "excluded the reversal action of the environment on the organism, and on the level of the cell, it assigned complete mastering to nucleic DNA on cytoplasmic material (proteins, mitochondria, etc.)" (Parisi 2007: 40). "Recently, biotechnologies such as mammal cloning have also raised questions regarding the Darwinian hereditary transmission of life defined by the Weismann barrier between the germline (nucleic DNA) and somaline (the cytoplasmic body of the cell)"(ibid.). In this ontological model of process, relation, and generation, the source of cause remains centered in but separate and insulated from externalities. This ontological distance occurs from holding an insurmountable difference between the germline and the somaline. As I am showing, the process ontology we require to encounter contagion cannot confine itself to strong ontological distinctions (ontological permanence), precisely because the ontology of contagion roots itself inextricably in anomalous contact and transgenetic mutation.

3 See Deleuze and Guattari's chapter titled "Geophilosophy" in *What Is Philosophy?* for an in-depth discussion of the imperative to escape history, and for history as

founding itself on negation: "What History grasps of the event is its effectuation in states of affairs or in lived experience, but the event in its becoming, in its specific consistency, in its self-positing as concept, escapes History. To think is to experiment, but experimentation is always that which is in the process of coming about—the new, remarkable, and interesting that replace the appearance of truth and are more demanding than it is. What is in the process of coming about is no more what ends than what begins. History is not experimentation, it is only the set of almost negative conditions that make possible the experimentation of something that escapes history" (Deleuze and Guattari 1994: 110—1).

4   For Deleuze and Guattari's concept of the cosmic as it relates to machinic becoming, see Deleuze and Guattari 1987: 142, 333, 347–56. For contagion see ibid.: 241–2.

5   See also Deleuze's discussion of reproduction and "the hereditary" (Deleuze 1990: 324).

6   This vision of anomaly resonates with Parisi's affinity for evolutionary processes theorized using "far-from-equilibrium notions of matter which omit entropic (loss, external negativity) dynamics of accumulation and discharge from their ontology" (Parisi 2007: 48). There is also resonation with Parisi's use of algorithmic information theorist Gregory Chaitin's notion of *Omega*, or, "incomputable algorithms at the limit of any computational process" (Parisi 2013: 7). In both cases, the possibility of mutation, or change in nature, through contagion, is intrinsic to ontology of process and relation.

7   For the conception of a surplus of touch see Mirt Komel's contribution in this book (Chapter 1).

8   For a detailed analysis of the role of touch in structuring topological borders and edges, see Gregor Moder's contribution to this book (Chapter 4).

9   I cannot touch on the entirety of scholarship concerning touch and vision here. For a synthesis of different perspectives on touch and vision, see Cathryn Vasseleu's work *Textures of Light: Vision and Touch in Irigaray, Levinas, and Merleau-Ponty*.

10 For a detailed anthropological analysis of the phenomenon of synesthesia in relation to the sense of touch, see Tomi Bartole's contribution in this book (Chapter 2).

11 For a variety of psychoanalytic interpretations of the scream, with attention to gender performance, see Dixon 2011: 437–9.

12 See Merleau-Ponty's essay "Indirect Language and the Voices of Silence" in *Signs* (Merleau-Ponty 1964: 4–1). "The whole of spoken language surrounding the child snaps him up like a whirlwind, tempts him by its internal articulations, and brings him *almost* up to the moment when all this noise begins to mean something. The untiring way in which the train of words crosses and re-crosses itself, and the emergence one unimpeachable day of a certain phonemic scale according to which discourse is visibly composed, finally sways the child over to the side of those who speak."

13 "Still, it is important to understand the affinity of the mouth, and the interior of the mouth, with meat, and to reach the point where the open mouth becomes nothing more than the section of a severed artery, or even a jacket sleeve that is equivalent to an artery … The mouth then acquires this power of nonlocalization that turns all meat into a head without a face. It is no longer a particular organ, but the hole through which the entire body escapes" (ibid.: 23–4).

14 See Rachel Aumiller's Contribution in this volume for a contrasting interpretation that argues the impossibility of escaping the history of the Mother Tongue (Chapter 7)

References

Colwell, R. (1996): "Global Climate and Infectious Disease: The Cholera Paradigm," *Science* 274, no. 5295 (1996): pp. 2025–2031.

Deleuze, G. (1990): *The Logic of Sense.* trans. M. Lester, New York: Columbia UP.

Deleuze, G. (2003): *Francis Bacon: The Logic of Sensation*, trans. D. W. Smith, London: Continuum.

Deleuze, G. and F. Guattari (1987): *A Thousand Plateaus: Capitalism and Schizophrenia*, trans. B. Massumi, Minneapolis: Minnesota UP.

Deleuze, G. and F. Guattari (1994): *What Is Philosophy?* trans. H. Tomlinson and G. Burchell, New York: Columbia UP.

Dixon, D. (2011): "Scream: The Sound of the Monstrous," *Cultural Geographies* 18, no. 4, pp. 435–455.

Dixon, D. and J. Jones III (2015): "The Tactile Topologies of *Contagion.*" *Transactions of the Institute of British Geographers* 40 (2015): pp. 223–234.

Dolar, M. (2006): *A Voice and Nothing More.* Cambridge, Mass.: The MIT Press.

Guilbeault, D. and S. Woolley (2016): "How Twitter Bots are Shaping the Election," *The Atlantic*, November 2016.

Guilbeault, D., J. Becker, and D. Centola (2018): "Complex Contagions: A Decade in Review" in *Spreading Dynamics in Social Systems.* Springer Nature.

Kahn, D. (2001): *Noise Water Meat: A History of Sound in the Arts.* Cambridge: The MIT Press.

Lovecraft, H.P. (2005): *Tales.* New York: Library of America.

Merleau-Ponty, M. (1964): "Indirect Language and the Voices of Silence" in *Signs.* trans. McCleary. Evanston: Northwestern UP.

Merleau-Ponty, M. (1968): *The Visible and the Invisible.* trans. A. Lingis, ed. C. Lefort. Evanston: Northwestern UP.

Merleau-Ponty, M. (1973): *The Prose of the World.* trans. J. O'Neill. Evanston: Northwestern UP.

Parisi, L. (2006): "Generative Classifications", *Theory, Culture & Society* 23: 32–35.

Parisi, L. (2007) "Biotech: Life by Contagion," *Theory, Culture & Society* 24, no. 6: 29–52.

Parisi, L. (2013): *Contagious Architecture: Computation, Aesthetics, and Space.* Cambridge, Mass.: The MIT Press.

Shah, S. (2016): *Pandemic: Tracking Contagions, From Cholera to Ebola and Beyond,* New York: Sarah Crichton Books.

Vasseleu, C. (1998): *Textures of Light: Vision and Touch in Irigaray, Levinas and Merleau-Ponty,* New York: Routledge.

Index